BY TOM DOYLE

The Glamour Chase: The Maverick Life of Billy MacKenzie

Man on the Run: Paul McCartney in the 1970s

Captain Fantastic: Elton John's Stellar Trip Through the '70s

Captain Fantastic

TOM DOYLE

Captain

Fantastic

ELTON JOHN's STELLAR TRIP THROUGH THE '70s

BALLANTINE BOOKS · NEW YORK

Published in the United States by Ballantine Books, an imprint of
Random House, a division of Penguin Random House LLC,
New York.

BALLANTINE and the HOUSE colophon are registered trademarks
of Penguin Random House LLC.

Photo credits can be found on page 281.

LIBRARY OF CONGRESS CATALOGING-IN-PUBLICATION DATA
Names: Doyle, Tom
Title: Captain Fantastic: Elton John's stellar trip through the '70s /
Tom Doyle.
Description: First edition. | New York: Ballantine Books, [2017] |
Includes bibliographical references and index.
Identifiers: LCCN 2016034659 (print) | LCCN 2016035358 (ebook) |
ISBN 9781101884188 (hardcover: alk. paper) | ISBN 9781101884201
(ebook)
Subjects: LCSH: John, Elton. | Rock musicians—England—Biography.
Classification: LCC ML410.J64 D69 2017 (print) | LCC ML410.J64
(ebook) | DDC 782.42166092 [B]—dc23
LC record available at https://lccn.loc.gov/2016034659

Printed in the United States of America on acid-free paper

randomhousebooks.com

987654321

FIRST EDITION

TITLE PAGE IMAGE: Anwar Hussein/WireImage
Book design by Simon M. Sullivan

To Brian Doyle and memories of 1976:
the Rover behind the shop,
Captain Fantastic . . . on a stolen tape,
burns on the dashboard,
fires to light

CONTENTS

Prologue   xi

1   **A Long, Long Time**   3

2   **Elton John Has Arrived**   19

3   **Reborn on the West Coast**   37

4   **A Well-Known Gun**   49

5   **Hope You Don't Mind**   63

6   **Hercules**   81

7   **No Superman Gonna Ruin My Plans**   101

8   **All Aboard the Starship**   119

9   **High in the Snowy Mountains**   135

10   **From the End of the World to Your Town**   149

11   **Drift of the Fantastic Voyage**   169

12   **Burning Out His Fuse**   179

13   **An Audience with the King**   197

14   **Floating into Space**   217

15 **Super Czar**   231

16 **Quack!**   247

Epilogue   259

Acknowledgments   269

Discography   271

Bibliography   279

Photo Credits   281

Index   283

PROLOGUE

IF YOU WERE TO TAKE a peek at random entries in his diary, 1969 seemed to have been a fairly humdrum year for Reg Dwight. A moon-faced twenty-one-year-old, going on twenty-two, from the northwest London suburb of Pinner, he cut a vaguely Beatleish figure in his bowl haircut and Lennon-inspired "penny round" glasses. His pleasures were simple: getting up early on Sunday mornings to play soccer; reading his collections of magazines on World War II and the Old Master painters; going to the cinema and returning home to jot down his thoughts on the films he'd seen.

> *January 17, Sunday: Saw:— "Lady In Cement"—good, "Secret Life of An American Wife"—lousy.*

Music, however, was his obsession. Reg's poky bedroom in the small flat at 30A Frome Court, Pinner Road, where he lived with his mother, Sheila, and stepfather, Fred, was a virtual record library—approximately fourteen hundred singles, three hundred LPs, and one hundred EPs, which he lovingly played and cleaned and cataloged. There was an expression for people like him, who were utterly entranced by the sounds magically emanating from revolving black plastic discs: "It's called vinyl in the blood," he'd proudly state. His mum laughed and called him an old hoarder. Reg wouldn't ever let anyone borrow any of his records, for fear of them being scratched. He would get annoyed if anyone else even touched them.

To feed his obsession, he helped out, unpaid, at Musicland, a large record shop on the corner of Berwick and Noel streets in Soho, the seedy and thrillingly boho heart of London. Reg would drop in, have a cup of tea, then get behind the counter. Often he'd wait there until late in the evening for the deliveries to come in, especially the American imports. In October '68, he'd hung around for hours to get his hands on a copy of Jimi Hendrix's head-spinning double LP *Electric Ladyland*. In April of that year, he stayed on until nine o'clock at night in eager anticipation of the arrival of Leonard Cohen's stark second album, *Songs from a Room*.

There was a fetishistic element to Reg's record collecting. He much preferred the thicker American cardboard covers to the flimsier British ones. He'd been delighted to discover that Laura Nyro's wildly eclectic, piano-driven *Eli and the Thirteenth Confession* came with a lyric sheet perfumed with scented ink. He'd admit to anyone that when he was a solitary child, records had been his friends, and so they remained.

Sometimes, the outside world wasn't so friendly. In a violent disruption of his unremarkable everyday existence, one night, returning to Pinner from Soho, diffident, bespectacled Reg had been beaten up.

April 12, Saturday: Went into Musicland. Got "duffed up" on the way home. Went straight to bed.

Ten days later, perhaps not coincidentally, he became the proud owner of a boxy vehicle, which would ferry him around in comparative safety.

April 22, Tuesday: Got home tonight to find that Auntie Win and Mum had bought me a car—Hillman Husky Estate— Superb!!

In reality, Reg's life wasn't as ordinary as it seemed. The year before, he'd begun living a strange, parallel existence as Elton John: his stage name—and increasingly exaggerated persona. Stepping out of the shadows of Bluesology, the band in which for three years he'd been an enthusiastic, if often teeth-grindingly frustrated, member, hammering away in the corner on his Vox Continental organ, he harbored a strong desire—highly unlikely you'd think if you were to take just one look at him—to become a pop star. Sometimes this shy and funny individual would suddenly erupt with excitement at the very thought.

"I'm going to be a star, do you hear me?" he'd loudly declare, with comic drama, as if assuming the role of a brattish character in a hackneyed rags-to-riches Hollywood biopic. "A *star*!"

But stardom was proving agonizingly tough to achieve. He had started off 1969 on a promising high with the release in January of his second single, "Lady Samantha," a ghostly heavy rock ballad centered on a sad, spectral female protagonist wafting supernaturally across the hillsides and spooking the locals, as dreamed up by his lyric-writing partner, eighteen-year-old Bernie Taupin. It had been what was termed a "turntable hit," pulling in an encouraging number of radio plays, before entirely failing to rouse the interest of the record-buying public.

There was an almost schizophrenic nature to the songs that Bernie and Elton had been writing for the past thirteen months as payroll employees of Dick James Music—the former on £10 a week, the latter £15, since he was required to sing and play on their demonstration recordings. Half of these songs were in tune with the post-psychedelic, head-in-the-clouds mood of the times, bearing typical "Wow, man" titles such as "A Dandelion Dies in the Wind" and "Tartan-Colored Lady." The other half were far straighter and more commercial-minded, written with a view to being sold off to chart singers looking for material. These, which the pair invariably viewed as "stinkers," were usually intensely lovelorn: "You'll Be Sorry to See Me Go," "There's Still Time for Me," "When the First Tear Shows."

One song from this latter crop, "I Can't Go on Living Without You," a frothy and upbeat pop soul track in the style of Dusty Springfield, was selected in February as a potential UK entry for the Eurovision Song Contest, that annual pancontinental clash of oom-pah tunes and overwrought ballads. "I Can't Go on Living Without You," in competition with five other songs from British writers, was performed by the diminutive Scottish singing sensation Lulu on BBC1 that month and witnessed by a televisual audience of close to twenty million.

It came in sixth out of six in the ensuing postcard ballot. Even more depressing, the winning entry, the gibberish lovey-dovey anthem "Boom Bang-a-Bang," went on to scoop the Eurovision prize for Britain. For Elton and Bernie, it was a sign that they were paddling in too-shallow waters. They resolved never again to write such pop pap.

Instead, they threw themselves into the making of what was to become the first Elton John album, *Empty Sky*. Recorded in nocturnal downtime sessions at the DJM studio in New Oxford Street, it was a happy time for all involved—plotting and scheming their bright shiny futures in breaks at the Wimpy restaurant along the road, eating dinner after hours at the Golden Egg café, walking through the near-deserted streets at four in the morning to doss down at the flat that producer Steve Brown's father was given as a perk of his job working for the Salvation Army. Reg always slept on the sofa, drifting off with a head filled with amazed wonder at how the tracks were shaping up.

Hearing the playback of the propulsive, faintly trippy title song of *Empty Sky*, eight and a half minutes long, took him aback. To his young ears, it was the greatest thing he'd ever done or possibly even ever heard. But, in truth, from the outside perspective, Reg still seemed to be fumbling to work out exactly who he wanted Elton to be. The songs bore obvious reverberations of the sounds of his vinyl collection back at Frome Court—the loose swing of the Rolling Stones, the wandering flute reveries of Traffic, the rootsy modernist Americana of the Band.

One song, however, the hymnlike "Skyline Pigeon," gently floating along on ornate harpsichord phrasings and churchy organ, stood out from the rest. Its lyric was inspired by the views from a twelfth-century clock tower in Lincolnshire that as a child Bernie would climb to watch the sun slipping below the horizon. It was written from the imagined perspective of a captive bird longing to be turned loose and to soar high and far away. As a pining ballad from a couple of jobbing songwriters who spent half their time chained down penning on-spec middle-of-the-road compositions, it was hard not to read it as a yearning for creative freedom.

Falling into neither of the fashionable musical categories of the time—woozy psychedelia and weighty rock—"Skyline Pigeon" was something else entirely. Perhaps it was a pre-echo of a time to come, a pared-down singer-songwriter approach that just might belong to the decade to follow.

Reg becoming Elton. The first photo session: Hampstead Heath, London, January 22, 1968.

Even if creatively reborn as Elton, in physical reality, Reg was still awkwardly coming to grips with his pop star guise. Shortish at five feet eight inches and prone to dumpiness, he struggled with his weight. His glasses constantly slipped down his snub nose. His stubby fingers looked nothing like those that might belong to a piano player.

The January before, he'd been photographed for the first time as Elton, looking like a bank clerk who'd experienced a drunken epiphany of sixties liberation before sweeping down Carnaby Street to randomly buy clothes for a "far out" makeover. A leopard print fedora. A flamboyant fur coat with a ludicrously hairy collar that looked as though it might have things living in it. He'd also taken to wearing shirts cut from nursery curtain material featuring popular children's book characters.

Yet remarkably, as 1969 progressed, his celebrity, in sometimes bizarre ways, appeared to be on the rise, as he incredulously noted in his diary:

April 30, Wednesday: Offer to open a carwash in Cricklewood—what!! Stayed in tonight. My glasses broke.

To promote "Lady Samantha," he'd been interviewed by the UK teen magazine *Jackie*. "I always wanted to be famous," he confessed, even though he wasn't really.

"He says he can be unbearably moody and self-pitying," revealed the uncredited *Jackie* writer, "but usually manages to laugh himself out of it."

Those around him knew this to be true. His black moods would suddenly descend, but they would blow away just as quickly. It wasn't hard for him to cheer himself up. Simple pleasures once again.

At the yearly Pinner Fair in the last week of May 1969, Reg amused himself at the various "roll-up roll-up" stalls. At one, where the challenge was to throw Ping-Pong balls into jam jars, ever competitive, he quickly succeeded twice, his prize being two unlucky piscine creatures cruelly forced to swim around in small transparent plastic bags of water.

May 28, Wednesday: Went to the fair with Mick and Pat: I won a coconut and two goldfish!!—John and Yoko!!

The next day, John and Yoko died. *"Very upset!!"* scribbled Reg. A week later, *Empty Sky* was released. It struggled to sell four thousand copies before, for now, disappearing completely.

EXACTLY FIVE AND a half years after that day at Pinner Fair—November 28, 1974—a limousine was gliding through the streets of Manhattan. Inside, heading for Madison Square Garden, were the now legally named Elton Hercules John and John Lennon. The latter was almost paralyzed by fear at the prospect of his first appearance onstage in more than two years. The mood in the car was heavy and silent, as if its passengers were traveling to a funeral rather than a sold-out gig.

John and Elton had first met the previous year, in October 1973, during what was to become known as Lennon's "Lost Weekend" in Los Angeles. Separated from Yoko Ono, he'd enjoyed a second adolescence—or perhaps suffered a premature midlife crisis—in the romantic company of the Lennons' personal assistant, May Pang, while getting out of his mind with the dangerously spirited likes of Keith Moon and Harry Nilsson.

Elton had been a brief visitor to the deranged sessions for Lennon's *Rock'n'Roll* album, where the band members were worryingly loaded on vodka and cocaine while producer Phil Spector, his temples throbbing from heavy amyl nitrate use, had grown frighteningly out of control. Elton had quickly left, realizing the scene was a "hairy" one. The recording of the album would later collapse after Spector terrified everyone by firing a bullet into the studio ceiling.

In these past few months of 1974, in New York, John and Elton had become collaborators and drug buddies: recording the former's latest single, "Whatever Gets You thru the Night," at the Record Plant on West Forty-Fourth Street and spending hours holed up in a suite at the Sherry-Netherland hotel on Fifth Avenue snorting cocaine, laughing their asses off, trading surreal wisecracks, and indulging in bitchy gossip about anyone and everyone.

At the same time, the pair were suffering the notorious paranoia-inducing side effects of the stimulant. One evening, there was a knock at the door. In his wired state, it felt to Elton as if it took him ten minutes to pad his way over to it and put his eye to the peephole.

"It's Andy Warhol!" he whispered to John in disbelief.

Lennon began waving his arms wildly. "Fuck off!" he exclaimed, though under his breath. "Don't let him in!"

Their paranoia was later ramped skyward when a group of cops arrived at the hotel suite and warned Elton about an anonymous call they'd received from a crazy person saying that he had a gun, he was in the hotel, and he was hunting for him. They warned the star to be super-vigilant. This utterly shook both John and Elton, but Lennon in particular, since he was preparing in less than two weeks to make such a high-profile public appearance at the Madison Square Garden show.

The reason Lennon was putting himself through such agony was because of a wager. At the session for the maddeningly catchy and dance-floor-ready "Whatever Gets You thru the Night," where Elton had contributed harmony vocals and thumping, funky piano to complement the ex-Beatle's lead vocal and guitar, he'd bet John that the record would be Lennon's first solo American number one. To Lennon, whose last big single had been "Imagine," in '71, which itself had reached only number three, it seemed like a remote possibility. Elton had made John promise that if he was proved right, John would appear with him onstage to perform the song. When the record reached the U.S. top spot on November 16, Lennon was forced to honor the deal.

To prepare himself, eight days ahead of the gig, Lennon and May Pang flew up the coast to check out Elton's show at Boston Garden, where to his ears the fevered cries of the fans sounded like an echo of Beatlemania. Having grown ever more cartoonish and outrageous in his stagewear, Elton had appeared onstage in a jumpsuit covered in multihued feathers that made him look like a chicken repeatedly plunged into pots of rainbow-colored paints. Topping it for his encore, he'd come out wearing a bikini adorned with an enormous heart, which, he fancied, made him look like an outsized chocolate box.

"Ah, so this is what it's fucking like nowadays," John said afterward, grinning.

Come the night of the Madison Square Garden show on Thanksgiving Day, sitting tensely in the limo, Lennon was forced to face the fact that his stage fright had grown acute in recent years, owing to his lack of regular live performance. He'd been vomiting most of the previous night and unable to sleep, following a failed attempt to numb his nervousness with cocaine and champagne.

As Elton and the band took to the stage, out front no one in the audience had a clue that Lennon was about to appear. No one, that was, except for Yoko Ono, sitting in a seat she'd requested where she couldn't be seen from the stage. Ono had sent good luck cards and a single white gardenia each to John and Elton backstage. Lennon affixed his to the lapel of his black suit jacket, before he was forced to once again throw his guts up through sheer terror. He didn't know that his estranged wife was in the crowd. He was relieved to think that she wasn't coming to the show.

"Otherwise I know I'd never be able to go out there," he admitted.

Eleven songs in, Elton, sitting at his glittering grand piano and daringly resplendent in tight white trousers striped in lime gold and mauve, affixed with suspenders pulled up over his surprisingly toned and hirsute chest, turned to the crowd. "Seeing as it's Thanksgiving," he began, his voice audibly shaky, "we thought we'd make tonight a little bit of a joyous occasion by inviting someone up with us onto the stage. And, uh, I'm sure he will be no stranger to anybody in the audience when I say, it's our great privilege and *your* great privilege to see and hear . . . Mr. John Lennon!"

In the wings, Lennon clung to Bernie Taupin, pleading with him, "You gotta come on with me." Then, addressing the roadies, friends, and hangers-on standing around him, John suddenly seemed resigned to his fate, as if he was a petrified World War I foot soldier readying himself to clamber up a trench ladder to face a storm of bullets. "Oh well," he cried, "here we go, over the hill."

The roaring response from the crowd as Lennon stepped onto the stage was instantly deafening. The walls of the Garden seemed to shudder with the volume of the squealing, cheering, hooting, and stomping. The PA system hanging from the ceiling swung hazardously. There followed an ovation, which took almost ten minutes to die down before the musicians could launch into the rattling introduction of "Whatever Gets You thru the Night."

Next, Elton introduced "one of the best songs ever written," "Lucy in the Sky with Diamonds," a faithful rendition of which, save for the addition of a reggae skank to its third chorus, was his current single. During the number, Lennon's tension showed and his voice sounded raw and constricted when Elton eased back from the microphone to allow him to take the spotlight in the later choruses. At the song's conclusion, John spoke to the audience for the first time.

"Ah . . . I'd like to thank Elton and the boys for having me on tonight," he said. "We've been trying to think of a number to finish with so as I could get out of here and be sick . . . and we thought we'd do a number of an old estranged fiancé of mine called Paul. This is one I never sang. It's an old Beatle number and we *just* about know it."

John and Elton and the band proceeded to thunder their way through "I Saw Her Standing There," track one on the first Beatles album, *Please Please Me,* released eleven years before. Back playing his beloved rock'n'roll, Lennon's performing spirit was reawakened. As he departed the stage, no one could know that it was for the very last time.

Elton and John Lennon (in his final live performance), Madison Square Garden, New York, Thanksgiving Day 1974.

From her vantage point in the crowd, Yoko had felt that her husband looked lonely up there. Too many bows, taken too quickly. Afterward Lennon felt guilty that he hadn't been as moved by the experience as those around him were. But as soon as Yoko stepped into the backstage area, as John later admitted, he felt his strong emotions for her stir once again. Two months later, the couple got back together, and Yoko immediately became pregnant. Elton was later asked to be godfather to their son, Sean.

Reg Dwight's goldfish were long dead and gone. But—

unimaginable five and a half years previously—Elton John, the coked-up, bikini-wearing superstar, had played a pivotal role in re-uniting the actual John and Yoko.

"How WEIRD IS that?" Elton marvels, his eyes widening behind sea-blue lenses as he casts his mind back down the decades. "I mean, who would've known?"

It was one of many highly surreal moments that typified his 1970s. "John was a force of nature," he states. "A *fucking great force of nature.*"

Four decades later Elton is sitting in the narrow dining room at the back of his townhouse in Holland Park, west London. On the walls surrounding him are a gallery's worth of modern art originals, including a framed white rosette by Tracey Emin bearing the pro-vocative legend "Action Cunt" and a thirteen-foot photographic print by Sam Taylor-Wood titled "Wrecked," a re-creation of Leon-ardo da Vinci's *The Last Supper* with the central figure of Christ replaced by a bare-breasted woman.

Enthusiasm pours out of him as he remembers the giddy highs of the first decade of his orbiting fame. He talks assuredly and fast fast fast, his words crashing into one another in their rush to escape his mouth. His voice is deep and rounded, bordering on basso pro-fundo. He is a prolific and enthusiastic swearer: No one says "fuck" with quite as much gusto. He is in decent shape, given the excesses of his past, the only apparent hangover being an unsettling gasp for air when he's at his most effusive.

Having spent the 1960s as an unfulfilled earthbound observer, in the 1970s, Elton achieved vertical takeoff. Once his delayed launch had taken place, from 1970 to '76, he was unstoppable, scoring seven consecutive number one albums in America, along with four-teen Top Ten singles.

It was a dizzying and unpredictable trip, which found him hang-ing out with old Hollywood royalty, traveling on his private jet the *Starship,* and becoming ever more extroverted as he increasingly relied upon cocaine to fuel his fantastic voyage. His 1970s story includes encounters and friendships with a supporting cast of characters such as Elvis Presley, Bob Dylan, Stevie Wonder, Mae West, Groucho Marx, Katharine Hepburn, and Princess Margaret.

"Fucking hell," he astonishedly notes at one point, "you could write books and books and books about it."

The series of interviews I conducted with Elton that are featured in *Captain Fantastic* were originally commissioned by Britain's biggest-selling rock magazine, *Mojo,* to take a retrospective look at the heady era that was his 1970s. Most of these conversations, rich in details and anecdotes, were never published, owing to page constraints. When I realized that I had to exclude so much great material from my articles—and that even Elton's story of meeting Elvis in 1976 (when both were suffering declines in differing ways) would have to go untold for the time being—the idea for this book was born.

To me, there were major aspects of Elton's life and career in the 1970s that had been subsequently eclipsed by his mainstream celebrity status. Not least that it has been generally forgotten that Elton was both as cool and as musically influential in that decade as David Bowie, Pink Floyd, Led Zeppelin, or the Rolling Stones—none of whom sold as many albums as he did during the seventies.

Much of his musical genre hopping during that decade can be credited to his wide-ranging and eclectic listening tastes. The mind of the music obsessive he remains to this day still boggles when he talks about the 1960s and '70s cultural big bang that he witnessed and then became a major part of.

"From the early sixties to the mid-seventies," he enthuses, "it was an explosion of incredible creativity that I don't think there's been in music, in art, in theater, in cinema, whatever. In those fifteen years, music just changed completely. There were ten or twelve albums a week that you could buy. You were listening to everything. You were listening to Ravi Shankar, you were listening to *Hot Rats* by Frank Zappa, you were listening to *Astral Weeks* by Van Morrison, you were listening to the Band, to Leon Russell, to the Grateful Dead, to Jefferson Airplane. It was fucking *astonishing*. It was like having a fucking injection of great drugs every two or three minutes with the music that was going on."

Having spent those nascent years lost in music in his bedroom at

Frome Court, when Reg became Elton and a star, in the United States he went on a determined pilgrimage to the various recording studio and concert hall locations of the music that had fired his imagination.

"One of the first things I did when I went to America was to go to Memphis and kiss the eight-track machine at Stax Records," he remembers. "I did my visit to Motown. I did my visit to the Apollo. I went to the shrines of where music had come from. Music for me is just as exciting, but there'll never be an exciting time like that again. 'Cause I was young and it was all happening. I was lucky to be born at that time."

WHEN YOU TALK to Elton, Reg is never far away.

Elton's success in the 1970s came at a time when many musicians were changing their birth names to something more starlike. But for some, including him, it proved far harder to change their personality.

"I didn't get any confidence until I started performing onstage and let that buried half of me come out," he confesses. "The timid boy that I was, I continued to be offstage. I was comfortable on the stage but not very comfortable off of it. Although I was having a ball, you're still stuck with the insecure, nervous person inside. Being successful doesn't cure it. In fact, it makes things a little worse because then the difference between your stage persona and your actual, normal persona is so far removed."

If he can rattle on and on with enormous enthusiasm about music, one to one, Elton still seems to find general small talk harder. This lingering shyness appears to be evidence that inside, he is still very much Reginald Kenneth Dwight, who never stopped being a reticent, slightly wary individual, despite having utterly transformed himself. "I thought I was getting rid of that shy boy," he states. "But you know what? You're still stuck with that shy boy. You're still stuck with the same shit inside of you."

This extraordinary metamorphosis, and the conflict between the dual sides of his personality, Reg versus Elton, were to characterize the star's entire early career. As the true successor to the Beatles in terms of sheer popular phenomenon, he experienced a thrilling but turbulent flight. *Captain Fantastic* traces the skyscraping accomplishments and plummeting lows of Elton's 1970s, from the height of his stacked heels to the depths of his depressions. It is the tale of the bashful kid who turned into a superhero.

"Fuck! My life," he says, revealing that familiar grin, "has been incredible."

Captain Fantastic

Reg (second from left) trying to look cool with the struggling Bluesology, London, July 22, 1965.

1 A LONG, LONG TIME

To fly all this way to California, across the Atlantic from England in a jumbo jet, to the land of freedom, adventure, and rock'n'roll, only to end up on a red bloody London bus. He'd wanted to roar off in a Cadillac or something, instead of trundling toward Hollywood, taking "fucking forever" to get there. He was totally embarrassed, totally pissed off.

He hadn't even wanted to come. It was his music publisher and record label boss, Dick James, who persuaded him to make the trip. Dick was fifty and an old-school music biz figure, with his bald head and business suits and thick-rimmed glasses. He'd made his fortune publishing the songs of the Beatles, so he knew a thing or two.

The problem was that Elton's second album, recorded at great expense and titled simply *Elton John,* had been released in April in Britain and hadn't fared much better than his first, *Empty Sky,* which had tanked. As the pages of the 1970 calendar began to blow away, he was running out of options.

He'd been sorely tempted to take up an offer from Jeff Beck, the swaggering star guitarist who had been kicked out of the Yardbirds in '66 for his repeated no-shows and fizzing tantrums. Since then, the drably named Jeff Beck Group had made two albums that sold well in America, before falling apart in a cloud of petty arguments and ego huffs.

One night in July at the Speakeasy club in London, the rock star hangout just north of Oxford Street, Beck had caught a show by Elton's new three-piece band. Impressed by what he saw, Beck came up with a proposal: Back me and we'll tour the States. Then Elton heard the terms of the deal—for every booking, Beck would take 90 percent of the $10,000 fee. Elton and the band would share just 10 percent.

Nevertheless, he thought, *Wow, a thousand dollars a night. Still sounds like a lot of money.*

Dick James talked him out of it.

"You'll be a bigger star in America than Jeff Beck in a year's time," he insisted.

"I thought, *Oh, Dick, you're so stupid,*" Elton remembers.

Now it was August and he'd touched down in Los Angeles, thrilled to his fingertips to actually be in America. Exiting the airport, he'd been greeted by the sight of the double-decker parked outside. His face fell and it quickly had to be explained to him by Norman Winter, his new U.S. publicist, that the bus was a surprise stunt he'd planned for him. It would carry Elton and the band into L.A. and fanfare his arrival in style.

A screaming message in huge white letters on a black banner ran almost the entire length of it: ELTON JOHN HAS ARRIVED.

Dutifully, Elton had stepped onto the rear platform of the open-backed London bus. It really didn't feel as though he'd "arrived." But if he had, it had taken him a long, long time.

THE VERY FIRST thing Reg could remember was sitting at the piano.

In his blurry memory, his gran Ivy lifts him onto her knee and he immediately starts banging the keys. In the days that follow, no one can keep him away from the seemingly captivating instrument. One day his infantile pounding somehow gives way to his working out the chords and elegant top line of "The Skater's Waltz."

His mum, Sheila, is flabbergasted. Reg is only three but it quickly becomes apparent that he has quite a gift.

"I just sat down," he remembers, "and I could pick out a tune very easily."

By the time he was four, in 1951, Reg had a mass of bubbly hair, which made him look cherubic and a bit like Shirley Temple. A typical preschooler, he was prone to tantrums, though the piano seemed to be a reliable source of calm for him. If he was kicking and screaming, his father placing him on its stool always cooled his hysteria.

There was music all around the house: from the wireless, from the cabinet-sized, varnished-wood-encased radiogram (part radio, part gramophone) on which Sheila and his dad, Stanley, would play their records. Stanley, who'd performed as a trumpeter in a dance-hall band called the Millermen, favored the cool piano jazz of George Shearing, the dreamy percussive melodies of Charlie Kunz. Sheila preferred the pop sounds of the early fifties: Johnnie Ray, Rosemary Clooney, Frankie Laine. Reg's favorite musician quickly became Winifred Atwell, the Caribbean pianist who could play anything from classical to honky-tonk. He was fascinated by how Atwell wasn't the least bit snooty when it came to her musical tastes. He'd excitedly listen to her finishing a piece on a concert grand and saying, "And now I'm going across to my other piano," which turned out to be a battered old upright bought from a junk shop.

By age six, Reg had developed quite a repertoire and was fast becoming the center of the entertainment. If Stanley and Sheila had friends coming over in the evening, they would put him to bed during the day for an afternoon nap so that he could stay up later and play piano for them all. He'd transpose the proto rock'n'roll of the Super-Sonics' "New Guitar Boogie Shuffle" and its B side, "The Sheik of Araby," into jaunty piano tunes. Then he'd slow the tempo into "Butterflies" by Patti Page, or "Wish You Were Here" by Eddie Fisher, before maybe picking the pace back up with Jo Stafford's "Diamonds Are a Girl's Best Friend."

But apart from all of this fun and showing off, there was unease at home. Reg never felt real love from his father.

Stanley had been a flight lieutenant in the Royal Air Force in the latter years of World War II, promoted to squadron leader in 1953. As a result, he was away from home for extended periods of time. Reg would dread his returning for the weekends. His dad seemed snobbish and stiff. He'd tell the boy off for kicking a ball around the garden, fearing he'd damage the plants. He wouldn't allow him to eat celery because the crunching irritated him. Reg grew up feeling suppressed by him and ultimately afraid of him.

Stanley and Sheila had met through the RAF, where she was

working as an office clerk. But even when Reg was still very young, their marital bond was already beginning to fray. Worse, their disputes seemed to be having a destabilizing effect on him. His mother described him as a bag of nerves.

"A bag of nerves?" he echoes. "Yeah, I was on tenterhooks as a child. Maybe because when your parents don't get on, you're always worried there's gonna be a row. So it drove me towards music even more. Sitting in your room listening to the radio. Looking at your records, *studying* them. Looking at the little numbers, writing them down, who wrote the B side. It was like having a university course in music. I was fascinated by watching records go round the turntable. I remember twelve-inch seventy-eights which classical music used to be on. You could break records in those days. It was a *tragedy* when you broke a record."

Looking to develop her son's natural talent, Sheila found a private piano tutor for Reg when he was seven. Mrs. Jones would teach him classical pieces and encourage him to practice for three hours each day. For the most part, he hated the passages he was forced to learn. He loathed the sad and dissonant night music of Bartók, though he found himself falling for the prettier melodies of Bach and Chopin.

That year, he gave his first public performance, of sorts, at the wedding of his soccer-player cousin Roy Dwight. The band booked to play at the reception turned up late, and to fill in, Reg sat at the piano and entertained the guests until the adult musicians arrived. There was a British law at the time forbidding anyone to play for a paying audience until the age of thirteen. It was a pity, really, thought Sheila, because otherwise Reg would quite likely be hailed as a child prodigy.

All the while, his father remained a remote and forbidding figure. Still, it seems that in some ways, Stanley tried to connect with his music-obsessed only son. For Reg's ninth birthday, his dad bought him a copy of Frank Sinatra's *Songs for Swingin' Lovers!* The boy wasn't exactly won over by this gift, however, indicating that the difficulties in the father-son relationship now cut both ways. Later, the tough-to-please Reg would moan that what he'd really wanted was a bike.

Pop music had dramatically moved on by the mid-fifties, and replacing the jazz standards and crooning balladeers was the souped-up sound of rock'n'roll. Shifting with the trends, in 1956, a year after it had been number one in Britain, Sheila brought home "Shake, Rattle and Roll" by Bill Haley and His Comets. As much as Reg loved it, he preferred its flip side, "A.B.C. Boogie," and another disc his mother had bought, the stark and eerily mournful "Heartbreak Hotel" by Elvis Presley. The same week he first heard these records, he was at a barbershop, waiting to have his hair cut and flicking through a copy of *Life* magazine, when he saw a photograph of the quiffed and impossibly cool Presley.

Now aged ten and beginning to buy records for himself, Reg was more compelled by the edgier, electrifying 45s of Little Richard and Jerry Lee Lewis, both wild-eyed and savage piano players with buzz-shocked hair. His mother found these sounds far too raucous and headache-inducing, and so Reg was forced to play the discs in his bedroom, miming in the mirror, a suburban preteen whose overfed reflection mock-singing back at him looked nothing like his skinny and snake-hipped idols.

Alone in his room, he'd stare at his records for hours. Most of the label designs were dark and dull, so he was drawn to the more colorful ones: the orange background and golden stars of Polydor, the yellows and blacks and bewildered-looking lion of MGM, the RCA Victor logo of a dog staring curiously into the horn of a gramophone as he whirled around the turntable.

But Sheila was worried that Reg seemed a self-absorbed and lonely child. Later, he'd admit that he'd longed for brothers and sisters and claim that his father was against the idea. To Sheila, the young Reg was a "terribly sad person. I used to sit there crying my eyes out when he was a child."

IT WAS MUSIC that rescued him. Turning eleven, Reg moved up to Pinner County Grammar School, a bustling high school facility housed in an Art Deco–style building where he had access to a proper Steinway piano and was invited by his music teacher to audition for a part-time scholarship at the Royal Academy of Music, the esteemed London conservatory founded more than a century before. Almost effortlessly sailing through the test, he was assigned to classes at the Academy in Marylebone, near Regent's Park, every Saturday morning.

There his music teacher, Helen Piena, was astonished when she performed a four-page Handel sonata for Reg and he played it back to her, note for note, having instantly memorized the piece. When it came to music, his mind was like a tape recorder. Yet soon it became clear that he really had no interest in sight-reading pages of musical notation. His talent was for playing by ear. He would learn the passages he was given to play, mentally dissecting their structures, before disobediently improvising his own embellishments to the melodies, already a songwriter in his soul.

At home, he played the piano for hours, until forced to stop by his parents or when the complaints from the neighbors became impossible to ignore. But as he grew older, a rebellious streak began to surface. Later he would boast that he'd regularly skip the classes at the Royal Academy and sit on a Circle Line subway train, looping around and around London, before coming back on the Metropolitan Line to the Northwood Hills station closest to home. In truth, if he had been a chronic truant, he'd have been thrown out of the Academy. Instead, lacking the discipline to learn the musical theory required to become a concert pianist, he remained just above average among the other precocious young musicians.

Rock'n'roll had dizzied his schoolboy head, and even as a tubby kid in short trousers and too-tight blazer, he would wow his fellow students at Pinner County Grammar by pumping out "Great Balls of Fire" on the Steinway. Having seen Buddy Holly perform in concert, he began wearing glasses in imitation of him in an effort to look hep. After eighteen months of wearing them constantly, he realized he couldn't see without them.

Stanley Dwight, meanwhile, really wasn't happy about the musical direction in which his son was heading. Reg was baffled by his vehement response—after all, Stanley had been a part-time musician himself; he should understand. Sent to an RAF post two hundred miles north of Pinner, where notably Reg and Sheila didn't follow him, he would pen stern and angry missives back to his wife warning her to tame the apparently gone-feral youth. "Reggie must give up this idea of becoming a pop musician," he wrote in one letter. "He's turning into a wild boy."

During Stanley's protracted absence, Sheila fell for an amiable and laid-back local painter and decorator, Fred Farebrother, whose name Reg, with his absurdist sense of humor (inspired by BBC Radio's surrealist comedy troupe the Goons), reversed, calling him Derf.

In the otherwise terrible winter of 1962 in England, remembered for years to come as the Big Freeze, Stanley and Sheila divorced, and at fifteen, Reg was free to be whoever he wanted to be.

IF IN 1963 you found yourself in Northwood, on the northwest edge of London, on a weekend evening and thirsty for some alcoholic refreshment, you may well have wandered into the large, detached Northwood Hills pub opposite the tube station. Inside, if you were brave enough to venture through the slightly more genteel saloon to the public bar, the domain of the more committed drinker, you would have discovered that it was packed. More so, a local could have told you, than it had been for a long time.

The reason would have become quickly apparent. At an upright piano positioned near the window, sporting a ginger-toned Harris Tweed sports jacket, his hair short and neat, you would see "Reggie," the Northwood Hills's resident piano player. He would be knocking out pretty standard pub song fare: rowdy wartime sing-along "Roll out the Barrel," music hall throwbacks like "My Old Man (Said Follow the Van)," maybe "When Irish Eyes Are Smiling" for the more boozily nostalgic or maudlin.

Then suddenly, amid the seething crowd, a pint accidentally spilled would lead to an angry word, which would lead to a punch thrown. "When there were fights, there were *fights*," Elton recalls. "So when I was singing, if there was a fight that did break out, I was out the window. Even though I was shit-scared, I knew I could jump out the window, wait for it all to calm down, and then get back as soon as possible. 'Cause music helps to sort these situations. At sixteen years of age and being quite insecure, it gave me an inner steel."

It also gave him an opportunity to extend his range. Often, between the crowd-pleasing tunes, he'd slip in something current, like Bruce Channel's recent number one, the howling "Hey Baby," or turn in something soulful, like Ray Charles's yearning "I Can't Stop Loving You."

Fred, or Derf, now introduced by Reg to everyone as his stepfather, attended these pub performances every weekend, his encouragement of the teenager's musical aspirations drawing them closer. Reg earned only a pound a night from the gig, but at the end of each set, Fred passed through the drinkers, pushing a money box under their noses and asking for tips for the young pianist. And so, nightly, Reg earned north of a tenner, sometimes totting up thirty-five quid a week (the equivalent of almost $400 today), at a time when the average weekly wage was only £12. "That paid for my amplifier and my electric piano," he remembers, "and gave me the experience of dealing on a solo basis."

He'd already been in a group, of a kind. Hanging out at the youth club in his local church hall back when he was thirteen and fourteen, he began to encounter like-minded sorts including Stu Brown, his cousin's boyfriend, who fancied himself a guitarist and singer.

Reg told Stu he was a piano player. Stu instantly erupted in cruel laughter, since rotund Reg looked far from the picture of a rock'n'roller. Hurt and annoyed, but determined to prove himself, Reg took to the keys and began to mimic Jerry Lee Lewis with surprising intensity and passion. Brown was instantly silenced, and together the pair began to hatch a plan to form a band.

Dumbfounding everyone, at the first gig played in the church hall by the freshly named Corvettes, Reg did his full Jerry Lee, aggressively heeling away the piano stool midnumber and standing up to play. The shocked reaction this provoked among the audience quietly thrilled and astonished him. From then on, kicking the piano stool away would become his signature onstage trick.

As TEENAGE BANDS often do, the Corvettes fell apart within a year and a half, owing to a lack of gigs, shoddy amplification, and a procession of woefully out-of-tune church hall pianos. Having experienced the highs of being part of a group, Reg was back playing alone at the Northwood Hills.

Within the year, though, he bumped back into Stu Brown, who—along with the Corvettes' bassist, Geoff Dyson—had deepened his knowledge of the blues, at the time acutely in vogue. Stu suggested to Reg that he come play with them. Armed with his recently bought Hohner Pianet electric piano and an amp to ensure he would be heard on a level way above a decrepit church hall piano, Reg joined his first proper band, completed by drummer Mick Inkpen. Cribbing and bastardizing their name from jazz guitarist Django Reinhardt's 1949 album *Djangology*, the quartet became Bluesology.

More in tune stylistically with the painfully hip rhythm and blues of UK singer Georgie Fame than the scream pop of the Beatles, Bluesology added brass to their lineup and, as time passed, bagged regular gigs at local pubs and then a host of cool clubs in Soho. A purist R&B and soul band, they would knock out numbers by Jimmy Witherspoon, and later Eddie Floyd and Otis Redding.

Reg switched from his Hohner Pianet to the more R&B-friendly Vox Continental organ. But he knew he was a fairly bad organist and, worse, the instrument kept breaking down. Often he felt like a fraud: weighing nearly two hundred pounds and stuck stage left behind his keyboard when all he wanted to do was be the lead singer—a role for the most part taken (aside from the odd Reg-sung number) by the taller, slimmer, more traditionally frontman-like Stu Brown. Soul and blues were all very well, but in his heart Reg still loved the manic charge of rock'n'roll.

He'd recently gone to see the Beatles perform live at London's Hammersmith Odeon and it had proved an intoxicating experience, witnessing the emotionally heightened scenes both outside and inside the venue. "Seeing the Beatles was kind of like seeing God in a way," he laughs. "Just actually seeing them live and being in their presence. Police in the street. It was just chaos everywhere they went. That was the exciting thing about it, just to have a glimpse at the moment. Being in an audience that frenzied. You couldn't hear anything for the noise."

Sick of school and more than ever dedicated to pop music, in 1964, Reg quit Pinner County Grammar School only two weeks before he was due to take his crucially important A-level exams. Longing to be in the eye of the capital's music scene, he managed to land himself a job as a mailroom clerk, delivery boy, and general dogsbody at Mills Music, a sheet music publisher on Denmark Street. He soon became a well-known face in the area, dashing up and down the parade of instrument shops and recording studios that was at the time London's equivalent of Tin Pan Alley.

It was here that he first encountered Caleb Quaye, an aspiring guitarist similarly working as a runner for Paxton's Music in Old Compton Street. The two immediately hit it off, though Caleb constantly ribbed Reg, nicknaming him Billy Bunter and telling him that he thought Bluesology's band name was pretentious. Like most, he couldn't imagine how this plump, myopic teenager, however funny and likable, could ever set foot on a stage.

But even if outwardly tentative, Reg was made of sturdy stuff. In the spring of 1965, Bluesology played a gig at the Elms Club in the northwestern London suburb of South Harrow, where they found themselves facing a crowd of hostile, greasy-haired bikers. Sneering at the band's soulful R&B, most of the rabble retreated to the back of the hall. Some of them then began angrily revving their motorcycles at the entrance, as if readying themselves to ride into the venue. Others threatened to smash the place up if Bluesology didn't play rock'n'roll. The shaken band plowed on regardless, though Reg was sorely tempted to launch into his beloved Jerry Lee Lewis or Little Richard numbers.

Bluesology were growing in confidence, and in July '65, they notched it up a gear. First, they released their debut single, having landed a deal with Fontana Records to put out an original song, "Come Back Baby," written—and, more significantly, sung—by Reg. The band sounded shaky and amateurish on vinyl, performing this loungy bossa nova with a generic lyric written from the perspective of a jilted, pining lover, although the song's ornate structural twists nonetheless revealed its writer's deft ways with an arrangement.

It was to prove a flop. But not before Reg heard himself on the airwaves for the first time. Driving in his car, he happened to catch a DJ on Radio Luxembourg give "Come Back Baby" a spin. "Hey, that's me singing, folks!" he exclaimed aloud. In a shrewd move, Reg had also managed to sell the song to his bosses at Mills Music for £500 ($5,500 today).

Then Bluesology landed a second lucky break. On July 22, they entered a Battle of the Bands competition at the Gaumont State cinema in Kilburn, north London. After performing, and while waiting for the results, they were approached by an impressed booking agent, Roy Tempest, who asked them if they'd consider backing U.S. soul artists on British tours. They immediately agreed, but were quickly deflated in the weeks afterward when the musical director for Wilson Pickett—just about to release his signature hit "In the Midnight Hour"—wasn't similarly impressed by their playing.

It was to prove a minor setback, however, and Tempest soon had Bluesology on the road, slogging away backing various American acts. The Chicago soul singer Major Lance was so taken by how meticulously the band parroted his songs that he found he didn't have to change a note. The hulking Washington, D.C., crooner Billy Stewart was a fine touring partner, although the band would often have to stop on the M1 motorway while he leisurely and copiously urinated like a racehorse. Georgie Fame, at the time riding high with a run of R&B chart hits, had recently covered Stewart's hit "Sitting in the Park." One night at the Ricky-Tick in Windsor, Reg watched, astounded, as the American soul man dealt with an infuriating heckler.

"Someone said, 'We want Georgie Fame!'" he remembers. "He fucking jumped off the stage and chased him. I thought, Fuck, you're a brave man shouting at Billy Stewart. He was *huge*. He must have been twenty-four stone"—more than three hundred pounds.

Meanwhile, Patti LaBelle and the Blue Belles provided a different sort of education—part musical, since the singer (who'd endured a hard-knocks upbringing in Philadelphia) was a tough taskmistress, and part social, when it came to the ways of the road. LaBelle often invited Bluesology to play cards with her and used her gambling wiles to win back their wages from them. Sometimes, overcome with guilt, she would take them back to the girls' rented flat and cook dinner for them.

Reg was quickly disillusioned by his time backing "Patti LaBelle and her Blue Bellies," as they were billed one night, finding himself playing dreary standards such as "Danny Boy" and "Somewhere over the Rainbow." It was a taste of a life as a cabaret musician, a life he was to come to despise.

Other bookings only served to show him how quickly musical stars could fall. Supporting the Ink Spots, who'd managed to carve out a fine career as a doo-wop group in the fifties, he'd watch younger audiences grow bored and wander off when they played their old hits.

Day by day, night after night, it amounted to a demanding, seemingly endless trek, even for a band with the boundless energy of teenagers. One long shift might find them schlepping between three bookings, from the Cavendish in Sheffield to Tito's in Stockton to the Latino in South Shields. Or they'd play a trio of gigs in different London clubs in the same evening: the Ready Steady Go to the All Star to the Flamingo. Another night, in Manchester, it would be the Oasis to the Twisted Wheel and then back to the Oasis for a late-night slot. Show after show after show with the latest American soul act arriving in the country—Arthur Alexander or the Exciters or Solomon Burke or Doris Troy.

Next it was off to Hamburg, shadowing the steps of the pre-fame Beatles, living in shabby rooms above seamy venues and playing nightly sets where Reg would sing rude words to his songs for any unsuspecting non-English-speaking Germans. And then to St. Tropez and the Papagayo Club, where Brigitte Bardot had been known to shimmy tantalizingly in a short dress on the dance floor and where Reg gave himself an electric shock with his faulty equipment, requiring a sedative shot in the ass from a doctor as the other band members stood around his bed.

Still, ever the record obsessive, his mind was on other, more musical shocks to the system. "I remember playing the Papagayo Club with Bluesology when *Revolver* came out and 'Reach Out I'll Be There' by the Four Tops," he says, his memory rewinding back to the hot August of 1966. "I couldn't believe both records were so brilliant. It was like, *Fuck . . . what?*"

By December, still only nineteen years old, Reg was appearing on the same stage as one of his formative heroes, opening with Bluesology for Little Richard at the Saville Theatre in London. Once again, though, the group faced an audience of enraged, blues-hating rockers, who threw motorcycle parts at them during their set while chanting, "Off . . . off . . . off!"

When the headliner took the platform, Reg was astounded to witness his idol at such close proximity, standing like a returning king atop his piano, pulsating with energy, a vision in sequins and light.

He decided right there and then. His mission from now on, however long it might take him, was to become a bedazzling rock'n'roll piano star.

STILL THE NEVER-ENDING road of exhausting gigs as a wage slave stretched out ahead of him. He'd share bills with other bands like the Move from Birmingham and sense their drive and determination and realize that Bluesology lacked these qualities, and were instead held together only by loyalty and a shared need to earn money as they motored, crammed in the back of the van, from one gig to another.

"We'd play in places like Balloch in Scotland," he remembers. "We'd arrive and say, 'Why's the stage ten feet tall?' And they'd say, 'So that the fucking people can't get to the band.' You'd see that there would be two sides to the audience. Everyone would be in two halves and you'd just wait for the fight to break out."

Into this hectic and road-weary scene stepped Long John Baldry. Earning his piratical nickname for his unusual height—six foot seven, almost a foot taller than Reg—Baldry was highly regarded as a singer and leading face of the British blues movement. His most recent venture, fronting the three-vocalist lineup of Steampacket alongside Julie Auger and Rod Stewart, had collapsed when the band had been offered a residency at the Papagayo Club in St. Tropez, and for financial reasons, Stewart had been cut out of the deal and left behind. Down in the south of France, the effervescent one-man party that was Baldry drank himself to a standstill, missing gigs by the second week. In the end, when Steampacket was sacked from the engagement, it was Bluesology who ended up stepping in.

After a subsequent Bluesology show back in London, at the swish

Cromwellian club in South Kensington, where there was gambling upstairs and dancing below, Long John Baldry began sizing them up as his new group. Their prospects at this point were not great: Their second Fontana single, the similarly Reg-fronted "Mr. Frantic," a potboiling R&B tune that in spite of its title sounded oddly listless, had failed to chart. And so they took up the offer to back Baldry, who reshaped them in the image of Steampacket, encouraging Stu Brown to drop his guitar playing to concentrate on vocals and bringing in another tall, blond singer, Alan Walker, to form a three-man front line. This reconfiguration reenergized the group. After the first few gigs, even Reg considered the new lineup to be not a bad little band.

Baldry was great company: a complete hoot, drinking and loudly playing his blues 45s on the record-player system recently installed in their van as they drove from here to there up and down the country. Onstage, eccentric and brandy-fueled, he would sometimes baffle the crowd by stopping a song to tell a joke or berate someone in the audience. He was also openly camp at a time when homosexuality was still illegal in the UK. Utterly naive, Reg didn't even realize Baldry was gay.

Though he was now making a living as a musician, playing the organ sidestage behind three charismatic vocalists, Reg remained quietly frustrated. He wanted to be a lead singer, but he realized that given his pudgy appearance, no one was likely to give him the job.

Maybe he should concentrate on writing songs, he thought. It might be the only way that he was going to get anywhere.

THE AD APPEARED in the June 17, 1967, edition of the *New Musical Express*. Reg was on tour in Newcastle when he picked up a copy and spotted it: "Liberty wants talent. Artistes/Composers, Singers-Musicians to form new group. Call or write Ray Williams for appointment or mail audition tape or disc to 11 Albemarle Street, London W1. Tel: Mayfair 7362."

He secured an appointment with Williams and went into the Liberty Records offices for an audition, nervously parking himself at their upright piano. Perhaps a touch bizarrely, given the fact that he'd already sung on two records with Bluesology, he fell back on his Northwood Hills pub routine, performing a selection of Jim Reeves songs including "He'll Have to Go" and "I Love You Because" and even exuberantly paddling out "Mammy" by Al Jolson.

Williams thought Reg had an unusual and interesting voice, no matter how plain and un-pop-star-like he appeared. Reg, for his part, had zero confidence in his own image. He later remembered that on that day he felt he looked like "a lump of porridge."

A test recording session was booked. Walking through the door of DJM Studio, Reg was met by the sight of Caleb Quaye, his one-time fellow music publisher runner, now a sound engineer, who at first didn't recognize "Billy Bunter" in his longer hair and slightly groovier getup. When he realized who the artist he'd be working with actually was, Quaye burst out laughing. But his merriment was cut short when he heard Reg sing. To Quaye's ears, his almost androgynous vocal tones sounded like Sandie Shaw.

Ray Williams played the recordings to his bosses at Liberty. They were not won over. Breaking the bad news of the rejection to Reg, he suggested an alternative idea.

He said, "Well, I've got all these lyrics on my desk from this guy in Lincolnshire."

"Bernie became the brother I always wanted." Elton and Bernie, the hopeful songwriters.

2 ELTON JOHN HAS ARRIVED

BEFORE THEY EVEN MET, they'd written twenty songs together.

Later they would look back and view the fact that they'd both responded to the Liberty ad as a twist of fate. Especially since Bernie Taupin hadn't himself even managed to mail the letter including examples of his song lyrics. He had got as far as stuffing them into an envelope and addressing it, but then left it on the mantelpiece at the Taupins' farmhouse in the small Lincolnshire village of Owmby by Spital (population: 300) in England's East Midlands. Somehow, the letter had been temporarily lost, tucked behind a clock, and lay there for two weeks before Bernie's mother found it and popped it in the post.

Like Reg, seventeen-year-old Bernie had always been something of a loner. As a boy he loved the poetry his mother and maternal grandfather would read to him. His childhood imagination was flooded by the long, fantastical verses of Coleridge's "The Rime of the Ancient Mariner" and the adventures of the gallant knight Lochinvar in Sir Walter Scott's "Marmion," causing him to charge around the hills surrounding his home wielding a wooden sword.

The Taupins were not a musical family, but Bernie's ears were caught by the sounds of Johnny Cash and Marty Robbins he heard by turning the radio dial to the American Forces Network station. Robbins's country-and-western murder ballad "El Paso" was a formative favorite, with its tale of a jealous cowboy who shoots his love rival in a tussle for the affections of the wicked Feleena. Bernie played Robbins's 1959 album *Gunfighter Ballads and Trail Songs*

until it was worn out. These were not just epic stories, but epic stories set to song.

Inspired by the words of these songs, eleven-year-old Bernie
penned what he fancied was a short book on the history of the
American West, albeit only six or seven pages long, and even sent it
to a London publisher. A representative gently responded with the
words "Dear Mr. Taupin, there's nothing we can do with your book
right now." Encouragingly, though, they added that the youngster
appeared to have a flair for writing and that he should pursue it.

Bernie kept these ambitions to himself and left school at fifteen,
falling into a procession of menial jobs, including working at a
printing press inking leaflets for local fetes and horse shows and laboring on a farm where he was tasked with forking the carcasses of
diseased chickens into an incinerator. All the while, back in the
kitchen at his family's farmhouse, he would *tap tap tap* away, writing poems on an old typewriter.

As 1966 turned to 1967, his verses of juvenilia began to take on
more psychedelic hues, with titles such as "Swan Queen of the
Laughing Lake" and "The Year of the Teddy Bear." Later he was
rightly to regard these as terrible rip-offs of the spaced-out hello-
trees-hello-sky lyrical fashion of the day. Significantly, though, the
week that Bernie spotted the Liberty Records ad in the *New Musical
Express,* the number one single in Britain was Procol Harum's "A
Whiter Shade of Pale," a faux-classical dream song with a lyric by
Keith Reid, a member of the band who wrote their songs' words
but—interestingly—didn't play an instrument.

Thanks to his mother's forcing Bernie's hand by sending the letter
to Liberty, Ray Williams got back in touch. "When you happen to
be in Mayfair," Williams wrote, "pop in and see me."

Of course, farm boy Bernie was never simply passing through
Mayfair. But he took Williams up on his offer and jumped on a train
to travel the hundred fifty miles south to London. Climbing the stairs
to the offices on Albemarle Street that Liberty shared with Gralto, the
company that published the songs of the Hollies, he was thrilled to
pass their singer-guitarist Graham Nash on the stairs, looking impressively with-it in his worn-out tweed jacket and high-waisted jeans.

Williams played matchmaker, giving Bernie's lyrics to Reg, who began to fit these screeds of poetry to music over the following weeks. Having spent years studying pop records, for him, turning words on a page into songs was a breeze. It quickly proved to be a highly productive hookup, which set in place the unusual remote writing approach that was to characterize their partnership.

During moonlighting demo sessions at DJM's makeshift office turned studio, nicknamed the Gaff by everyone who frequented it, Reg would record these collaborations, with Caleb Quaye behind the mixing console. At one session in late July 1967, Bernie turned up, arriving unfashionably early, intimidated by the prospect of meeting Reg and hanging out with these "swinging London" types. In an effort to mask his insecurity and perhaps to fit in, the diminutive lyricist, just short of five feet five, hid his eyes behind trendy sunglasses. One musician he encountered there turned to him and said, "Great shades, man, can I try them on?" Bernie had no idea what he was talking about.

Reg turned up and invited him for a coffee around the corner at the Lancaster Grill on Tottenham Court Road. Bernie was surprised to discover that his songwriting partner was not the deeply cool figure he'd imagined him to be. "He was definitely not Granny Takes a Trip," Bernie laughs, referring to the modish King's Road boutique of the day. "Just *Granny*. I was expecting someone very hip, plugged-in. And sure, he was out there playing in all those great clubs of the time, backing all these wonderful American artists. But he had none of the pretensions or the airs of many of the other people that circulated around at that time.

"I just thought he was a really nice guy," he adds. "He was very, very friendly. A little shy. Very caring, but very awkward. We were *both* very awkward. It very much eased me because I thought, *Oh good, I'm not feeling sort of substandard here*. 'Cause I was pretty green. I was very much a fish out of water."

Reg himself, not yet emboldened by his Elton persona, was typically tentative and hellishly nervous about meeting his co-writer. "I was wondering who would turn up," he says, "what he would be like, whether he would be fucking horrible or would I like him. He was incredibly young. We hit it off straightaway. It was like a kismet thing."

Back in the studio, hearing songs that featured his words actually coming out of the speakers, Bernie was utterly enthralled. He thought to himself, *Wow, this is, like, the real thing.* The first creatively successful product of the collaboration was "Scarecrow," a midpaced and lightly bouncy piano ballad given a skeletal arrangement with badly played shaker and tambourine. Although the lyric was convoluted and largely nonsensical, with clunking lines such as "like moths around a lightbulb, your brain is still bleeding," it was a start.

Encouraged by the work of his new songwriting team, Ray Williams pressed a few copies of "Scarecrow" onto acetate discs with a view to possibly selling the rights to his office neighbors Gralto. Bernie took a copy back to Putney, south London, where he was staying with his aunt and uncle, and proudly played it for them. "That's a memory you can't erase," he enthuses. "I mean, it was so exciting."

Other recordings followed: "Velvet Fountain" with its earnestly delivered opening line "Do you believe in fairies?"; the fanciful full-band treatment of the self-consciously trippy "A Dandelion Dies in the Wind" with its "purple clouds" and "golden rain." Reg and Bernie quickly took up an after-hours residency at the DJM studios while learning their craft and defining their roles. It was clear that Bernie was no musician—Caleb Quaye howled with laughter during one session when the lyricist tried to play a tambourine, wildly out of time, looking as if he was trying to swat a fly. Similarly, Reg, who admitted he had always struggled with having the confidence to express his feelings on the page, was no lyric writer, as proved when he offered up a self-penned song called "The Witches' House": "I go to the witches' house / I go there when I can / Me and Molly Dickinson in my delivery van."

Session by session, they strove onward, secretly recording at the studio without the knowledge of the staff at DJM. Until, fatefully, they were caught. The studio was housed on the first floor of the building at 71-75 New Oxford Street above a branch of the Midland Bank. An arrangement had been put in place where the security guard downstairs at the bank had to be notified if there was to be a nocturnal session in the offices above.

One night, for whatever reason, the message wasn't relayed and the security guard was forced to call and wake up Ronald Brohn, DJM's studio manager, to alert him to the goings-on. Brohn raced over there. Caleb Quaye looked up from the mixing desk to see the enraged Brohn standing in the doorway of the control room. The engineer quickly hid his joint and was loudly bawled out.

The next morning Quaye faced what he would come to refer to as the Great Purge. Dick James and his son and employee Stephen demanded to know what the hell had been happening. Quaye, certain he was about to be sacked, not least since he had been furtively requisitioning checks to pay for rented equipment and session musicians, nervously began to list the names of the artists and bands he had been recording.

"That's it," barked Dick James. "I'm throwing them all out. It's over."

"Well, you can throw them out and you can sack me if you want," Quaye replied. "But I've got these two guys . . . I think you ought to listen to their stuff."

Sweating, Quaye threaded the tape onto a reel-to-reel machine and played a selection of Reg and Bernie's songs. Five or six tunes in, Dick James's mood turned from enraged to intrigued. Never one to miss a potentially rewarding business opportunity, he asked Quaye to set up a meeting with the pair.

It felt to the sheepish Reg and Bernie as if they were being summoned to the headmaster's office. Astonishingly, though, Dick James offered to sign them to a deal as songwriters. On November 7, 1967, they inked their names to the contract.

Bernie immediately moved in with Reg at Frome Court so that the two could concentrate on their writing. Notably, though, their collaborative process didn't change. Each preferred to work alone: Bernie would write or type lyrics, Reg would take them away and come up with the chords and melodies.

"It was one of the happiest times of my life," remembers the singer. "We were inseparable. He turned me on to different music, I turned him on to different music. We were buying records, we were going to the cinema, we were going to gigs. It all revolved around artistic things.

"For me, he became the mate that I could hang out with, and the brother I always wanted."

MEANWHILE REG WAS still out on the road for sporadic dates with Long John Baldry, as part of an expanded nine-piece lineup that now included Caleb Quaye on guitar, a sax player named Elton Dean, and Marsha Hunt, the future face of the musical *Hair*, on additional vocals. Together, they performed as the Long John Baldry Show.

By this point, Baldry had turned his back on the blues and refashioned himself as something of a crooner, remarkably scoring a number one hit in Britain with the hokey orchestrated showstopper "Let the Heartaches Begin," sung in a trembling, croaky voice in imitation of Tom Jones or Engelbert Humperdinck, after he had downed a copious amount of Courvoisier in the studio.

Onstage, wearing bottle-green suits and frilly-cuffed shirts, the band would be forced to mime to a tape of the hit, since it was impossible to re-create its string-soaked arrangement in the live environment. Reg hated every minute of it. Having gone from playing in chic clubs on the UK circuit, he now found himself in far cheesier cabaret venues, setting up his equipment during bingo sessions and performing while people were eating fish and chips.

His changeable outlook was not improved by the fact that he had begun popping amphetamine-based diet pills in an effort to slim down. Baldry found they made Reg aggressive and short-tempered, as well as increasingly huffy and prone to perfectionism. If anyone messed up onstage or played out of tune, Reg would boil over. During the sets, he made catty comments behind Baldry's back, though loud enough for the others to hear, causing them to break up with laughter. One night, he stood up midshow and started moaning and ranting and kicking his malfunctioning amplifier while dressed in an enormous fur coat. To Quaye's eyes, Reg looked like a furious Winnie-the-Pooh, storming around the stage and attacking the gear.

Then, on Christmas Eve 1967, someone came along to brighten Reg's mood. At the Cavendish club in Sheffield, he met a local girl, Linda Woodrow, an ash-blonde three years his senior and four inches taller.

In matters of the heart, Reg was still a naïf. He'd had one girl-friend, or at least love interest, back in his pub-piano-playing days at the Northwood Hills when an older girl, a twenty-year-old blonde named Nellie, had taken a shine to him. More exotic still, it transpired that she was a gypsy, living in a caravan that was moved on from place to place by the police every few weeks.

He visited her on-site, following her direction to "turn left at the third field" on the approach into Southall in west London. Bucking his preconceptions about those who chose an itinerant life, he found her caravan clean and Nellie herself very welcoming. Though not as welcoming as he'd have perhaps liked. After their dalliance, he remained a virgin.

Linda Woodrow was a more sophisticated individual than Nellie—privately educated, fond of high fashion, and well known on the Sheffield music scene, thanks to her shifts spinning records at the local ice rink. Her companion at the Long John Baldry gig at the Cavendish was another DJ, Chris Crossley, nicknamed the Mighty Atom by virtue of his vertically challenged stature of four feet eight inches. Mingling with the crowd and chatting at the bar after the show, the band members assumed Crossley to be Linda's boyfriend. That was until the others noticed that she and Reg were deep in conversation.

They became friends, then a romantic item. In London, the relationship quickly intensified, with Linda visiting Reg on the weekends at Frome Court. A lack of privacy ensured their romance had certain limits, however, since Reg was of course living there with Sheila and Fred, not to mention sharing the bunk beds in his small room with Bernie. Before long, though, Linda had moved to London and rented a flat of her own.

During these first months of 1968, Reg's frustrations with touring life as a bit-part player in the Long John Baldry Show began to deepen. He even briefly considered quitting as a musician altogether and started scanning the small ads in the papers looking for a job, working in a record shop, or doing anything really apart from being a supper-club organist.

At the same time, Stephen James had been shopping Reg and Bernie's songs around the record companies with a view to having them covered by name artists. In their reactions to the tapes, more than one A&R man voiced an opinion that surely the singer on these recordings—with his smooth delivery and impressive range—was strong enough to front the songs himself. It seemed an interesting idea to Stephen James, which he conveyed to his father. As a result, DJM offered to sign Reg as a recording artist to a five-year deal.

Reg was overcome with happiness. But there was one aspect of the arrangement that troubled him—namely, the thought that few people were likely to buy a record by a singer with the acutely un-glamorous name of Reg Dwight.

Flying back down from Scotland after a gig at Green's Playhouse in Glasgow, Reg was restless on the plane. He wandered up the aisle toward sax player Elton Dean. "I'm leaving the band," he bluntly announced. "To become a pop star. Is it all right if I call myself Elton Dean?"

Dean was flummoxed. "That's a bit strong, Reg," he replied.

On the airport bus taking them back into London, Reg was scribbling names on a piece of paper. If he couldn't be Elton Dean, he thought, then maybe he could borrow the first name of his current frontman and use it as a surname.

He was later to view it as a eureka moment. That was it. He would become Elton John.

"I was never happy with the name Reg anyway," he says. "It's an old-fashioned name. It wasn't the name I wanted as a kid. Changing it was just, psychologically, a big boost for me."

Not that, initially, it made much difference to his commercial fortunes. Stephen James cut a two-single deal with Philips, licensing the DJM recordings to them, and the first Elton John single, "I've Been Loving You," was swiftly released, on March 1, 1968. Although the song was credited to both Elton and Bernie, in truth, the latter's credit came as a result of the former's generosity, since he'd written both the music and lyrics himself. But it showed. "I've Been Loving You" was not too much of a stylistic stretch from Long John Baldry's "Let the Heartaches Begin," a ho-hum easy-listening ballad that quickly sank.

Everything was moving fast for him, however, both professionally and personally. Linda Woodrow had found a basement flat for her and Elton to share, at 29 Furlong Road, Islington, north London.

"Furlong Road . . . the first time I moved away from home," he ruminates. "Really didn't enjoy that much."

In truth, it proved to be one of the most painful periods of the singer's life.

To help pay the rent, Bernie came as part of the household setup, moving into the bedroom, while the newly domesticated couple inhabited the living room.

Elton and Linda made an odd pair—her with the posh accent and stylish clothes, him trying to dress like a rock star on a limited budget with his enormous fur coat. There were other, more problematic differences that set them apart. Linda didn't seem to share Elton's absurdist sense of humor or, worse, his taste in music. He'd later claim she'd constantly dismiss the songs he was writing, destroying him inside. She preferred the passé pop jazz of Buddy Greco and Mel Tormé.

But, at twenty-one, he finally lost his virginity. Not long after, according to Elton, Linda told him she was pregnant. Overcome with a sense of old-fashioned propriety, though not exactly getting down on one knee, he mumbled to her, "Well, I suppose we should get married, then." A date was set, for the third week of June.

As time passed, Elton began to view the impending wedding as an oncoming train, speeding toward him while he was tied to the tracks. One afternoon in the kitchen at Furlong Road, he turned on—but didn't light—the gas oven. He placed a pillow inside and rested his head on it.

Bernie found him. "I ended up pulling his head out," he remembers.

It was, says Elton, only a semi-serious attempt to take his own life: "Um . . . kind of half and half. I'd backed myself into a wall by saying I was gonna get married. I didn't want to get married. It was a cry for help. You know inside you're making the wrong move. You deal with it by being preposterous." As suicide attempts go, it was indeed preposterous: He'd only turned the gas oven dial to "low," and he'd left the windows open.

It didn't stall the plans for the wedding, however. On a half-hearted stag night in the first week of June, Bernie and Long John Baldry took Elton to the Bag O'Nails club in Soho. The three proceeded to get uproariously drunk. Baldry, who was supposed to be best man at the ceremony, asked Elton if he'd even yet booked the hall for the reception. Elton broke down in tears.

Baldry seized the opportunity to speak his mind. "If you marry this woman, you'll destroy two lives, yours and hers," he warned him. More importantly, Baldry, an unashamedly gay man, sensed there was a deeper root to his friend's dilemma.

"He said, 'For fuck's sake, you're more in love with Bernie than you are this woman,'" Elton recalls. "'For God's sake, come to your senses.'"

Elton and Bernie woozily stumbled back to Furlong Road sometime around four in the morning, waking Linda. Then Elton, with drunken bravado, decided to tell her that he wanted to call off the wedding. Bernie hastily retreated to his room and locked the door as the argument between the unhappy couple exploded on the other side. A little while later, Elton knocked and said, "I'm coming in there with you." He spent the rest of the night on the floor.

In spite of Long John Baldry's assumptions about Elton and Bernie, both insist their relationship was never a sexual one. But the incident seemed to strengthen their brotherly bond. The morning after the bust-up with Linda, Fred Farebrother arrived in his van to pick up their belongings, and they returned together to Frome Court.

"It was," says Elton, in remembering the lucky escape he had from choking domesticity, "a turning point in my life."

FROM HERE, THE two continued to spend their days hacking away in the studio, trying to write songs that would keep Dick James happy. Their own, more esoteric offerings were meanwhile piling up: the groovy sixties swinging "The Angel Tree," the mournful psych melodrama of "Tartan-Colored Lady," the surrealist romance of "When I Was Tealby Abbey," the brazenly Beatlesque "Regimental Sgt Zippo." Bit by bit, they were getting somewhere, even if none of these recordings were ever to be officially released.

Elsewhere, with their pop songs designed to be hawked to other artists, there was little but frustration. Tune after tune was rejected and the pair would despondently take the train back home to Pinner, growing increasingly disillusioned with the music business. "There were tremendous, tremendous highs and lows," Bernie says, "where we got our hopes up, only to have them dashed."

Sometimes they found themselves so near to greatness but yet so far. When playing on a session at Abbey Road for the novelty troupe the Barron Knights, a starstruck Elton, with Bernie in tow, met Paul McCartney, who sat down at a piano and sang for them the next Beatles single, "Hey Jude." It blew their heads apart. "It was like, *'Eeeeee!'*" says Elton. At the same time, says Bernie, "it was kind of disheartening to see all the movers and shakers existing in this fabulous world that we weren't really a party to."

But there were at least a few promising signs that the pair's fortunes might be on the rise. A new promotions man at DJM, Steve Brown, a comparative longhair in a company of "straights," heard what Elton and Bernie were doing and urged them to write from their hearts. Taking this approach, they came up with "Skyline Pigeon," which both felt was their greatest songwriting achievement yet. Further reinforcement came from Roger Cook and Roger Greenaway, writers of hits for the Fortunes and Gene Pitney, who tried to bring attention to the John/Taupin songs. Cook covered "Skyline Pigeon" and released it on Columbia in August 1968. The very same month, another version of the song was recorded for Pye by the clean-cut would-be pop star Guy Darrell.

Night shifts at DJM produced Elton's debut LP, *Empty Sky*, unsuccessfully promoted by ads on the backs of a hundred London buses. It wasn't a complete failure, however. In America, the California group Three Dog Night, an outfit always hungry for songs, virtually photocopied "Lady Samantha" for their second album, *Suitable for Framing*, released in the summer of 1969 and bringing in some much-needed funds for Elton and Bernie. When the album reached number ten on the *Billboard* chart, Elton got his hands on a copy of the trade mag and proudly underlined the entry.

The flopping of *Empty Sky* didn't dampen the hopes of Dick James, who firmly believed that he had found someone special in

Elton. Instead, he chose to up the ante. The next Elton John record, he decided, would be recorded with a far higher budget of £6,000, and at a better-equipped studio.

There was already a new song to hang the next album on. One morning at Frome Court, over breakfast, Bernie had rapidly scribbled a lyric that read like an intimate, almost bashful message to an unnamed object of his affections, accepting his failings and even poverty and instead offering up only these lines on the page. "It's the voice of someone who hasn't experienced love in any way," he says. "It's a very virginal song." Betraying its swift execution as part of an everyday routine, the piece of paper on which he wrote "Your Song" was stained with egg.

On Monday, October 27, 1969, it took Elton only ten minutes to conjure up its chords and melody. "Your Song" was quickly demoed with him alone at the piano, at a faster clip than the version that would be released and sung in a hushed tone that was almost feminine.

It was clearly an enormous step forward, and it galvanized the DJM team. The relatively inexperienced Steve Brown stepped aside as producer, approaching Gus Dudgeon, who had recently overseen the imaginative production of David Bowie's first Top Five hit, "Space Oddity." Dudgeon had already heard of Elton, having been aware of the *Empty Sky* advertising campaign.

"I remember seeing ads on the backs of buses," he recalled. "That kind of registered with me. Hello, we've got a record company that's actually working hard on the behalf of an artist. So when I got the call I thought, *Oh, this is the guy that they're pushing really hard.*"

Dudgeon set to work by drafting in the arranger of the inventive strings on "Space Oddity," Paul Buckmaster. Sessions were booked at the state-of-the-art Trident Studios tucked away in St. Anne's Court in Soho, where the Beatles had decamped from Abbey Road to record "Hey Jude" and parts of *The White Album,* drawn there by its eight-track tape machine.

Elton was told that the plan was to record the songs live with an orchestra. Naturally, this added a nervy edge to the proceedings. "I had to play the piano with all these brilliant session musicians," he says. "And if I fucked up . . . The fear element was great."

There was a sonic leap between *Empty Sky* and the album that was to become *Elton John*. Most of this aural advancement was centered on the pristine and sparkling piano sound. With it, and these new songs, Elton seemed to catch something that was in the air: the burgeoning trend for piano balladeering at the dawning of the 1970s. It was a sound that was suddenly appearing all around him, on the records he was listening to both before and after making *Elton John*—the glassy piano textures of Joni Mitchell on *Ladies of the Canyon,* the grandeur of Larry Knechtel's playing on Simon & Garfunkel's *Bridge over Troubled Water,* the delicacy of Leon Russell's meandering arpeggios and gently pulsing chords on "A Song for You."

On *Elton John,* you could hear the Saturday mornings of the musician's youth spent playing the works of the great composers. The classical influence was heavy, and unusual for the times. In contrast to the shoestring budget of his first LP, the making of this second album was meticulously plotted, Elton remembers, "like a military operation," making full use of the latest developments in studio technology. It was a time when recordings were becoming lusher and the possibilities in hi-fi sound were opening up.

Coloring the picture, Paul Buckmaster's orchestral arrangements were inspired and unorthodox, lending soaring drama to the schoolboy crush tale of "First Episode at Hienton" and an adrenaline rush to "The King Must Die," Bernie's monarch-toppling homage to the vibrant historical novels of Mary Renault. Elton was captivated by watching the eccentric figure of Buckmaster at work, particularly when the producer made strange mouth noises to convey the odd buzzing string effect he was after for the beginning of "Sixty Years On." The result sounded like a chorus of wonked-out wasps.

Lyrically, Bernie's contributions went from high to low. The words of the rousing "Take Me to the Pilot," he would later admit, meant "fuck all." In contrast, he painted a vivid picture of a devilish southern harlot who "milked the male population clean" in "No Shoe Strings on Louise," as brought to life on the microphone by Elton in an overly chewy impersonation of Mick Jagger.

For the most part, everyone's inspirations flowed freely. Even Elton felt moved to put pen to paper, adding the lines of racial solidarity to the coda of the brilliant and powerful gospel epic "Border Song." Released as the first single from the new album, vexingly, it floundered. But not before Elton was invited to perform it on BBC1's *Top of the Pops*. On the Thursday night the show aired, he watched it on the color television in Dick James's office, sweating anxiously as he viewed this broadcast version of himself. Still, it was amazing. This was really happening. He was on TV.

A music industry showcase at the Revolution Club in London's Mayfair launched *Elton John* two weeks before its April 10 release, where the singer appeared as part of his new trio along with drummer Nigel Olsson and bassist Dee Murray. Elton, in his Mickey Mouse T-shirt and round John Lennon glasses, tried his hardest, kicking away the piano stool, battering the tambourine off his butt. But the response from the music business cognoscenti was muted.

"He's got no chance," one invited booking agent was overheard saying. "I just can't see him onstage at Madison Square Garden."

Following this first proper attempt at flight, Elton landed with a bump. It was back to the day job. Unable to earn a living wage from his own songs and recordings, he was forced to pay the bills by resorting to anonymously singing an array of cover versions on cheap hits compilation albums for budget labels—most prolifically for Hallmark's *Top of the Pops* series, the covers of which featured a parade of young ladies whose clothes appeared to be in the process of falling off.

At the very least, it spotlit his versatility. He convincingly belted out Stevie Wonder's "Signed, Sealed, Delivered (I'm Yours)." He aped the quivering tones of Bee Gee Robin Gibb's mawkish solo single "Saved by the Bell," in perfect imitation of its dreadful warble. In spite of his skin color, he enthusiastically threw himself at the Heptones' ska version of "To Be Young, Gifted and Black." So distinctive was his voice that any listener familiar with Elton's own records could easily have identified him within a line or two.

Still, for a few months, everything was an uphill struggle. When they performed in Paris, opening for the smooth bossa nova grooves of Sérgio Mendes and Brasil '66, the crowd booed and lobbed tomatoes at Elton and the band. A stand-alone single—the only half convincing Stonesy hip-thruster "Rock and Roll Madonna"—was released in June and instantly died in the light.

Booked to perform on August 14, 1970, at the Yorkshire Folk, Blues & Jazz Festival in Krumlin in the north of England, Elton, Nigel, and Dee arrived on the makeshift site, in a valley in the middle of rural nowhere, to discover the organizers in hippie disarray. Despite its being the height of the British summer, it was bitingly cold. In front of the stage, most of the twenty-five-thousand-strong crowd lay stoned on the ground, cocooned in sleeping bags or failing to maintain their core temperature under thin sheets of plastic. No actual running order of groups had been arranged. Pink Floyd was said to have been booked, but they in fact knew nothing about it. Backstage, the Pretty Things and the Groundhogs were squabbling about who was going on when.

An exasperated Elton declared, "Oh, I'm going to go on now!" It was eight in the evening, and almost as soon as the trio walked onto the stage, the heavens opened. In yellow overalls, aluminum-colored boots, and a Donald Duck–style bib, Elton rose to the sodden occasion, passing out cups of warming brandy to the drenched front rows. He realized that if he jumped around, really not caring what he was doing, then at least he would keep his own ass warm.

The audience roared at the sight of this bespectacled court jester dancing in the rain. He booted the piano stool away and they howled even louder. The wilder he was, the more they loved him.

It was the moment he knew he was on to something.

Seven days later he flew to America, ready to take on anything.

EARLIER THAT YEAR, Russ Regan, the U.S. executive of Uni Records and the man famed for rebranding the Pendletones as the Beach Boys, was at the Continental Hyatt on Sunset Boulevard one morning, having breakfast with Roger Greenaway. He looked up to see Lennie Hodes, DJM's New York representative, wandering over.

"Russ, wow, I've got a package for you," Hodes said, disappearing up to his room to grab it. On his return, handing over a record mailer containing a copy of *Empty Sky,* he explained to Regan,

"Now this artist was just released by Bell Records and we've shopped him around and so far we haven't got any offers to pick up his contract."

Greenaway obviously knew whom Hodes was talking about. He told Regan that Elton John was going to be a star.

In truth, Bell Records had turned down the opportunity to release *Empty Sky* before five other East Coast American labels did the same. After Regan coaxed the full truth out of Hodes, he thought to himself, *Well, if it's been turned down by people, forget it.* He really wasn't interested. But as a favor to Lennie, whom he liked, he played *Empty Sky* when he got back to the Uni office.

"Y'know, I'm not gonna say I thought he was a superstar at that moment in time," Regan states. "But I said, 'This guy's really good.'"

Regan called Hodes, who told him that he could license Elton's records in the States for no advance. It seemed like pretty much a no-lose deal. In the weeks that followed, as the company began making plans to release *Empty Sky*, the just completed and far slicker *Elton John* arrived.

"I listened to it in my office," says Regan. "I looked up and I said, 'Thank you! Thank you! How lucky can one man get to have a piece of product like this?' I put the phones on hold. There were about thirty employees at the time at Uni Records. I said, 'Everybody, come on in, you gotta hear something.' So they all came in. They all sat on the floor. And after the album was over it was like, 'My God, what?! This is unreal.' We were so elated to have this product . . . and that was the beginning."

Regan wanted to bring Elton and the band over to Los Angeles and have them play a string of shows at the Troubadour. He insisted it had to be done on DJM's money, though. The trip would cost around £5,000—the equivalent of $46,000 today.

Back in London, weighing up the proposition, Dick and Stephen James looked at each other and made a decision: It's our last shot on Elton.

AND SO IT was he found himself on the trundling red London bus, heading for Sunset Boulevard and the Continental Hyatt. He and the band were so mortified by this gimmicky arrival that they were trying to duck below the windows out of sight of passersby.

Russ Regan, on the bus beside them, was effusive, constantly beaming and repeatedly declaring, "I love you guys." Elton, his sulkiness giving way to nervousness and babbling, kept launching into his *Goon Show* voices to break the tension.

As they pulled toward West Hollywood, their saucer eyes were met by the vision of the America they'd grown up watching on television: gas stations, hamburger stands, doughnut joints, 77 Sunset Strip.

It was true that Elton hadn't even wanted to come. But now he was here, and even if the trip turned out to be a dud, at least he could go shopping for records.

"I didn't feel the time was right, and I was completely and utterly wrong," he admits. "When I got to America, the last thing I expected was what happened at the Troubadour."

"I was leaping on the piano. People were going, Oh my God." Wowing the Troubadour, August 1970.

3 REBORN ON THE WEST COAST

IT WAS THE TWENTY-FIRST DAY of the eighth month of the new decade. The second year of Nixon's doomed presidency and the fourth week at number one for "(They Long to Be) Close to You" by the Carpenters. The temperature in Los Angeles was hovering around 75 degrees.

Up and down Sunset Strip, past the Continental Hyatt where Elton and the others were checking in, moved the everyday parade of the supercool, the misfits, and the bums, while here and there hippies on the sidewalks hawked copies of the *Free Press* for twenty-five cents to cruising drivers: "Don't be a creep, buy a *Freep*."

Nine miles southeast of the Hyatt, at the Hall of Justice, the Manson trial was into its second month. Weirding out those forced to attend it, glazed female members of the Family hung around outside the building, wearing sheathed hunting knives, Xs burned with a soldering iron onto their foreheads in imitation of the facial carvings of their dark-eyed leader. By night, they slept in bushes or a parked van.

The day before, August 20, Manson, who'd spent the past two months either staring for hours at Judge Charles Older or making wild, head-game proclamations, had taken the stand for the first time. Unstrung and angry, he'd railed about his treatment in jail, calling it humiliating and "like kicking a dead man." Today the prosecution revealed they had two witnesses who would testify that on March 23, 1969, Manson had visited the home of Sharon Tate at 10500 Cielo Drive, then occupied by the record producer Terry Melcher, before the killings twelve months ago. The revelation blew a hole in Manson's defense. He'd claimed he'd never been anywhere near the place.

Elsewhere in the city, unrest was stirring over Vietnam. Eight days later, fourteen miles southeast of the Hyatt, in Laguna Park, police would tear-gas Mexican American antiwar protesters, resulting in a riot breaking out in the surrounding streets. Amid the fog of violent confusion, four people were killed.

As edgy and dangerous as it was, the atmosphere in L.A. didn't affect Elton in his music-headed bubble, his eyes filled with stars and stripes. Eight of them had flown over from London, lining up in front of the red bus for a photo opportunity. Elton stood in the foreground, smiling sheepishly in his beard and tight-fitting jeans. Down the line ran a procession of faces whose expressions ranged from sunny grins to mild bemusement or insouciance: Bernie, Dee Murray, a kneeling Nigel Olsson, and the London-chic and slightly dandified trio of DJM sleeve designer and photographer David Larkham, Steve Brown, and Elton's now manager Ray Williams, over whose left shoulder road manager Bob Stacey peeked at the camera.

For weeks, the people at Uni had been forcefully pumping up expectation in the city ahead of Elton's appearance. Publicist Norman Winter had adopted a bold strategy: Let's treat him as if he's Elvis opening in Vegas rather than an unknown artist hitting town for the first time. Amazingly, it had worked, and as a result, Elton was all over local radio, with posters in every record store.

That night, Elton went to the Troubadour, the five-hundred-capacity hipster hangout on Santa Monica Boulevard, to check out the Dillards, the Missouri bluegrass group who'd recently gone electric. Forever the fanboy, he was "knocked out" by them, but shocked to learn that his support act at the club was to be David Ackles, the former child actor turned purveyor of intense theatrical songs delivered in moody baritone. Elton, a huge admirer, immediately tried to have the bill inverted, but to no avail. "We could not believe we were playing over David Ackles," he says. "He was one of our heroes."

With a few days to kill before the opening Troubadour show on Tuesday, the first of a mind-boggling six-night residency, Elton rented a Mustang convertible to get around. His main priority was to visit record stores and stock up on American discs actually bought in the United States. Meanwhile back at the hotel, more mundane matters prevailed. Nigel Olsson, lacking a hair dryer to blow-dry his long and carefully tended locks, had Ray Williams call a friend, Joanna Malouf, to ask to borrow one. She wasn't at home, but her flatmate Janis Feibelman was. Soon after, Janis arrived at the Hyatt with her sister Maxine in tow, who instantly caught Bernie's eye.

The next day, everyone, apart from an increasingly nervous Elton, went on a road trip to Palm Springs. Alone and stewing in his hotel room, his anxiety pulling his mood downward into an almighty huff, he called Dick James in London and—quite rightly—moaned that Ray Williams had abandoned him.

He didn't have long to fret, however. As a Uni Records artist, Elton now shared the roster with Neil Diamond, and so the company arranged for him to go and visit his new labelmate at his house off Coldwater Canyon for some encouragement before the first Troubadour show. Upon his arrival, Elton's nervousness began to get the better of him and he seemed painfully shy and socially awkward. Diamond thought: *This kid is never going to make it.*

Day by day, the pressure in Elton's mind had been building. The night before the show, he suddenly blew, standing up in the middle of a packed restaurant and saying that was it, he was going home. The enormity of what he'd let himself in for was throwing his head into severe turmoil.

Not that he really needed to worry. Sound-checking at the Troubadour the next day, his mood changed. He instantly felt at home. The band was clearly polished and more than ready for the show.

"We were like a new engine," he says. "We'd done our mileage. We were run in."

Here he was onstage at the venue where Lenny Bruce had been arrested for obscenity in '62, where the Byrds had found one another in '64, where Joni Mitchell and Neil Young had made their starmaking debuts, and where he was now playing a piano that Laura Nyro had touched only two weeks before. Everything around him seemed to blur his twin realities as fan and performer and serve to both unnerve and empower him. Reg may have been feeling jumpy and wired about the whole affair, but Elton was now supremely confident.

Walking into the venue midafternoon, Uni marketing man Rick Frio was taken aback: "The three guys were onstage and the first thing I thought was that they were playing the record behind them. There was so much music coming out of those three fellas that it was incredible." He immediately called Russ Regan back at the office. "I said, 'We're home free, it's gonna work.' 'Cause up till that point, we were doubtful. I mean, we had never seen them, had never even met them, and all we had was the record. It was gangbusters from then on."

THE NIGHT OF the show, the Troubadour was packed. Uni's determined push ensured a respectable smattering of celebrities seated around tables in the club, including Quincy Jones, Mike Love of the Beach Boys, Gordon Lightfoot, Danny Hutton of Three Dog Night, and the formidable folk blues singer Odetta, all waiting for the appearance of this twenty-three-year-old nobody Elton John.

"It was very hot and smoky and a great vibe," he says. "I honestly think they weren't expecting what they were gonna see."

Come ten o'clock, Neil Diamond walked out onto the stage to say a few introductory, if oddly noncommittal, words. "Folks," he began, "I've never done this before, so please be kind to me. I'm like the rest of you—I'm here because of having listened to Elton John's album. So I'm going to take my seat with you now and enjoy the show."

Then Elton stepped into the light, colorful and alive and a startling contrast to the half-lit and glum-looking individual on the cover of his eponymous LP. He sat down at the piano in an outfit designed by Tommy Roberts of London's Mr. Freedom boutique: yellow bell-bottomed coveralls with a grand piano appliquéd on the back, a long-sleeved black T-shirt bearing white stars, and, to complete this outlandish look, white boots affixed with green bird wings.

At first, the crowd did get what they'd perhaps come expecting to see, as he launched solo into "Your Song" before Dee and Nigel slid in to join him on the third verse. But as early as the second number, he began to transform amid a pummeling and gutsy-voiced "Bad

Side of the Moon." He was up and away. In his mind, he was com-
peting with the Rolling Stones, not mild-mannered singer-songwriters
trapped behind a piano. By song three, "Sixty Years On," which
dramatically built from delicate piano arpeggios to thunderous instrumental passages, a far cry from their more introspective stylings
on vinyl, he knew he had them.

"With a three-piece band," he points out, "there's no way you
can just sit there and interpret those songs à la record, because it
was an orchestral album. So we went out and did the songs in a
completely different way and extended them and extemporized and
just blew everyone away."

As the show rolled on, he fueled the intensity, through "Border
Song," "Country Comfort," "Take Me to the Pilot," and then, to
make the point explicit that here was an apparently meek character
with a rock'n'roll heart, "Honky Tonk Women." Firing into the set
closer, "Burn Down the Mission," he kicked the stool away and
lunged into the vamping sections, launching his heels into the air for
a series of handstands as he stretched the song over the ten-minute
mark with detours into Elvis's "My Baby Left Me" and the Beatles'
"Get Back." A shocked Neil Diamond was cheering so loudly that
he spilled his drink.

"I was leaping on the piano," recalls Elton, still thrilled by the
memory. "People were going, 'Oh my God.' Right place, right time,
and you seize those opportunities."

IT WAS THE performance that made him. Russ Regan was amazed to
discover that within the space of forty-five minutes, he'd landed
himself a star. "I knew we were going all the way," he says. "I just
knew it." The Troubadour's owner, Doug Weston, was similarly astonished. Having witnessed scores of landmark debut performances
at his club, he reckoned "no one had captured the town as completely and thoroughly."

But still, afterward in the dressing room, Elton fell to earth and
some of Reg's awkwardness returned. Uni publicist Norman Winter
brought Quincy Jones backstage and introduced Elton to him as "a
genius." Elton was horrified. Later he angrily tore a strip off Winter:

"Never do that to me again." People were telling him he was the greatest. But inside, he didn't feel like the greatest.

"I don't think I ever believed the hype," he says.

Crashing down to earth backstage at the Troubadour.

The day after the show, he was interviewed by *Rolling Stone* for the first time and came across as self-effacing and "oddly sub-dued . . . almost fragile" to writer David Felton. "I don't want the big star bit," he declared. "I can't bear that bit. What I want is just to do a few gigs a week and really get away from everything and just write, and have people say, 'Oh, Elton John? He writes good music.'"

Of course, he protested too much. But this strange admission did reveal the schism that was to widen as his career progressed: the desire for musical credibility versus the bright lure of the showbiz spotlight.

. . .

THE SECOND NIGHT, he looked up from the piano halfway through "Burn Down the Mission" and there in the second row sat the long-silver-haired figure of Leon Russell staring back at him. "I nearly fucking shit myself," Elton laughs. "Leon was such a striking-looking man and my biggest influence at the time, without question."

Meeting him in the dressing room after the show, Elton was relieved to discover that instead of being annoyed that he'd cribbed some of his eccentric rock'n'roll piano player act, Russell was friendly and complimentary and even invited Elton to his house the next day. He turned up suffering with a throat that was ragged from two nights of belting it out. Russell gave him a tip: Mix one spoonful of honey and one spoonful of cider vinegar with the hottest water you can take, gargle it for a minute, spit it out, then do it again and again. "I've done it from that day," Elton says.

On the morning before the third show, August 27, came the confirmation, via the printed word, on page 22 of the *Los Angeles Times,* that something vital had happened that first night at the Troubadour. Their highly regarded rock critic, Robert Hilburn, had submitted a review of the show that no one could ignore:

> Rejoice. Rock music, which has been going through a rather uneventful period recently, has a new star. He's Elton John, a 23-year-old Englishman whose United States debut Tuesday night at the Troubadour was, in almost every way, magnificent.
>
> His music is so staggeringly original that it is obvious he is not merely operating within a given musical field. He has, to be sure, borrowed from country, rock, blues, folk and other influences, but he has mixed them in his own way. The resulting songs are so varied in texture that his work defies classification into any established pattern.
>
> Beyond his vocals, melodies and arrangements, there is a certain sense of the absurd about John as a performer that is reminiscent of the American rock stars of the mid-1950s. Only someone with that wild, uninhibited view of his music would dare ask the

audience to sing along—something that is almost never done any more—or drop to his knees, like Jerry Lee Lewis used to do. The audience . . . roared its approval.

By the end of the evening there was no question about John's talent and potential. Tuesday night at the Troubadour was just the beginning. He's going to be one of rock's biggest and most important stars.

Elton was floored. "It was a turbo review," he says. "It spread to New York, Chicago . . . it really kick-started our career and in a hugely quick way."

Calls started coming in from the promoter Bill Graham, and from the producers at *The Ed Sullivan Show*.

The review didn't just cement Elton's reputation. Its glowing praise bolstered his confidence and reinforced his self-belief. From the third show on, he came further out of his shell, displaying a campiness onstage that he had previously hidden from view.

That day he'd enjoyed a trip to Disneyland, where Uni had managed to lay on the celebrity treatment for him, ensuring he was whisked to the head of the lines. He left having bought a pair of Mickey Mouse ears. That night at the Troubadour, in combination with a pair of shorts, he wore them to perform "Your Song." It was a glimpse of the Elton of the future.

IN THE DAYS that followed, the Los Angeles music community further embraced Elton and Bernie. Danny Hutton arranged for them to visit his friend, the drug-damaged Brian Wilson, at the time slowly reconnecting with his music by writing seven of the twelve songs on the Beach Boys' upcoming album *Sunflower,* set to be released on the last day of August.

As they arrived with Hutton and his girlfriend, the actress June Fairchild, at the gated entrance of Wilson's Bel Air mansion, Elton's and Bernie's minds were reeling. Danny pressed the intercom and Brian answered, jokily singing the hook of "Your Song" manically sped up: "I-hope-you-don't-mind-I-hope-you-don't-mind-I-hope-you-don't-mind."

"He was not well at the time," says Elton. "His wife, Marilyn, was fabulous: 'You wanna hamburger, Brian?' We had dinner and the dining room was filled with sand. He went upstairs to introduce us to the kids, woke them up. 'This is Elton John, I-hope-you-don't-mind.'

"Bernie and I were freaking out. I'm from Pinner, he's from Lincolnshire. We hadn't taken a drug in our lives."

After dinner, Brian led them into his home recording studio to play them the master tape of "Good Vibrations." Not more than ten seconds in, he pressed the Stop button, confusedly, saying, "No, that's not right." Then he tried to sell Elton his grand piano. At four in the morning, they left, completely disoriented. "I mean, we were absolutely in awe of this man," Elton says, "but freaking out because we'd never been in such a weird situation."

Weirdness abounded throughout this eye-opening California trip. Another night, Elton drove in the Mustang up to Hutton's place high on Lookout Mountain Avenue in Laurel Canyon, the oh-so-hip artistic enclave that in the past had drawn the likes of Orson Welles and Natalie Wood to its leafy calm and in recent years had provided creative dropout sanctuary for the Byrds, the Mamas & the Papas, Joni Mitchell, and Crosby, Stills, Nash and Young. In these worrying and jumpy times, though, as the hippies were tipping toward dangerous hedonism, the Canyon had increasingly become a magnet for unsettling freaks and drug-peddling criminals. Worse, the collective drug paranoia of these overindulging artists had been rendered horrifically real by the brutality of the Manson murders.

Blissfully tuned out from these disturbing frequencies, there at Hutton's house Elton met Van Dyke Parks, the cerebral, bespectacled lyricist for the Beach Boys' aborted *Smile* album. They had dinner and Elton played Hutton's piano to entertain them. They stayed up all night, and sometime after seven in the morning, he got back in the Mustang.

Driving down the hill on Laurel Canyon Boulevard, heading home to the Hyatt, Elton felt strangely energized. His time spent in Los Angeles had seen him grow up and get wise. He'd met some of his heroes, but he'd also rubbed shoulders with people he considered to be "con men and hipsters." Elton realized he could see through them. Inside, he pledged never to end up like these sad music-biz hustlers.

He thought to himself: *God, I was so naive a week ago. And you know what? It's really weird. I've never stayed up till seven in the morning in my life. I really feel good. I must be excited.*

"Years later," he says, "Danny told me that they'd put cocaine in my food. I'd no idea the first time I did cocaine."

The trio that sounded like an orchestra: (left to right) Nigel Olsson, Dee Murray, Elton.

4 A WELL-KNOWN GUN

BERNIE TAUPIN'S HEAD was full of western stories. The allure of frontier days had begun for him in the fifties with the flickering black-and-white TV images of Roy Rogers, the Lone Ranger, the Range Rider, and Lash LaRue, all saving the day and riding into the sunset. Beamed into his home on a rural English farm, these evocative visions made a powerful childhood impression, bringing adventure, as he puts it, to "the dreariness of your upbringing." Later, outgrowing the more cartoonish capers of these on-screen heroes, he'd been drawn more toward grittier tales of the American West— trailing the intrepid gold prospectors through the snow in Johnny Horton's 1960 hit record "North to Alaska," or discovering that sometimes, as in the songs of Marty Robbins, the outlaw might be hanged.

For his part, Elton absolutely hated westerns. They bored him to tears. If a cowboy film came on TV, he would immediately switch it off.

But Elton of course loved the Band and their romantic visions of bygone America, and so he could relate to Bernie's lyrics about the West: the stagecoach fugitive caught by the Pinkertons in "Ballad of a Well-Known Gun," the Confederate army enlister of "My Father's Gun," the hopeless fiery uprising of the poor and broken folk in "Burn Down the Mission." These were clearly written in homage to Robbie Robertson's songs for the Band, though, brimful of Elton's musical character, they could hardly be dismissed as plagiarism. "I wouldn't say it was a blatant rip-off," says Bernie, "because, God, if only I could have ripped off so well."

So rich were Bernie's impressions of the United States that he had actually penned these lyrics before ever setting foot on American soil. Song by song, they made up Elton's third long-player, *Tumbleweed Connection*. Thanks to the tough contract with DJM, which required two LPs a year, even by the time Bernie and Elton reached America, they had another album in the bag.

It had been recorded in March 1970, at Trident Studios, almost dovetailing with the sessions for *Elton John*. In contrast to that record's lush orchestrations, however, *Tumbleweed Connection* was a more pared-back and earthy affair. The main reason for this was the involvement of Caleb Quaye's new band, Hookfoot (including *Empty Sky* drummer Roger Pope), who lent the songs their hard-edged country rock swing and rolling soul grooves. "Even though it had some orchestration," Elton points out, "it was far more funky."

The only track on *Tumbleweed Connection* that echoed the baroque arrangements of the *Elton John* album was "Come Down in Time," which delicately swelled from harpist Skaila Kanga's gently plucked introduction into an elaborate Paul Buckmaster score for strings and woodwind. Bernie's eerie and almost otherworldly lyric concerned potential lovers who never quite manage to meet—kept apart by either physical remove or the distance of time or, perhaps, given the way the female character seems to haunt the narrator, bereavement. Subtle and open-ended, these were Taupin's most sophisticated stanzas to date. " 'Come Down in Time,' " says Elton, "is an *astonishing* lyric for someone who's not even twenty."

For the most part, though, *Tumbleweed Connection* was soaked in American influences. "Where To Now St. Peter?" drifted along on dreamy California verses reminiscent of Joni Mitchell. "Amoreena" was a yearning country soul love song with images of cornfields and cattle towns and a heart as big as Texas. "My Father's Gun," both lyrically and musically, made the reference to the Band explicit, coming across like a slowed, if no less rousing, take on "The Night They Drove Old Dixie Down," complete with Preservation Hall–style brass. "Burn Down the Mission" was the epic six-and-a-half-minute closer, moving from gospel verses and choruses into the driving up-tempo instrumental passages that Elton used to full effect in his live show.

Given that Bernie had never been to America when he wrote the words for these songs, there was the odd anachronism, particularly in "Country Comfort," which convincingly sounded as if it was born in the southern United States, except for the glaringly British inclusion of a hedgehog in the final verse. Similarly, the sepia-toned gatefold sleeve of *Tumbleweed Connection* depicted Elton and Bernie hanging out together on an old-time train platform, as if beamed back to pioneering railroad days. Only on closer inspection did the station's metallic plate ads for the *Daily Telegraph,* Swan Vestas matches, and Cadbury's chocolate reveal the scene to be a very English one, shot by David Larkham on the Bluebell Railway steam train heritage line running through the southern English county of Sussex.

Nonetheless, even if it was recorded in London in the cold spring of 1970, where the winter snow had turned to icy drizzle, *Tumbleweed Connection* was very much an album with its soul in America—and one set to resonate with the country's vast populace of record buyers.

AFTER THE HEAD-REELING highs of the Los Angeles shows in August, Elton, Bernie, and the touring party flew up the coast to San Francisco for a comparatively muted date before an audience of the city's music biz tastemakers at the Bay Arena on September 8 and then jetted across the country for two East Coast gigs, in Philadelphia at the Electric Factory on the eleventh and twelfth.

Surprisingly, even following the triumphs of the Troubadour appearances, there was a lingering doubt in some quarters at Uni Records as to whether Elton had the stuff to turn the hype into record sales. Russ Regan tried to tune out the naysayers who questioned his comparatively lavish spending on his newly favored artist. They had even begun to call the British singer-songwriter "Regan's Folly." On the road in Philly, Regan was on the phone to Uni's financial controller back out west when the latter let slip this derogatory in-office nickname. Regan exploded, furious, and yelled at the guy. Later, he'd say he felt he was on the verge of dropping dead of a heart attack, right there and then in his room at the Philadelphia Holiday Inn.

Come showtime at the Electric Factory, Regan was no less pumped up. Neither was a gung-ho Elton with, in his mind, nothing to lose: "We just blew the place apart." The audience response was immense, and physical. Midway through the show, Uni's Rick Frio worried that the floor of the fifteen-hundred-capacity venue might collapse: "It felt almost dangerous. I'd never been in a concert like that where you thought the floor was gonna cave in." Regan, flying on adrenaline and vindication, grabbed the promoter by the neck and shouted, "You see what I mean?!"

If the Troubadour gigs had wooed the critics and Elton's fellow musicians, the Electric Factory shows were the moment when it became clear that he could equally captivate a real ticket-buying audience. Around eleven o'clock the morning after the first show, Regan was awoken by a call from someone in the New York offices of MCA, Uni's distributor, wondering what the hell had happened in Philly. They'd just had orders from various record stores totaling five thousand albums. Regan fell back asleep, only to be woken again two hours later by another call saying orders had just come in for another five thousand.

A swift comedown from their Philadelphia buzz, New York, a week later, was a downer. Booked to play a lunchtime promotional show at the Playboy Club, Elton turned up late, midafternoon, and ended up performing in this chichi environment to a thinning crowd of journalists, most of whom had gone back to work. It was a disaster. Emotionally drained after the performance, he burst into tears.

For Bernie, New York was terrifying, a far cry from the sunlit, if paranoid, L.A. He felt as if he had descended into "the bowels of hell." The first night they arrived, booked into the Loews Midtown, the police shot someone outside his hotel window. "For me," Taupin says, "with my background and upbringing, just learning to come to terms with New York was absolutely devastating." The next day, shocked and numbed, he wrote a lyric, "Mona Lisas and Mad Hatters," which seemed to scorn the city and its swarming occupants, dwarfed by what he saw as light-blocking skyscrapers.

"If you dissect it," he argues, "it's not a put-down. It's a song about being pretty scared of New York."

It was also the sound of an alienated farm boy trying to get his head around his new circumstances and surroundings, a theme he would return to again and again.

ARRIVING BACK IN London, Elton was supercharged. The first public display of this newfound confidence was at his opening slot for folk-rockers Fotheringay on October 2 at the Royal Albert Hall.

The wheels for this pivotal London show had been set in motion three months earlier, in the dark and uncertain days of July in London when he'd thought about giving up—which, after America, already seemed an age ago. Elton had been booked as a pianist and singer on a jobbing session for the Warlock Music publisher. Headed by Joe Boyd, Warlock's Boston-born owner and producer who'd done much to advance the progress of hippiefied folk with Fairport Convention and the Incredible String Band, the sessions were an attempt to rerecord some of the Warlock writers' songs in a more commercial vein, with a view to selling them to other artists.

Elton was keen to get involved, being particularly fond of the achingly melancholic songs of Boyd's troubled protégé Nick Drake. He turned up for the two-day session at Sound Techniques Studio in Chelsea and efficiently laid his contributions down on tape, rendering in particular Drake's "Time Has Told Me" and "Saturday Sun" in a country rock style close to that of the recently recorded but still unreleased *Tumbleweed Connection*. The other singer booked to appear on the recordings was Linda Peters (later to marry Fairport Convention's Richard Thompson and become his artistic partner). Peters had never been in a studio before, and to calm her jangling nerves, she proceeded to get wasted on Valium and wine. "I don't remember much about it," she later admitted. "Except that Elton had to hold me up to the microphone."

Also playing on the session was Jerry Donahue, the guitarist who'd recently joined with Fairport Convention's departed vocalist Sandy Denny to form Fotheringay. Chatting to Donahue at the session, Elton asked about the possibility of his being first on the bill at the band's upcoming show at the prestigious Albert Hall. Donahue felt Elton was a "sensitive" player and talked the other members of the group into giving him the gig. He would come to sorely regret the fact that Fotheringay knew very little about Elton's stage show: "We had no idea what he had in mind, that he was going to do the most incredible rock'n'roll show."

Walking tall after his American adventures, Elton barreled onto the stage and took command of the venerable domed Victorian venue with his stool-kicking, piano-bashing act, upstaging Fotheringay even before they'd managed to reach the stage. After his set, a reeling and shaken Sandy Denny approached Elton backstage with the words "How are we supposed to follow that?"

The truth was they couldn't, and they didn't. Fotheringay's whimsical electric folk sounded hopelessly weak in comparison to what had come before, and the show was one of the chief factors in their subsequent breakup three months later. That night, understanding the awkward situation he'd created, Elton slipped out of the building before Fotheringay had even begun their ill-starred set.

HE WASN'T OVERLY cocky, though. He knew that his return to America later that month would prove whether the ripples created by the Troubadour and Electric Factory shows would turn into significant waves, or dissipate as quickly as they had appeared.

In October in the States, "Take Me to the Pilot" was released as the next single, with "Your Song" bafflingly banished to the B side in favor of the more up-tempo A side. In the end, radio DJs made their own decisions about the tracks, flipping the single to air the far more affecting ballad. Russ Regan was driving on the Hollywood Freeway when "Your Song" suddenly popped up on the local AM radio station KHJ. He was so moved that he had to pull the car over. "I cried like a baby," he says. "It was just very emotional to me that I felt that I was gonna be vindicated."

That same month, the *Elton John* album entered the U.S. chart and began a slow climb. Elton was thrilled to see his name in the *Billboard* listings, alongside George Harrison's post-Beatles triple album splurge *All Things Must Pass*. Harrison even sent a telegram congratulating him. To Elton, with success came "a sigh of relief."

This second U.S. jaunt started out on a flat note, however, with a series of poorly attended shows at the street mission turned rock hall, the Boston Tea Party, on October 29–31. Undeterred—and finding his road legs that would never seem to tire—Elton criss-crossed the States, sharing stages with Leon Russell, the Byrds, Poco, the Kinks, and Eric Clapton's new, dangerously drugged-out group Derek and the Dominos. There was much in the way of touring life camaraderie with the other musicians, but also fierce, if friendly, competition.

"Every time I was second on the bill," Elton remembers, "whether it was with Leon or the Kinks or whoever, my thing was, 'I'm gonna go on and you're gonna have to follow me, 'cause we're gonna tear the fucking house down.' And I would say ninety-nine percent of the time, everyone who came on and followed me *did*. And I stood there and went, 'Fuck, yeah.' You think you're good and then they go on and they're even better than you are.

"Derek and the Dominos were on fire by that time. But I remember playing in Chicago at the Auditorium Theatre and *we* were on fire. Then Eric came on and I thought, 'Well, good luck.' And they were *fucking* incredible and your respect for someone goes up so much."

Every day seemed to reveal a jaw-dropping moment, not least when Elton and the group returned to the Electric Factory in Phila-delphia in the first week of November. Unbeknownst to them, the Band, playing on the seventh in Worcester, Massachusetts, put their stage time forward so they could fly down the coast in their private plane to catch Elton's show.

That night, he was in feverish form, ripping up his shirt and throwing the torn pieces to the crowd. Afterward, as he was cooling off, the members of the Band casually wandered backstage. The sight of them seemed so utterly unreal that Elton turned woozy.

He felt he might lose control of his bodily functions and perhaps suffer a potentially calamitous, bowel-loosening mishap similar to his reaction when he'd spotted Leon Russell in the audience at the Troubadour. Repeating one of his graphic favorite phrases, Elton recalls, "I nearly shit myself. They just walked into the dressing room. They were *such* a huge influence."

Tentatively, he put a copy of the freshly pressed *Tumbleweed Connection* on a turntable. It was clearly a record that was very much in debt to the Band. They told him they loved it. Talk turned to whether he'd maybe like to come up to their spiritual home of Woodstock to record, maybe write a song for them. Elton managed to play it cool, but inside, Reg was screaming with joy. It seemed as if it was in a different life that he'd excitedly waited behind the counter at the Musicland record shop in London to bag a copy of the Band's self-titled second album. In reality, it had been only fourteen months before.

WHEN ELTON RETURNED to Los Angeles, it was for the coronation of the piano king. Upscaling from the Troubadour, he headlined the three-thousand-seat Santa Monica Civic Auditorium, with Ry Cooder and Odetta opening for him.

Elton arrived onstage in rectangular shades and a towering brown top hat and a black cape. Throwing it off to reveal a yellow jumpsuit adorned with a huge Donald Duck badge and a smaller pink-faced, red-nosed plastic clown mask just above his groin, he sat down at the piano and started solo and slowly, with "I Need You to Turn To" and "Your Song" before gearing up through "Bad Side of the Moon," "Country Comfort," and "Sixty Years On." He was so keen to perform a dramatic new song, "Indian Sunset," which Bernie had been moved to write after visiting a Native American reservation, that he read the words from a piece of paper as he sang. A film crew was in attendance to capture every moment, their cameras almost blocking the view of the paying audience.

Under the hot stage lights, Elton was boiling, performing under layers of clothing that he discarded as the show progressed, in a comedic striptease, taking off his jumpsuit to reveal another underneath before he peeled it away to end up in a long Fillmore West sweatshirt matched with mauve tights that Bernie's now girlfriend Maxine Feibelman had dared him to wear.

During "Burn Down the Mission," enthralled by his handstand acrobatics and silver-booted keyboard kicking, the audience rushed to the lip of the stage, overwhelming the security guards. When the crowd howled for an encore, Elton was forced to return to the stage, instill calm, and then explain that he had nothing left to perform. He ended by busking his way through a cover of John Lennon's "Give Peace a Chance."

Elton had brought the house down. But not everyone was bowled over by this arch and outlandish display, which was sometimes at odds with the serious tone of the songs. In his review for *Billboard,* Eliot Teigel perceptively reasoned, "Elton John faces a major decision in his short career. Does he abandon his valid musical skills in favor of being a 'stage freak' using unnecessary physical tricks?" Even Robert Hilburn worried that the theatrics were in danger of overshadowing the music, cautiously revising his effusive write-up of only two months earlier in the *Los Angeles Times:* "Some felt John was trying to use gimmicks to further his career. They felt he should stick to the music, that the fancy clothes and exaggerated Jerry Lee antics were signs of a desperate desire for success."

Later Elton defended himself against the accusation of careerism. "It wasn't desperation to be successful," he countered. "I just wanted to get away from the things that everyone else was doing. I could have come out on the stage in a pair of Levi's and a cowboy shirt. But I would have been bored to death. I just couldn't do it."

In truth, this determined dive into the dress-up box was a reaction against his shy and restricted childhood and the inferiority complex of his teens. He was making up for lost time and freeing himself. At the age of twenty-three, he was only now really beginning to live.

Moreover, by playing up the theatrics and not taking himself too seriously, he was having a ball.

"I went the more humorous route," he reasons, "because (a) I was stuck at the fucking piano and (b) I never saw myself as a sex symbol."

THE STARS WERE aligning for him in other ways as well. The airwaves were suddenly alive with his music. The rise of stereo FM radio—a high-fidelity sonic wonder compared to the tinny qualities of AM—was, as luck would have it, perfectly suited to the glossy production values of his records. Giant steps had been made in the field of studio production in the past few years, with the rapid move from eight- to sixteen-track recording. Gus Dudgeon's recording skills ensured that both *Elton John* and *Tumbleweed Connection* were on the cutting edge of these audio advances, with their pristine piano and orchestra reproductions and Elton's warm, full-bodied vocals.

"We were there when FM started to break," says Elton. "You put it on in the car and you went, 'Fuck, this sounds so much better than AM.' It was innovative. It was in stereo, and they didn't have a playlist like the AM stations. It was a changing time and it was fucking exciting." Soon, a name was coined for this new, FM-friendly musical genre—Album-Oriented Rock, or AOR. It was to prove vital to Elton's career.

In the States, live-to-air FM performances were becoming the vogue, making listeners feel as if they were in the studio or concert hall rather than on the receiving end of remote, crackly transmissions. Elton had already played live on KPPC in Pasadena, the first FM underground rock station in California, but it was on the East Coast that he would give his most memorable radio performance, on New York's WABC-FM.

November 17 saw Elton, Dee, and Nigel gather at producer Phil Ramone's A&R Studios on West Forty-Eighth Street, the three wearing headphones, as if making a record, albeit in front of an audience of more than a hundred invited guests. The station's silky-voiced DJ, Dave Herman, made the introduction: "Would you welcome, very warmly, those of you at home, those of you here, Mr. Elton John."

At first, there were sound problems in the studio, which Elton addressed in very polite, almost affected English tones after "Your Song": "Can you turn the piano down? It's very loud and I can't hear what I'm singing in the cans." He quickly loosened up, however, teasing the listeners at the end of "Country Comfort" by saying that Bernie "did the Palais Glide during that number naked throughout the audience. So if any of you heard squeals of delight, it was Bernie there."

Later, he further lightened up and revealed more of his self-deprecating humor, explaining after "Border Song," "We've played that so much, now we call it the 'Boredom Song.'" After kicking into "Bad Side of the Moon" and a gutsy-voiced "Take Me to the Pilot," he sounded genuinely overwhelmed by the reaction of the audience, whose collective cheers and whoops sounded as if they were produced by a far larger crowd. As WABC quickly took the decision to cancel commercials, cancel the news, allowing the band to run straight through, "Burn Down the Mission" passed the ten-minute mark, segueing into the full-tilt rock'n'roll mash-up of "My Baby Left Me" and "Get Back." At the end, having hammered his fingertips raw through the sheer force of his playing, Elton left blood on the piano keys. To quote Herman's closing assessment of this storming performance, it was "outtasight."

The WABC gig exists as a sonic document of the excitement stirred up by Elton's 1970 live shows. Initially, as a key indicator of how popular he was becoming in America, enterprising souls taped the show from the radio and it was widely bootlegged on vinyl in various editions with titles such as *Very Live, Knockin' 'Em Dead Alive,* and *Live E Jay.* In the end, DJM Records was forced to attempt to nullify these counterfeits with its own release of the show, titled (because of the differences in date stylings) *11-17-70* in the United States and *17-11-70* in the UK. In keeping with its cool-giving black-market origins, the cover was intended to look like an actual bootleg, with an unfussy monochrome image of Elton in mid-flight, standing bent over the piano.

"It was never meant to be a live album, it was meant to be a broadcast, but the playing on it was phenomenal," Elton points out, with none of the immodesty this statement suggests, and more the buzzed enthusiasm of a fan. "It's one of the best live albums I've ever heard."

Three days after the WABC show, he opened for Leon Russell at two shows at the Fillmore East on the Lower East Side. Startling Elton, from the opening line of "Your Song" it was apparent that the audience knew every word, which they sang back at him. Although neither Elton nor Bernie was aware of his presence during the show, in the crowd that night was Bob Dylan. Later, possibly their greatest idol came backstage to say hi. "Bernie and I were just like, 'Fuck!'" says Elton. "Dylan said, 'I love that song about My Father's Gun.' We were like, 'Uh . . . uh.' Dylan has an aura about him. It's not frightening. It's just . . . foo, blimey."

Nigel Olsson was a witness to this overwhelming encounter: "They went nuts. They couldn't believe it. Bernie was almost in tears. Bob's there with a little briefcase and glasses and looked like an accountant."

The next night, an impressed Dylan returned, bringing along his wife, Sara, Paul Simon, and John Phillips of the Mamas & the Papas. The news reached Britain and a *Melody Maker* report appeared the next week with the cred-bestowing headline DYLAN DIGS ELTON!

Meanwhile the demand on the West Coast was such that two more shows were booked in California for early December, at the Anaheim Convention Center on the fourth and the Swing Auditorium in San Bernardino on the fifth. It was all happening so fast. Astoundingly, Aretha Franklin released a powerful cover version of "Border Song," fully realizing its gospel intent, and it entered the Top Forty. Elton was approached by director Hal Ashby, who'd seen him in concert, to star as the death-obsessed Harold Parker Chasen in his next film, the black comedy *Harold and Maude,* which the singer felt was an ambitious step too far for him to contemplate. "To do films properly," he reasoned at the time, "you've got to work at it full-time, devote all your energy to it."

To cap the year, Elton was invited by NBC TV to appear on *The Andy Williams Show,* in the same episode as another of his formative heroes, Ray Charles. Williams was quietly amazed that Elton turned up wearing a cape and an earring. Elton performed "Your Song" alone before, for the show's finale, side by side, he and Charles, respectively playing black and white grand pianos, traded verses on Stevie Wonder's "Heaven Help Us All" along with the host and a kaftan-wearing Mama Cass, the audience clapping in time.

He had turned his fortunes around in a way that had been unimaginable at the beginning of 1970, the year that changed everything for him. The words of the opening song of *Tumbleweed*

Connection were ringing loud and true: In Old West parlance, he was now a well-known gun.

Walking down the street together one day in New York, unrecognized by passersby, Bernie turned to Elton, offering him sage words:

"I think you'd better savor your anonymity now," he told his friend. "It'll be gone soon enough."

The bashful star returns home. Elton with his mother, Sheila, and stepfather, Fred, Frome Court, Pinner, 1971.

5 HOPE YOU DON'T MIND

IN AMERICA, it was easy to feel like a star. But back under the rain-cloud skies of London, surrounded everywhere by reminders of who you'd been and who you truly were, it was a lot harder. In reality, it was Reg standing on the pavement outside the forbiddingly trendy indoor Kensington Market in west London, afraid to enter. Inside lay stall after stall of seventies fashion hipness manned by the unapproachably cool staff—racks of regal-looking red velvet coats edged with gold brocade, a sea of suede jackets with shiny sovereign buttons, piles of corduroy caps in whatever color you fancied.

His friend June—wife of his pal Marc Bolan, who in the first month of 1971, after years of sideline sixties struggle, had finally risen to number two in the UK chart with T. Rex and "Ride a White Swan"—grabbed Elton and forced him to walk through the doors. "I was so self-conscious," he says. "June would take me by the hand."

In Britain, in terms of real fame, Elton was still pretty much nowhere. Leaving Los Angeles, he'd enjoyed a send-off from a group of fans at the airport. Arriving back at Gatwick, he'd walked down the quiet corridors entirely unnoticed. It was the suddenness of it all that took him aback. At the same time, he now harbored a real determination to make it work for him back home.

He wouldn't have to wait long. Word of Elton's U.S. triumphs had crossed the Atlantic, not least with the *Melody Maker* report of Dylan gracing him with his presence in the audience in New York. When the weekly music paper duly ran an interview with Elton in their first issue of 1971, the bitingly funny character that his friends knew, possessed of a mercilessly sharp tongue, first surfaced in print. Discussing his favorite subject—new records—he passed catty comment on the current exploits of the former Animals singer Eric Burdon, now fronting an almost all-black American funk band called War. "Have you got Eric Burdon's new one, Black Man's Burdon?" Elton was quoted as saying. "There's one track I like. But he should have been born black and given us all a rest."

What followed suggested that Burdon didn't take the comment at all well. Three weeks later, Elton and the band were booked to appear at MIDEM, the yearly European music business shindig held in Cannes on the French Riviera. Preceding him on the bill were Burdon and War. Both acts were assigned strictly timed fifteen-minute showcase slots. But, rebelliously digging deeper and deeper into their soulful grooves, and despite the screaming efforts of the organizers to halt their set, War went on, and on, finally leaving the stage after more than an hour. Pacing around, fuming, Elton stormed out of the theater.

The next night, he was persuaded to return. But before the trio could finish their short appearance, a too-hasty backstage operative stupidly brought the stage curtain down in the middle of their last number. Embarrassed for a second night running, Elton's fury boiled over. He hacked his way out in front of the curtain and seethingly addressed the audience.

"Whoever organized this thing is a fucking idiot!" he bawled into the microphone, to the sound of sympathetic applause.

As Reg, he'd kicked his amplifier onstage back in his days with Long John Baldry. But this was his first public temper tantrum as Elton. It wouldn't be his last.

FEBRUARY 1971 PROVED he wasn't a flash in the pan in the States, with *Elton John* hitting number four in the first week, followed by *Tumbleweed Connection* reaching number five the next. Now that he had two Top Five albums in America, British radio DJs were forced to take notice. By the middle of the month, "Your Song" was sitting at number seven on the UK singles chart and he was back (with a proper hit this time after the phantom pregnancy of "Border Song") on *Top of the Pops*.

"Thank God we did happen in Britain as well," he says. "It would've been horrible to happen in America and not happen in Britain, because obviously that's where you were born and that's where you live. But it all fell into place."

Not without a cost, however. In order to capitalize on the surge of interest in Elton, the first third of the year saw the singer hurtling north, south, east, and west, all over the UK, to fulfill the demand in bookings. Given what he'd just undergone in the States, it proved too much for him to handle. A slew of Scottish and Welsh dates were blown out in February, followed by a cutting back of the schedule for March. These were his first gigs canceled, on medical orders, on account of stress. "I was on the edge of a nervous break-down," he admitted at the time. "Now I've got to have three holi-days a year."

The centerpiece of these shows was a high-status headliner at the Royal Festival Hall on London's South Bank, on March 3, featuring an orchestra conducted by Paul Buckmaster. If there was a lingering suspicion that some writers in the British music press had decided that Elton was getting above himself following his U.S. success and with his perceived level of onstage pomp, then it was confirmed when *Melody Maker* ridiculed the Royal Festival show: "Elton John has shown what a musical dwarf he is . . . it was sad, the man, this living myth, darling of the Americans . . . struggling like a pygmy."

Sometimes, his growing flamboyance did in fact make him look faintly ridiculous. Closing the interrupted UK tour at the Fairfield Halls in Croydon, Elton stamped and hopped around the stage in too-tight red coveralls with a spangly purple bow tie held with a ribbon around his neck. This ill-fitting getup gave him less the ap-pearance of a cutting-edge, fashion-advancing rock star than of a toe-curlingly overkeen children's entertainer.

A film crew from London Weekend Television captured the show for a half-hour program focusing on Elton and Bernie, aired as part of the *Aquarius* arts series. Backstage, either a bit stoned or affecting the air of someone who was, Taupin falteringly tried to sum up his unstarry role in the operation: "Yeah, well, I live in a fantasy world," he offered. "I'm just sort of happy the way I am. And I want to stay that way, y'know. I don't want to sort of be anything pr . . ." He paused to think. "I mean not that I don't want to be prolific, but I don't want to be the sort of savior of modern writing. I just want to write what I want to write and if it's appreciated, y'know, people don't have to know me."

Bernie really meant what he said. He was genuinely happy to remain in the shadows. One subsequent scene in the documentary showed Elton standing center stage, presenting the visibly reluctant lyricist to the crowd. "I thought it only fair that I should introduce Bernie Taupin who never really faces his public," he announced. "And without Bernie there wouldn't be any songs anyway." Hiding a bottle of beer under his plaid coat, his eyes shielded behind shades, Bernie lifted them momentarily to eyeball the audience before grinning, bashfully waving, and then getting offstage as quickly as possible.

It was becoming a unique and strange existence for Bernie, more or less constantly touring with Elton and living a rock star lifestyle without—the odd introduction to the audience aside—ever being under the stage lights. Bernie insists he didn't ever crave fame, even if he enjoyed its offstage perks. "Truth be known," he says, "I was probably more interested in living that grass roots rock'n'roll-style life than Elton actually was. Only I was living it without having to perform."

While Elton was driving on with his career, Bernie had the space and freedom to get on and enjoy his life. Only eight months after he had met Maxine Feibelman in L.A. on the first U.S. trip, their relationship had moved to a significant new stage. In April, two days before the next U.S. tour was due to begin, they were married, at the Holy Rood Catholic Church, back in the Lincolnshire village of Market Rasen.

The wedding day was a clear indication of how quickly Bernie and Elton had become rock star news. The bride and groom wore white, though Elton outshone both in a suit bejeweled with rhinestone flowers in yellow, red, and blue and a silver silk top hat. Photographers and reporters pressed together outside the church as policemen tried to direct the flow of traffic and fans hung around hoping for autographs. It was a measure of how so much had changed in such a short time. Only a year before, no one in the media would have known them or cared.

Dick James bought the happy couple a silver Mini Cooper as a wedding present, and together the newlyweds were due to move to nearby Tealby into a two-bedroom semidetached cottage that Bernie whimsically named Piglet-in-the-Wilds. The couple honeymooned in the States—fishing on the Mississippi, visiting Civil War battle sites, driving to Dodge City and Tombstone.

A three-month American tour lay ahead and, already exhausted before it began, Elton's mind turned to thoughts of quitting. But he'd come so far. There was no stopping now.

AT THE SAME time, he was in danger of blowing it by flooding the market with too many albums, released too closely together. Before the American tour of spring '71 came another, the soundtrack to director Lewis Gilbert's film *Friends*. Concerning a young couple, Paul and Michelle, who meet on a flight to France, become lovers, and unsuccessfully try to set up a home together, the movie was panned at the time for its apparently gratuitous sex scenes. The soundtrack had been rush-recorded in three weeks by Elton at Trident Studios in London the previous summer, squeezed into the break between the first two American trips.

Bernie had skimmed through the script and, before Elton had even seen it, written three lyrics. There were five new John/Taupin songs featured, which cut between the orchestrated pop of *Elton John* and the country soul of *Tumbleweed Connection*—the title track, "Seasons," and "Michelle's Song" were serviceable but a tad schmaltzy, and "Can I Put You On" and "Honey Roll" were both the Band–style rock swingers. Adorning and blending the songs together were Paul Buckmaster's arrangements and symphonic instrumentals, but taken as a whole, *Friends* amounted to an unremarkable effort.

Paramount Pictures was keen, not least because of Elton's growing status in America, to put out the *Friends* soundtrack LP on their own label. As producer, Gus Dudgeon felt that it should be issued as a five-track "maxi single" at best, but it was released as a full album in a lurid fuchsia sleeve featuring an illustration of the film's kissing protagonists. Elton hated the cover and described it as a "fucking pink massacre" that to his mind might be the garish color of a dress worn by the showy English romantic novelist Barbara Cartland. The album sold poorly in the UK, and even though it scraped into the U.S. Top Forty, as far as its creators were concerned, it was a flop.

"They issued about six hundred thousand copies," Elton said of Paramount Records in the United States. He then quipped, "Little did they know that they were going to get five hundred and ninety-nine thousand of them back."

It was an album too far. He'd put out four LPs in the States in a year, three of them in the previous six months. Nevertheless, he was still riding high, with *Elton John* and *Tumbleweed Connection* both certified gold. This American tour, beginning in April, would take them everywhere, from the coasts to the heartland.

They began in New York, with three nights in the familiar environment of the Fillmore East, before setting out for Maryland, Illinois, Michigan, Ohio, Nebraska, Oregon, California, Arizona, Colorado, Texas, Louisiana, Florida, Missouri, Tennessee, Kentucky, and Georgia. "We covered everywhere," says Elton. "We did a lot of stuff in the south and a lot of [musicians] wouldn't go there."

He may have been worn out but there was a steely resolve within Elton. If he was going to truly break through in all parts of America, he knew the only way to do it was to put in the hours and the road miles. "You get up," he says, "and you do every radio broadcast, you do every print interview. There was so much going on. You worked so hard. Anyone can be successful in New York and in Los Angeles and Chicago. But there's a lot of country in between."

It wasn't, however, an ascent without rough moments in sometimes choppy air. Fame, for Elton, or maybe for Reg, was difficult to acclimate to. If a fan approached him when he was shopping in a record store, offering his compliments, he would say thank you, shuffle uneasily, and go red in the face. Others were more troubling in their gushing displays of love. He had worryingly begun to attract crazier and more disturbed devotees. As he was leaving the San Francisco Civic Auditorium after a gig there on May 9, one unhinged male fan clung to his car, pleading, "I must go home with you! Let me be a person!" Helpless and upset, Elton watched the poor guy sobbing on the ground as they drove away.

As the tour progressed, it was clear that in some quarters of the press, the knives were out for Elton. The hype had come to haunt him. In the *Seattle Post-Intelligencer,* after catching a show at the city's Arena on April 24, the critic Stephen Chensvold lambasted it as "glossed-over and well-promoted garbage . . . ludicrous." In *Melody Maker,* the paper's Los Angeles correspondent, Jacoba Atlas, went further, claiming that the latest tour was nose-diving fast: "Elton John seems to be having trouble with the middle part of the USA. His concerts have not been selling out, and in the words of one observer, 'He's dead in New York. And everyone knows New York is the center of popular opinion.'"

Those last words inflamed the promoter Bill Graham, who felt he had to bluntly and unemotionally respond by writing a letter to the music paper: "The report that Elton John was dead in the USA is not true. Elton was alive and well at the Fillmore East. He played to three packed houses in April. I consider Elton one of the truly great entertainers working today."

Counterattacking the cynics, Elton made the cover of *Rolling Stone* on June 10, 1971, gazing up at the camera in shorts and star-patterned boots and a T-shirt that tipped the hat to his songwriting partner with the legend BERNIE TAUPIN FUNKY MONKEY. Inside, among various articles characteristically aimed at "heads"—one examining the aftermath of the shooting of unarmed student protesters at Kent State University the year before, another lamenting a "5-Ton Grass Bust on the High Seas" in San Francisco Bay—Elton cut a comparatively straight and uncontroversial figure. The feature cast him as a celibate hard worker, someone too preoccupied by his daily travails and domestics to even think about rock'n'roll indulgences or a sex life.

"I've got no time for love affairs," he claimed in the article. "You wake up in the morning—even if you have a day off—and the phone will ring: 'Can you come into the office? There's something I want to talk to you about.' Your solicitor will phone you up, for a start, or your accountant, or your manager, or your publicist—somebody will phone you up. Then you have the day-to-day things to worry about, like your car will go wrong so you have to take it in. Or the stove will blow up. It's amazing how many things go wrong in life."

Elsewhere, his quotes further revealed his downcast mood, his glass seemingly half empty. He couldn't come to terms with the sales or acclaim, and worse, couldn't imagine his career lasting. "I've got to do everything in three years," he insisted. "After three years you just have to assume it's gonna go down. Realistically I don't think I can be any more popular than I am now. And I don't want to sort of work that hard while I'm, you know, going down and getting less money and working myself dead. I just want to quit at the top. Not quit, but quit working hard." This wasn't the kind of admission typical of a performer whose popularity was still rapidly on the rise. Already, Elton was sounding hopelessly weary.

For now, there was no sign of the hard work letting up. Crowning the tour were two shows at Carnegie Hall in New York on June 11 and 12, on the days immediately after the *Rolling Stone* cover hit the newsstands. Unknown to Elton, his mother had flown over from England for the gigs. The first that he knew about it was when he looked up to see Sheila dancing at the side of the stage. Afterward there was a party thrown in a suite decked out with carnival-themed decor at the Essex House hotel on Central Park South. Guests including Bette Midler and the rarely seen Sly Stone, resplendent in his voluminous Afro and gold lamé suit, toasted Elton's success.

It had been a challenging tour, and still it wasn't over. There were another four dates left—Cleveland, Providence, Columbia, Harrisburg—before he could finally go home.

HE RETURNED TO the UK, and fifteen million television screens, in an oddly low-key way. Unannounced and unexplained, he appeared with Marc Bolan and T. Rex on *Top of the Pops* as they ripped through "Get It On," set to be Bolan's second British chart topper of the year—although the record was renamed "Bang a Gong (Get It On)" in the States, where it was Bolan's sole Top Ten hit, to avoid confusion with a then current song of the same name by the U.S. jazz rock band Chase.

Stage right at the *Top of the Pops* appearance, Elton enthusiastically mimed the piano part for a record he hadn't actually played on, as the curly-mopped Bolan peacocked and licked his lips, in silver jacket and pink jeans, a star of glitter glued to his left cheek. Elton appeared to be in his element, up there onstage with his cool friends, and he ended the song standing upright after having nudged, rather than kicked, the piano stool away, possibly not wanting to be seen to be even trying to upstage the luminous Bolan.

It was the dawning of glam rock and Elton was there to witness it firsthand. It was also the beginning of a playful sales rivalry between the two rising stars. "A wonderful, brilliantly inventive man," Elton says of Bolan. "When Marc was coming in at number one, he'd say, 'Darling, I sold a hundred thousand records in an hour today!' He was so competitive, but in a nice way."

Music trends were moving fast, which played well with Elton's high-octane creativity and low boredom threshold, but sometimes made it hard for his audience to keep up with him. At the Garden Party, a one-day outdoor festival held at the Crystal Palace Bowl, south London, playing on a bill alongside Yes and Fairport Convention, Elton bamboozled and ultimately bored the rapidly dwindling crowd by playing nine new and unheard songs set to appear on his next album. "I remember it dying a death," he said later with a cringe. "People said, 'Oh God.'"

His career and creative decisions were becoming slightly chaotic. He was in effect a man without a plan, maniacally trying to cope with his touring schedule and the demands of his two-albums-a-year contract with DJM. Someone needed to oversee everything and plot the day-to-day scheduling. Since breaking away from his manager, Ray Williams, on his return from the first U.S. trip, it had been left to Dick James to provide nominal representation for Elton. Now he needed a devoted manager. As it turned out, the answer lay in someone who was already very close to him.

Elton had first met John Reid the year before when he'd dropped in to the London offices of EMI Records in Manchester Square to cheekily scrounge free vinyl copies of the latest releases. Reid was a music-obsessed Scot, at twenty-one two years younger than Elton, who had managed to transcend his upbringing as the son of a Paisley laborer to become the head of the UK operation of the EMI-distributed Tamla Motown Records. He made quite an impression on the singer.

Reid was clearly driven—he'd quit Scotland and his studies in marine engineering to pursue a career in the music industry. Once in the capital, he'd sold suits at a branch of Austin Reed tailors before landing a job at EMI's Ardmore & Beechwood publishing wing. Obviously a bright spark, he'd quickly progressed to Motown, where part of his job was deciding which releases from the American label would have the best chance of charting in the British market.

He'd enjoyed an early win in February 1970, picking the three-year-old and at the time largely forgotten "The Tears of a Clown" by Smokey Robinson and the Miracles out of the back catalog, releasing it as a single, and then watching it sail to number one in the UK. Blindsided by this development, Motown in the United States was then forced to reissue the track. Reid evidently had good ears, and his eyes were firmly fixed on the bigger picture.

Elton next saw Reid when he came along to the anticlimactic Revolution Club showcase for his second album in March 1970. But it was in San Francisco in September of that year, high on the victories of the Troubadour shows, that he first spent real time with the young label manager, in California on a work trip to attend the tenth anniversary celebrations for Motown. It was in this liberated city that the pair's growing friendship took a perhaps surprising turn.

Privately, Elton had always suspected he was gay. Traveling from Pinner into London's west end on underground trains in his days as a jobbing writer for DJM, he would find himself eyeing the guys, but not the girls. His relationships with the opposite sex had always been slightly awkward and doomed to failure. He was developing a conspicuous taste in ever campier attire, both onstage and off. In a fumbled, clumsy way, as was revealed much later, he had even once tried getting it on with his songwriting partner. "He made his affections known," Bernie coyly admitted years after the fact. "When I started laughing, it sort of broke the ice. He got over it very quickly."

It took Reid to confirm Elton's sexual proclivities. Returning from a highly significant night with the Scot in San Francisco, he admitted to Steve Brown, "I'm definitely gay." Elton had clearly fallen hard for the man from Tamla Motown, whom Ray Williams and the others had mischievously nicknamed Pamela Motown.

It was wholly liberating for Elton, at the relatively late age of twenty-three, to finally accept the true nature of his sexuality. Bravely, he didn't attempt to keep it hidden from those closest to him. When he got back to London, he came out to his family. Elton remembers that Sheila wasn't particularly shocked.

"Not really," he says. "She said, 'Yeah, well, we thought so, anyway.' Coming out to your parents is always traumatic. But they're not stupid. Parents are not daft. They know. But it's still traumatic. I had no resistance at all from any of my family members and from my friends, only support.

"That's all I cared about. I said, 'If my mum can accept it and my family can accept it, then I don't give a toss about anybody.' I was extremely lucky because other people don't get that sometimes. Y'know, a lot of people come out to their parents and they get rejected. But my mum has always been a modern-thinking woman. She's always been supportive, all the way through."

In London, Elton and Reid set up home together, arousing no suspicion in anyone outside the inner circle. It wasn't, after all, unusual for two young men to share a flat. Elton didn't carry himself with the mincing, limp-wristed demeanor of the archetypical "comedy" 1970s gay man, and his often colorful dress sense was easily attributed to his pop star status. He wasn't, for instance, nearly as conspicuously effeminate as the married Marc Bolan. Reid, meanwhile, was entirely straight in his appearance, with his short, side-parted hair and business suits.

Their flat at 384 The Water Gardens, a stylish apartment block on Edgware Road in west London, was a discreetly elegant and fashionable abode: modernist furniture, expensive piano, carpeted lift that opened directly into the living space. Showing her approval,

Sheila supported her only son in leaving the parental sanctuary of Frome Court and beginning this new life. "We've helped him all we could," she told an inquisitive reporter in October 1971, before revealing that she was sometimes embarrassed by Elton's flamboyance. "I did nag him about his clothes and his hair, but then I had been living in this suburban place. Now I go up to London and meet his friends and he looks fine."

In fact it was Sheila who first suggested to Elton that John Reid might become his manager. Reid, for his part, was initially reluctant to take on the role: He had a highly promising career within EMI and great things were expected of him. Eventually he relented, quitting his tenure at Motown and becoming a salaried employee of DJM.

Dick James was very happy about the whole affair, quipping to his son Stephen, "Who else can we rely on to get Elton out of bed in the morning than the guy he's in bed *with*?"

Stephen James was slightly more wary of Reid and his increasingly hawklike manner. He suspected that as each contract option came up, Reid would seize more power as manager in his renegotiations: "I felt he was only out for himself and that we weren't going to get any loyalty from him." James Jr. also noticed that Elton was becoming more confrontational, emboldened by his personal and professional relationship with Reid—"If we said black, he'd say white."

Even though he'd assumed the role of manager, as far as Reid was concerned, he'd been thrown into the deep end: "It was ridiculous. I was twenty-one at the time. I didn't have any money, I had no real experience." Looking on, their friends noticed changes in the couple as their tastes in clothes and hairstyles began subtly to morph. For a time, Elton even combed his thinning locks into a Reid-ish side flick.

But although he now had a boyfriend, there was a side to Elton that still felt very much alone. The singer was so driven and passionate when it came to his career that somehow he couldn't quite settle into the personal partnership. "Even though I was in a relationship with John Reid, I felt lonely," he admits. "All I had in my life was my music. Not a bad thing to have. But, yeah, there was a loneliness."

. . .

IT WAS TIME to go back into the studio, and for the first time, the songs had been harder to come by. On the eponymous LP and *Tumbleweed Connection,* Elton and Bernie had been working from a stockpile of material. For the next full studio album, the evocatively titled *Madman Across the Water,* they'd had to start from scratch.

The unrelenting touring, particularly in the States, where he'd completed three treks in twelve months, had two audible effects on the new record. First, many of the songs featured Elton singing in a sometimes overly mannered American accent. Second, Elton had clearly been influenced by having shared the stage with heavier-sounding bands during his recent tours, and the resulting album was in parts more in tune with the fashionable progressive rock of the time.

Madman Across the Water endured a troubled birth. Elton was tired and overworked, but he also felt that the normally dependable Paul Buckmaster was distracted during the sessions at Trident. The arranger turned up at the studio with no score penned for the grandly sweeping title track. For those songs he had actually prepared for, Buckmaster seemed to be bungling, knocking a pot of ink over his sheet music with eighty session musicians sitting waiting as Elton nervously bit his nails.

The singer finally flounced out of a session in a fit of pique after an argument with Dick James, who reckoned that one of the tracks had lost its direction and could benefit from being rerecorded. A week later, Elton turned up at DJM, shamefaced, with a cassette of the reworked track in his pocket to play for James's approval.

In spite of the difficulties involved in its making, *Madman Across the Water* proved that Elton and Bernie were still very much on a creative roll. An album of weighty ballads and midpaced rockers, lyrically it came over as a travelogue that documented—sometimes directly, sometimes obliquely—Elton and Bernie's experiences touring throughout the States. "Holiday Inn" read as if it had been scribbled on a scrap of paper midflight, with its detailing of landing in Boston, then moving from gate to limo to hotel, filled with ennui yet somehow strangely beyond fatigue. The episodic "Tiny Dancer," set to become one of the duo's most enduring songs, was Taupin's open love letter to Maxine, its title inspired by how his petite wife, now employed on the road as a stagewear seamstress, would stand gently swaying to Elton's performances. Though set to become a future Elton John standard, it was slightly marred on record by its singer's chewy vocal approximation of a southern American accent.

Elsewhere, the album was populated by a cast of imagined and decaying American characters, from the aging wino "Razor Face" to the homeless and ever moving onetime criminal and druggie in "Rotten Peaches." More tangential was the odd tale of the fictitious Alvin Tostig, who names his son "Levon," and employs him to sell balloons in town, as depicted in a David Larkham illustration in the lyric booklet stapled into the record's gatefold sleeve. Intriguingly, "All the Nasties" featured Elton, through the words of Bernie, addressing the press and ruminating on whether they might ever inquire about a private matter not made explicit in the lyric. No one picked up on the fact that it was a song hinting at the secret of Elton's sexuality.

But it was the expansive title track of *Madman Across the Water* that proved the standout. Unfolding over close to six minutes from its opening piano and trippy reverse reverb acoustic guitar effects into a hypnotic groove, it gradually built its intense atmosphere, ebbing and flowing and aided by Buckmaster's stunning orchestrations, to the high drama of its chorus, before fading to nothing and beginning again. The playfully elusive lyric—seemingly the scattered thoughts of someone with failing mental health—was wide open to interpretation, not least because Taupin refused to explain it. Some listeners were later to erroneously believe that the madman across the water was Richard Nixon.

Wrapped in expensive and elaborate artwork depicting its title and the name of its artist embroidered into denim, the look and sound of *Madman Across the Water* chimed with the fashions of 1971. Moreover, its warm and detailed production was very much suited to the burgeoning desire among record buyers for top-quality hi-fi sound. Even more importantly perhaps, it was FM radio ready.

Unbelievably, then, it stiffed in the UK, not quite reaching the Top Forty of the album chart, while far more successfully peaking at number eight in the States. In Britain, it seemed, the press backlash against Elton—seen to be sucking up to the Americans by spending most of his time there—had affected his sales. Appearing on BBC TV's newly launched *The Old Grey Whistle Test,* designed to show-case more serious rock as opposed to pop music, he couldn't help but gripe. "During the year I've had my fair share of bitchiness, which I really can't stand," he moaned on the show.

In his homeland, the lackluster performance of *Madman Across the Water* was viewed as the plummeting fall of Elton John after the rapid rise. "I like the songs on the album," he later commented. "I don't like my vocal performance. I knew after that album there had to be a change."

AT THE SAME time, those close to him believe this is where Elton first floated off on his star trip, pulling away from the band on the road, shielded from them by the increasingly protective John Reid. In truth, though, there was an element of survival instinct in his sudden remove and apartness. Particularly whenever he returned to the American West Coast, his arrival seemed to attract a swarm of push-ers and groupies and music biz hangers-on. These were days of lax security at concert venues and sometimes it seemed as if anyone could just wander backstage and into the dressing room. "It really was a sort of open-door situation," says Bernie. "Between the wheel-ers and dealers and the guys in the satin jackets from the record companies . . . it was just such a scene."

A very different scene greeted them when they flew south across the equator in October for the first tour of Australia. Instantly, Elton felt that the island continent was behind the times compared to Eu-rope and America. Touching down in Perth, having had his hair dyed orange with touches of green behind his ears, in a look that was more proto-punk than glam, Elton and the touring party began to attract stares and hostile comments. As they stood in line at cus-toms, one local woman cried out, "What's this? A bloody traveling circus?"

They were more welcome in other quarters. No less unlikely a figure than the Dean of Perth (a leading cleric of the Anglican Church of Australia) invited them all to a reception to be held that evening. Elton was hopelessly beat after the long flight, and so someone from his camp made a call wondering if the function could possibly be moved to the following night. The next anyone heard was when the local TV news channel broadcast a damning item declaring, "Elton John snubs the Dean of Perth."

It was a bad omen for what would turn out to be a disastrous tour. Antipodean promoters, it seemed, hadn't yet got to grips with how to stage modern rock shows, and so the venues for the gigs were random and strange—a soccer stadium in Perth, tennis centers in Adelaide and Melbourne, a detour to New Zealand to play a speedway track in Auckland.

More bizarrely, at the airport in Sydney ahead of the final show, Elton was treated as a threat to polite society. He arrived wearing a denim jacket on which were pinned and stitched dozens of badges and patches—a sheriff's star, an insignia with the words SUPER SCHMUCK, images of Donald Duck, Mickey Mouse, and Porky Pig. But the authorities took exception to a large white button bearing the meaningless and daft legend, in growing sizes of font, BITCH BITCH BITCH, along with others they considered to be sexually suggestive. In the end, Elton agreed to cover them up with Band-Aids to "save hassle." Nevertheless, the luggage of these apparent freaks was thoroughly searched while they were aggressively interrogated about whether any of them were marijuana smokers.

Their last gig, at the Randwick Racecourse on October 31, was the worst of a terrible run. A canopy of canvas over the top of the stage collapsed and blew away in high winds and the show had to be put on hold. Ever the troupers, Elton and the band, freezing in overcoats, then performed "Waltzing Matilda," regarded as Australia's unofficial national anthem, to a chorus of accompanying voices rising up from the crowd as the rain battered down.

OVERRELEASING AND OVERTOURING made 1971 a tough year for Elton. At the end of it, his nerves shot, his fingers raw, he felt "like a plate of jelly."

Shopping in London's upmarket food and department store Fortnum and Mason in the first week of December, he threw another hissy fit in public. The sales assistant at the till recognized him—wow, it was Elton John. She then took a look at his checkbook, which had of course been issued under the name of Reginald Dwight, and wouldn't allow him to make the transaction, unaware that that was actually his real name. The matter was quickly resolved, but still, he felt angry and embarrassed. "Fuck this," he snapped, stepping out onto the pavement and turning to John Reid. "I'm going to change my name."

On December 8, Dick James arranged a meeting for the singer with his lawyer to make the application for a name change by deed poll. Asked if he wanted to give himself a new middle name, he said, on impulse, "Hercules."

When Elton broke the news to his mum, she went berserk. It hadn't been a problem telling her he was gay. But this was changing, forever, the birth name she had given him.

"You can call me Herc, if you like," Elton teased her.

"Fancy calling yourself after Steptoe's horse," she huffed, referring to the long-suffering nag in the BBC's then popular sitcom *Steptoe and Son,* about two rag-and-bone men who lived in a junkyard.

But her son was determined to make the name change absolute. From here on in he insisted that everyone call him Elton. He would even tear up any letters that arrived in the post addressed to Reg Dwight.

But as he points out: "Changing your name, it doesn't alter anything."

Nonetheless, in future times, when Reg would have a wobble, he would take psychological strength from having legally assumed the identity of his far more glamorous, far more self-assured alter ego: Elton Hercules John.

Opposites—and outsiders—attract. Backstage at the Shaw Theatre in London: Princess Margaret and Elton (with her husband, Antony Armstrong-Jones, the Earl of Snowdon, in the background).

HERCULES

IF, IN 1972, YOU PEERED through its spiked iron gates at its weathered, ivy-clad stone walls, you wouldn't immediately think that the Château d'Hérouville had the makings of a hit factory. But the gently decaying property, built more than two centuries earlier, already held a place in French artistic folklore. Lying twenty-four miles northwest of Paris, the château in the Val d'Oise made its first impression upon a creative work as the Castle d'Hérouville in a hunting scene in *Modeste Mignon,* the 1844 novel by Honoré de Balzac. Around the same time, the Polish-born composer Frédéric Chopin and his lover George Sand, the promiscuous, androgynous female writer, often met there in secret. Adding to the myth of the château, after their deaths, their ghosts were said to haunt its halls.

Toward the end of that century, in the last torturous weeks of his life in the summer of 1890, Vincent van Gogh could sometimes be seen from one of its picture windows, painting in the surrounding fields. Reportedly he daubed a lost image of the château itself, but it was certainly in this pastoral setting that the tormented artist produced his last great work, the vivid if gloomy *Wheatfield with Crows.* It's believed it was in these same fields that Van Gogh shot himself on July 27, before stumbling to the nearby village of Auvers-sur-Oise and dying two days later.

Most recently, in the 1960s, the château had been bought by the French film composer Michael Magne, who transformed the top floor of its south wing into a recording facility he named Strawberry Studio. The location had become something of a magnet for the sixties counterculture in northern France. Jane Fonda, in the country filming *Barbarella* in 1968, brought Magne a sapling that he planted in the garden, which was now growing into a twisted tree.

The summer of '71 saw the Grateful Dead staying at the château when the California psychedelicists were booked to play a nearby festival. The gig was canceled, and so instead they staged an impromptu show on the grounds of the château for the local villagers. Less than keen, for obvious drug-related reasons, to have French police attend this "happening," the band made arrangements through the mayor to have fire officers provide security for the event. A welcoming meal was laid on for the firemen. Mischievously, and potentially dangerously, the Dead spiked their wine and fruit juice with LSD.

A splendid time, however, was apparently had by all. The night ended with naked firefighters frolicking in the château's outdoor swimming pool.

HOW ELTON CAME to discover the Château d'Hérouville was purely through financial necessity. Now that the money was pouring in, he was being subjected to the British government's punishing taxation of high earners at the marginal rate of 75 percent. His accountants advised Elton that writing and recording overseas—the same trick the Rolling Stones would pull in '72 by making *Exile on Main Street* in Villefranche-sur-Mer—would ease some of the financial pain.

Besides, Elton believed that getting out of London and fixing his mind on his creativity might alleviate some of the stresses he'd experienced making *Madman Across the Water*. In this way, he was to prove a pioneer of what was to become known as residential recording—making music in a beautiful place out in the country. It was an experience that both Dylan and the Band in the Big Pink house in West Saugerties, New York, and Traffic in rural England had previously benefited from. "I think we were inspired," says Bernie, "by Traffic going off to make records in little cottages in the country."

As producer, Gus Dudgeon was sent to France to scout potential locations. He initially chanced upon a villa in the south of the country, which he figured he could turn into a makeshift studio. In fact, he'd already ordered a hundred fifty mattresses to sonically deaden its walls when someone told him about the château outside Paris. "The minute I arrived there," he remembered, "I thought, *This has got to be the place. This has got to be ten times better than renting a villa and basically building a bloody studio in the middle of it.*"

Elton and the band arrived there in January 1972 with a new addition to the lineup, guitarist Davey Johnstone. The twenty-year-old Scot, who already looked the hirsute rocker part with his long wavy blond hair, was an impressively versatile musician—a brief member of the progressive folk group Magna Carta who'd gone on to play acoustic guitar, mandolin, and sitar on *Madman Across the Water*. Elton was keen to use his touring band on an entire album for the first time, and to pare back the orchestrations for a more focused sound. Having added Johnstone to the faithful core of Murray and Olsson, together the augmented group traveled to the château.

Once there, Elton and Bernie settled into a songwriting modus operandi that was both spontaneous and intense. The château was divided into two wings: one housed the studio, the other the living quarters. It was in the latter that the communal breakfast area became an improvised writing zone for Elton, with a piano and drum kit and amps dotted around the dining room. The duo arrived at the château with only two songs prepared, but within three days they had written another nine, at a breakneck pace that would come to define their albums made at Hérouville. Dudgeon remembered one morning watching Elton—within the space of half an hour—virtually autocompose a gorgeously atmospheric new song from a lyric Bernie had written called "Rocket Man."

"All the gear would be set up near the breakfast table," Elton remembers. "Bernie would be typing upstairs."

"Our approach was very, very immediate," says Taupin. "I remember sitting on the edge of my bed just scrolling out stuff and tearing it off and going on to something else."

"Bernie would bring down the lyric, I'd write the song," Elton explains. "The band would get up, join in with me and then we'd go over the courtyard to the studio and record it. It was a pretty sensible way of doing things. It was very, very casual and very quick. It was such a creative hive of industry."

It was also sometimes an acutely spooky environment to work in. Visitors to the château were convinced that the place was indeed haunted. Later, when David Bowie recorded *Pin Ups* and *Low* there, he was terrified by the eerie atmosphere in the master bedroom, particularly one cold and dark corner of it that seemed to suck in any natural or electric light.

"It had a very strange vibe about it," says Bernie of the château. "It was beautiful and tranquil, but at the same time there were definitely some sort of ethereal things in the air around there."

"It *was* haunted," believes Davey Johnstone. "Almost every day somebody would be tapped on the shoulder when they were walking down the giant staircase."

The heavy imbibing of marijuana by the band members likely enhanced their tuning in to these peculiar vibes. Not for the still drug-free Elton, though, even if he would join the others in indulging in fine French wines.

"The band were doing drugs . . . puffing," he says. "And we'd have a glass of wine. But we couldn't afford not to be reasonably clean-living. We were doing too much work."

It was an idyllic setup. Elton found himself playing the studio's Steinway piano beneath a thirteenth-century chandelier while occasionally glancing up to take in the lovely rural scenes outside the window. No matter how loud the band played, with no neighbors nearby, they could open all the studio's windows as they blasted away. Once a take had been completed, they enjoyed rib-rattlingly loud playbacks through the enormous speakers.

It was a loose and productive time, in what they came to call their honky château. As the recording progressed, it was clear that these new songs were so strong that they wouldn't need to be embellished by strings. The singer, privately relieved, was thinking, *No one can turn around and say, "Oh, it's Elton John with his hundred-piece orchestra again."*

ALL THE SAME, the first thing he did when he returned to London was to make a second, already booked appearance at the Royal Festival Hall on February 5 with a full army of classical musicians.

Whereas his previous performance there eleven months before found him backed by many of the string players who'd appeared on his Trident recordings, this time around the plan was for him to up the ante by fronting the eighty-piece Royal Philharmonic Orchestra.

As it turned out, the show was something of a trial. Elton suspected that the classically trained musicians weren't giving their all because they considered a pop show to be unworthy of their talents. Conducting them, Paul Buckmaster found himself the subject of snippy remarks during rehearsals.

"Can I please have a bit of quiet?" Buckmaster asked the musicians at one point.

"Well," came the sneering reply from one of their number, "if you got your fucking hair cut, perhaps you could *hear* quiet."

That night, Elton, sparkling in a silver jacket made up of rhombus shapes, opened the show solo before being joined by the band—including Davey Johnstone in his debut performance—for a more traditional rock set. After a break, having undergone a costume change, he reappeared in a cream-colored long-tailed tuxedo to much applause and whistling before doffing his silver top hat. He sat down at the piano in front of the orchestra and slipped into "Your Song." It was stirring stuff, but not everyone onstage appeared moved by it. As he led into "Take Me to the Pilot," some of the orchestra members sat around looking snooty and bored. Conscious of their hostile attitude, Elton became tense and uncomfortable, backed by what he perceived to be an ensemble of musical snobs. He ended an hour later with a lovely orchestrated version of "Goodbye," the closing track of *Madman Across the Water*, but he left the stage feeling deflated.

Afterward, now irate, once again Elton said more than he should have to the press. "I thought the orchestra were a bunch of cunts," he snapped at one journalist. "They made snide remarks. I sunk a lot of money into that concert and I'll never do it again." Ray Coleman in *Melody Maker* reckoned that the show was contrived: "Majestic occasion though it was . . . not the mindblower we perhaps expected. And it raised the hoary question: does pop want, need, or benefit from such an uneasy hybrid?"

It was a fair point, and clearly a dilemma that Elton was tussling with himself. Fifteen days later, he turned in a more stripped-back performance at the Shaw Theatre in Euston, at a benefit for the National Youth Theatre attended by Princess Margaret and her husband, Lord Snowdon. Elton and the Queen's younger sister hit it off immediately, prompting her to invite the singer and the band to dinner at Kensington Palace. Margaret had a reputation for enjoying a drink and was a heavy smoker, but more significantly, perhaps, was said behind closed doors to have a wicked sense of humor. As such, she and Elton were a natural fit, in both their shared love of hooting laughter, and likely in another way that wasn't at the time publicly apparent. "I always felt she was very lonely," Elton says. "She wasn't wild. She loved music, played the piano. I found her to be kinda lonely and always very, very sweet to me."

If this blossoming friendship would in the years to come usher Elton behind the private doors of the royal family, it was further evidence that no matter how the critics turned their noses up at him, he was fast becoming a key figure in popular British culture. A hero's welcome greeted him at his virtual homecoming show at Watford Town Hall, seven miles north of Pinner, on February 24. But with this rising profile, Elton also became a target for those with dangerous agendas.

Two days earlier—and only three weeks after the notorious incident known as "Bloody Sunday" in which twenty-six unarmed civil rights protesters were shot in Derry, Northern Ireland, by British soldiers—the Irish Republican Army had carried out a revenge attack by detonating an incendiary device hidden in a car parked outside the UK army barracks in the small Hampshire town of Aldershot, southwest of London. Seven civilian staff were killed. Now Britain was nervous and on high alert.

Partway through the Watford Town Hall show, with the gig in full swing, an organizer walked onto the stage and whispered into Elton's ear that a call had been made to the venue by someone claiming to be from the IRA, warning that a bomb had been planted in the building. Elton was anxiously forced to step away from the piano stool to make way for a policeman, Inspector O'Connor, who sat down and announced to the suddenly panicked audience that the hall had to be evacuated. As was often the case in those tense and uncertain days, though, the threat proved to be a hoax.

Fame was sometimes frightening, sometimes frustrating, but while he was now shining brightly, Elton refused to forget those musicians from his past now left in his shadow. By 1972, Long John Baldry had become a mess, drinking more and more as his career increasingly lost its direction. The previous year, both Elton and Baldry's other protégé, Rod Stewart, had individually produced tracks for a new Baldry album, *It Ain't Easy*, designed to get the singer back on track. It turned out to be Baldry's most successful record, not least when the grinding single "Don't Try to Lay No Boogie-Woogie on the King of Rock and Roll," reconnecting him with his blues roots, became an airplay hit on FM radio in the States. On a subsequent tour of America, though, Baldry, trying to mask his insecurities, hit the bottle even harder.

A subsequent, patchier album, *Everything Stops for Tea*, found Elton and Rod taking a vinyl side apiece in terms of production, with the former overseeing a novelty take on the New Orleans standard "Iko Iko." Such was their loyalty to their former bandleader that both far more famous singers appeared on *Top of the Pops* to perform the song with Baldry. At an after-show party, he was approached and interviewed by a writer from *Disc* magazine and was generous about Rod before—with affection but likely a touch of jealousy—poking fun at Elton.

"I always knew Rod was going to become something very, very special," Baldry pronounced. "But how could one predict that a boy with an overweight problem . . . I mean he is a bit broad across the beam, our Reg. Who would have thought that this strange boy with his myopic lenses and fat arse . . . could turn out to be one of the pop sensations of all time?"

Of course, Elton dealt out his share of bitchy comments about other people to the press, so he had to take it. He couldn't stop himself, it seemed, from blurting out wicked put-downs of other artists. Though it was surprising when one of his targets became his former hero numero uno, Jerry Lee Lewis.

In April, he caught a show by Lewis at the London Palladium.

Excitedly, Elton turned up in his drape jacket, only to be jeered at by the aging Teddy Boys in the crowd who recognized him. Ironically, after a run of flop singles in the sixties, Lewis had at the time abandoned rock'n'roll and detoured into a country music career. To Elton's eyes, when he stepped onto the Palladium stage, his idol had turned jaded and toothless. "He could have wiped the audience out," he said afterward. "But he just sat there and played country-and-western numbers as if to say, 'Fuck you.'

"All these old rock stars are the same," he added, dismissing the thirty-six-year-old. But indeed Jerry Lee Lewis must now have seemed practically antique to the twenty-five-year-old Elton—someone belonging to the past, just as he was looking to the future.

WHEREVER HE WENT now, Elton always had to deal with a certain degree of hassle. If it wasn't Teddy Boys mocking him at a gig, it was airport security personnel meticulously pulling apart his luggage looking for drugs. When he touched down in Los Angeles in April ahead of his next U.S. tour, four pairs of his eight-inch-heeled platform stage boots were dismantled in the belief that he was using them to smuggle illegal substances into the country. "It's just that it's such a new style, we haven't caught up with it yet," one customs agent apologized to him, before telling a reporter that the star had been "very cooperative."

As he hit town, "Rocket Man" was released as his next single. It was soon filling the radio airwaves. Driving one day down Sunset Boulevard, Elton heard a DJ on KHJ compare it to Rod Stewart's latest release, the strutting rocker "You Wear It Well."

"That's Rod Stewart's new record," the announcer said in his link. "He surely must be the number one male vocalist around at the moment. I've had lots of phone calls saying that Elton John is. Well, I think Rod Stewart just about beats Elton John."

Sitting at the wheel as he cruised the Strip, Elton was fizzing. Rightly so, perhaps, since the two records were completely different. "You Wear It Well" was a cocksure groover. "Rocket Man" was something else entirely, filled with alienation and a sense of sad adventure.

Its lyric had come to Bernie as he was motoring through the Lincolnshire countryside to his parents' house, the first lines arriving fully formed in his head. Immediately the rest of the song began to flash through his mind. He quickly pushed the accelerator to the floor to get to his destination to grab a pen and paper before he forgot them forever.

A vividly evocative mid-tempo ballad, lent further atmosphere by David Hentschel's plaintive synthesizer parts and Davey Johnstone's eerie, echoing slide guitar (not to mention the band members' meshed harmonies, which were to become a sonic trademark of Elton's subsequent records), "Rocket Man" was set in an imagined future where the narrator's day job involves lonely flights to Mars. Of course, it might have been one long metaphor, with its references to being "high as a kite" and "burning out his fuse" easily interpreted as drug references.

In this way, "Rocket Man" of course echoed David Bowie's veiled tale of the astronaut as mind-fried junkie in "Space Oddity," released three years before and also produced by Gus Dudgeon. But for Taupin, its inspiration had come from the forlorn, pollution-choked commentary of "A Day in the Life of a Tree" from the Beach Boys' 1971 album *Surf's Up*. However, he did later admit that he cribbed the title from the mournful song "Rocket Man" by Florida's baroque pop band Pearls Before Swine.

None of this, however, calmed an apparently livid Bowie, not least when—after "Rocket Man" rose to number six in the United States—"Space Oddity" (which hadn't initially been a hit in America) was rereleased in 1973 and didn't fare as well, reaching only number fifteen. It was unfairly judged by many to be an Elton rip-off. Bowie's wife, Angie, tried to cool his fury with the words "Other people can sing about space travel too."

"Rocket Man" seemed to be everywhere, not least because Uni Records had linked its release to the launch of Apollo 16. Cleverly, if opportunistically, the record label took out music trade press ads that read: "On the morning of April 16, 1972, Apollo 16 was launched into orbit on a journey to the moon. A few mornings earlier Uni Records launched a new Elton John single into the worldwide orbit. What a trip! Both launchings bound to set new records."

The publicity stunt tie-in prompted an invite from NASA for Elton, Bernie, and the band to visit their Manned Spacecraft Center in Houston, Texas, on April 28, the day after the Apollo 16 spacecraft splashed down in the Pacific Ocean. For four hours, the party were shown around the Center by Apollo 15 Command Module Pilot Al Worden and even given the opportunity to "fly into space" in a simulator.

"Rocket Man"—with its bracketed LP addendum "(I Think It's Going to Be a Long, Long Time)"—set up the arrival of Elton's fifth studio album, titled *Honky Château* in tribute to the French hideaway. Not only was it a far less ornate and more direct offering than *Madman Across the Water,* it also exhibited Elton's knack for musical genre hopping, opening with the infectious Louisiana swing of "Honky Cat" and closing with the glam rock swish of "Hercules." In between, it often sounded like a record made in New Orleans rather than northern France—"Susie (Dramas)" could have been written and produced by Allen Toussaint, "Amy" had some of Dr. John's voodooish swampiness, and "Salvation" (originally earmarked as the first single) was rousing, multivoiced, light-seeking gospel.

Elsewhere, the lyric of "Slave" revisited the violent uprising of "Burn Down the Mission" from a shackled perspective, and the aptly named, slow-lane "Mellow" featured the keening electric violin of the French musician Jean-Luc Ponty, as if channeling the ghosts of the château.

One track, however, stuck out through its sheer daftness. "I Think I'm Going to Kill Myself" belied its fatalistic title by being a jaunty tongue-in-cheek moment of light relief in which the singer cast himself as a teenager imagining the reactions to his death after he shoots himself. To highlight the incongruous frivolity, its middle section featured the sound of the hairy alumnus of the Bonzo Dog Doo-Dah Band, "Legs" Larry Smith, merrily tap-dancing.

Elton, like the Beatles before him, who had cast the lampooning ensemble in a strip club scene in *Magical Mystery Tour* in 1967, was a huge fan of the band their aficionados called the Bonzos. Having mutated from a rabble of art schoolers playing twenties jazz into a surrealist rock band, by 1972—in part because of the deep depressions and heavy tranquilizer use of their frontman, Vivian Stanshall—the Bonzo Dog Doo-Dah Band was effectively over, after a final and wryly named contractual obligation album, *Let's Make Up and Be Friendly*.

"Legs" Larry Smith, given his nickname as a result of his early appearances with the band, clacking around in tap shoes as the self-invented character Mr. Wonderful, had subsequently become the group's drummer. Now he was at loose ends. Fortuitously, looking to inject some humor into his upcoming American shows, Elton called him up and invited him on tour.

"I said, 'But, darling, I don't have a thing to wear!'" Smith remembers. "And Elton said, 'Well, look, go and do what you wanna do and bring it over to the States and away we go.' So I got two outfits made up and I flew over first-class to New York."

Smith, with his mock-effete actorly demeanor and acute sense of the absurd, was to further bolster Elton when it came to the flashy peculiarities of his stage costumes. "I'd already been established as a kind of flamboyant eccentric with my clothes," Smith says. "He was still in the closet in terms of gaydom." But with Larry's help, albeit in the guise of camp theatricality, Elton was able to throw those doors wide open.

Arriving in the States and at Elton's hotel, Larry paraded around in the outfit he'd already dreamed up for his tap-dancing appearance in the show for "I Think I'm Going to Kill Myself." He called it the Triple Wedding. "I had a shiny chrome crash helmet with a wedding cake couple glued on the top, and another two, one on each shoulder. A three-quarter-length tunic-waisted jacket. White flares with diamanté running down the seams. Wonderful silver lamé shoes from Chelsea Cobbler, beautifully made with diamanté round the platform soles. Silk gloves, a naughty doggy dog shit tattooed on my chest and, flowing off of each shoulder, forty yards of white netting."

It was quite a getup, and one that clearly tickled Elton. From then on, Larry was Elton's closest companion on the mammoth American and British tour that would run, on and off, for the next seven months. "He was the only person who kept me sane," Elton said of Larry in '72. "I get terribly bored when things are too serious. I want to get into funny things, so I might as well have a bit of comedy in my act."

Larry encouraged Elton to position a framed photograph of the sugary-sweet Hollywood legend Doris Day on top of his piano, which at a certain point in the set the singer would clamber up to kiss. Going further, Smith wondered if he could devise a "Singin' in the Rain" song-and-dance duet for the pair of them.

"You must be mad," Elton told Larry. "They'll wonder what the fuck's going on." It could easily have pushed a rock audience too far and sent them heading for the beer and hamburger stands, or worse, the exit doors. But Smith pointed out that "Singin' in the Rain" now had an added resonance, having been featured in Stanley Kubrick's *A Clockwork Orange* the year before, most notoriously in a rape scene. By featuring it in the show, Smith argued, they could be "double hip." Elton decided to give it a go.

As it turned out, the audiences laughed and roared and lapped it up. In the routine, tour manager Marvin Tabolsky sat at the piano and mimed to a prerecorded backing tape as Larry and Elton, in macs, capes, and fedoras, performed a skit reminiscent of the golden days of screen musicals, albeit with added risquéness.

"Gee, Larry, I wish I could dance like you," Elton said onstage to his partner. "I'm sure I'd get all the girls."

"Gee, Elton," Larry responded. "I wish I could play the piano like you. Because I know I'd get all the boys."

"Which he loved, of course," Smith points out. "Because he was still inside that closet with the door firmly locked."

IN OVERSIZED YELLOW glasses spelling out Z-O-O-M!, back in Britain, Elton appeared on *Top of the Pops* as "Rocket Man" made number two, his biggest UK hit yet. Backstage there was much cause for celebration since, after all his trials in Britain, here was proof that Elton was now a bona fide pop star.

For Davey Johnstone, it was quite an event, coming only five months after he'd joined the band. "We're all in one of these cheesy dressing rooms," he remembers, "and John Reid says, 'Let's have some champagne.' So he's opening it and talking at the same time and the cork goes straight up his nose. It was brilliant. It was like one of those great Spinal Tap moments."

His status upped, and outgrowing the London flat, Elton moved with Reid to a large two-story bungalow with an outside swimming pool at 14 Abbots Drive in the showbiz enclave of the Wentworth Estate in Virginia Water, Surrey, west of London. Here he enjoyed filling the house with the spoils of the high-earning star: Pricey artworks covered the white walls, a fifties jukebox sat in the game room, a suit of armor guarded the stairway, and the driveway was soon crammed with nose-to-tail luxury cars, including a de rigueur Rolls-Royce.

Far from being a messy rock star abode littered with empty bottles and overflowing ashtrays, the bungalow was conspicuously spic-and-span. Visitors noted that it seemed almost like a show home. Sheila and Fred married in May and moved into a property in the garden. The idea was that his mother and now legal stepfather could look after the house (which Elton, in a familiar theme, had taken to calling Hercules) and the two dogs he'd recently acquired—Brian, a spaniel, and Bruce, a German shepherd—whenever Elton was away, which was of course often.

After the painless birth of *Honky Château*, the making of the next album turned out to be a slog. Everyone else was raring to go, but Elton wasn't in the right frame of mind. The workhorse was worn out, and in June, he almost had to drag his bones back to the château.

Once he got there, Elton remained in a very peculiar state, as if he was moving in slow motion. He felt he was on the verge of a nervous breakdown. He said to Gus Dudgeon, "I can't make this album." The producer was unflappable. He told the exhausted singer, "All right, we'll do it in September."

But once relieved of this commitment, Elton changed his mind. He was planning to go on vacation in July and he thought, *Let's get it over and done with before then*. Even so, he knew it wasn't a particularly healthy way to approach a creative endeavor. For most of the recording, his temper was foul, and he was constantly quarreling with everyone. There were angry phone calls made to Dick James back in London. He and Elton didn't talk to each other for four months afterward.

Even Bernie, who'd completed his lyrics for the new album beforehand, stayed away from the studio for the most part this time around. When he arrived one day, without warning, Elton was walking across the château's lawn and nearly jumped out of his skin when he saw Taupin sitting behind a bush, enjoying a moment of quiet contemplation in the garden. Still, he was a welcome visitor to what had been a rough session. The band delighted in seeing Taupin's reactions to the new songs as they blasted out of the studio's speakers.

"Bernie might've thought, 'This would be a ballad' and it'd be a steaming rocker," says Davey Johnstone. "Or he might think, 'This'll be really up-tempo,' and it'd be the opposite. We all would be watching him."

At the end of a trying month, Elton's sixth album was in the can, even if he'd made it in a numbed daze. Running on fumes, he landed back in Los Angeles for his planned vacation, ranting worryingly as he walked through the airport. Those around him suspected he was cracking up before their eyes. He was subsequently diagnosed with glandular fever.

"I just was exhausted," he says. "It was plain exhaustion from working nonstop. You move so fast your body after a while says stop it. I never had any breakdowns in that time. If I was ill, I was ill. I was just ill because I was fucking working hard. It was a wake-up."

He cooled his aching mind on the coast, at a beach house he'd rented in Malibu. Joining him for the summer was Bryan Forbes, the British director of films including *Whistle Down the Wind* and *Séance on a Wet Afternoon*. Forbes, who also wrote scripts and novels, was a polymath who owned a bookshop back in Virginia Water. One day Elton had wandered in and they'd struck up a conversation that quickly turned to a friendship. Elton became a regular visitor to the house nearby, Seven Pines, that Forbes shared with his actress wife, Nanette Newman, where the singer admired the older couple's books and art and elegant décor.

Sometimes, suburban-born Reg felt—as is often the case with the nouveau riche—that he lacked refinement. Under the influence of Forbes, he began to cultivate his tastes. At the same time, 1972 marked the year that Elton truly began to spend, spend, spend— a compulsion that would come to publicly define him in the minds of some. Over the summer he daily went on money-burning shopping trips around Los Angeles. At the end of the holiday, he'd managed to fill sixty-seven suitcases and thirty-two trunks with his purchases of records, books, clothes, and jewelry. What's more, there were clearly still piles of money heading his way. In July, *Honky Château* became his first number one U.S. album.

Making the most of his first break in ages, Elton, with Bernie in tow, went to see Alice Cooper at the open-air Hollywood Bowl. They were astounded by how ridiculously and thrillingly large-scale the show was. A helicopter flew over and rained hundreds of pairs of paper panties from the sky. Bernie remembers himself and Elton "acting like kids in the audience. They threw posters out at the end and we were jumping up trying to get them."

Through Forbes and his film industry connections, Elton threw himself into L.A. life, even mixing with stars of old Hollywood. He was introduced to the still raunchy and sharp Mae West, then on the cusp of her seventy-ninth birthday. Elton would take her out for afternoon tea and together he and West would marvel at the people who'd come up to her, showering her with praise. "It was very touching," he remembers. "I sat there while Mae West was talking, thinking, *Fuck, I can't believe where I am.* All I did was listen. You don't interrupt."

Then one day Bryan Forbes told Elton that he had a surprise guest coming over for dinner that evening. Although it was the height of a baking summer, the visitor was insisting the fire be lit for his arrival. It was Groucho Marx.

"Groucho arrived in an overcoat and was *so* not friendly," Elton remembers. " 'When are we gonna eat? It's too cold in here.' We're all thinking, *Oh fucking hell.* Very uncomfortable for about half an hour. Then suddenly, of course, it was a big joke."

Once everyone had relaxed, Groucho said to Elton, "They tell me you're number one. But I'd never heard of you until I went into my office this morning and said I was having dinner with Elton John. They all fainted. After that I lost what remaining respect I have for you."

Even at eighty-one, Groucho's sense of humor was as razor-edged as ever and there was still very much a twinkle in his eye. Although his silver screen heyday was far behind him and he'd suffered a patchy career as a TV host throughout the sixties, he remained an open-minded individual who moved with the times. In 1968, in preparation for a role in the panned hippie satire *Skidoo,* in which he played a mob boss named God who tuned in, turned on, and dropped out, Marx had taken acid with writer and onetime Merry Prankster Paul Krassner. At one point during their trip, they were listening to Bach's Cantata No. 7 when Groucho began hallucinating "beautiful visions of Gothic cathedrals." He asked Krassner, "Do you think Bach knew he was doing that?"

Marx was still a provocative figure. In 1971 he caused a furor when he gave an interview to the underground San Francisco paper *Take One* and declared, "I think the only hope this country has is Nixon's assassination." While it made him a hero to the country's war-protesting youth, it also ensured that he had an FBI file opened on him as a potentially dangerous subversive.

That summer, Elton and Groucho got along so well that they ended up hanging out together on a number of occasions. One night, the singer and John Reid took Marx to see a theater performance of *Jesus Christ Superstar.* "Along the way," says Elton, "he stopped in a bar and picked up two girls. He was the biggest flirt I've ever met." As the theater lights dimmed, Marx barked, "Does it have a happy ending?" Later, during the crucifixion scene, he loudly declared, "This is sure to offend the Jews."

"Funniest fucker," Elton says. "He never could figure out why I was called Elton John and said I should be called John Elton. I've got a Marx Brothers poster signed by him—'To John Elton from Marx Groucho.' "

As their friendship developed, Elton often found himself impaled on the sharp end of Groucho's jokes. One night, laughing but exasperated, Elton held up his hands in mock surrender. "Don't shoot me," he protested, "I'm only the piano player."

Elton thought to himself, *That's a good line.* He stored it away for later.

THE U.S. TOUR resumed at the end of September. Inspired by his Hollywood summer, Elton and Larry had added even more razzle-dazzle to the show by the time it made its way back to California for two arena gigs before a total of thirty-five thousand people at the Forum in Los Angeles. There was also added intensity to Elton's playing, as he forcefully battered the piano keys, resulting in his bursting a finger wide open on the second night and having to rush backstage to stem the bloodflow.

He returned to massed cheers and offered the words "Even if I had only one finger left, I'd play for you." He then thanked the audience for the "most fantastic night of my life."

For "I Think I'm Going to Kill Myself," "Legs" Larry Smith made his entrance onstage followed by two little people dressed as U.S. marines holding his wedding train. "I came out blowing kisses," Smith recalls, while also remembering that during the number,

Singin' in the glittering rain of confetti: Elton and "Legs" Larry Smith cackling among the chorus girls.

twenty thousand dollars' worth of confetti showered on the performers. "I was in heaven," he says. "It was just a joy to do."

Not everyone in the band thought these preposterous theatrics were a great idea, though. "Our attitude was always *Oh God . . . cringe,*" Davey Johnstone admits. "We're going, 'What? He doesn't need this . . .'"

All the while, on the road, Legs was whispering into Elton's ear: "It's wonderful . . . carry on . . . get bigger . . . get crazier."

Elton certainly would. He was only just getting going.

Writing, always writing. The ever prolific Elton and Bernie, London, 1973.

7 NO SUPERMAN GONNA RUIN MY PLANS

THE QUEEN MOTHER HAD NEVER SEEN anything like it. From her vantage point in the royal box of the London Palladium on the evening of Monday, October 30, 1972, she applauded politely as she watched Elton emerge from the wings in teetering stacked-heel boots, white hexagonal glasses, and a silver suit patriotically striped in red and blue. He took a bow and sat down at a white grand piano.

"Did I hear a snigger from the audience?" he said into the microphone, suddenly aware of how outlandish he must have appeared in such a stuffy environment as the great British upper-crust tradition of the televised Royal Variety Performance.

He'd been advised that he should play a couple of his best-known hits—maybe "Your Song," maybe "Rocket Man." Elton thought, *Boring!* He was in a mood for mischief. Nine years before, back in '63, John Lennon had urged the poshos to "rattle your jewelry." Elton planned to offer up something more bizarre.

He began by pumping out the opening chords to "I Think I'm Going to Kill Myself" before launching into its oddly happy-go-lucky suicidal lyric. Then, in the instrumental break that followed the first chorus, Legs swanned onto the stage in his Triple Wedding outfit, his fists gripping bunches of multicolored balloons. He released them, untied, into the audience and they flew erratically around the stalls making farting noises. From where he was sitting, Elton could see women in tiaras mouthing, "Ooh, ooh."

Legs, in his long brown locks and Zapata mustache, crash helmet, and white wedding shoulder veils, beamed and tap-danced, then blew kisses and waved and disappeared sidestage. Behind his humongous drum kit, Nigel Olsson, who considered Smith a "bloody twit," shot a withering look across at Dee Murray and thought, *I hope this is a dream.*

Next, Elton introduced one of the songs he'd written and recorded during his depleted summer at the château. "This is about all the rock'n'roll records of the 1960s," he announced, "and it's called 'Crocodile Rock.'" It was his new single released three days before—a kitschy and naggingly catchy take on the dance craze singles of the past.

At its close, Elton and the band, including a returning Legs—who'd respectfully removed his crash helmet—lined up at the front of the stage to collectively bow to the audience and, as was the tradition, in the direction of the royal presence. It looked as if they'd thoroughly enjoyed themselves. In truth, Elton had found the whole affair "horrendous."

"Princess Margaret has told me she thinks it's four hours of boredom," Elton indiscreetly told a reporter later. "I know what she means."

They'd all had to fly home from California especially for this royal appointment, since there was still another month left of the American tour. Jet-lagged backstage at the Palladium—with its limited space and a full roster of acts: the Jackson 5, the British female impersonator Danny La Rue, and the toothy, tickling-stick-wielding Liverpudlian comedian Ken Dodd among them—Elton was forced to share a dressing room with Jack Jones and Liberace. The latter gave him a demonstration of how he could light up his suit with a hidden button. Now *there* was an idea. There seemed to be no limit to how brilliantly ludicrous stage costumes could be.

THAT TIRING AND testing evening aside, Elton was keen to focus his sights back on Britain, feeling that he'd neglected his native land in recent years with his virtually incessant American touring. "Driving to Bolton isn't quite as glamorous as driving to Santiago," he pointed out to the *New Musical Express,* strangely choosing a South American city he'd never actually visited to illustrate his point. "But we have to get our finger out."

His success in America was obviously hugely rewarding, but Britain in 1972, with the rise of glam rock, was really where it was at in terms of trailblazing music and fashion. In August, at the Rainbow Theatre in north London, Elton had witnessed David Bowie's biggest show yet in his futuristic incarnation as Ziggy Stardust, supported by the equally outré sci-fi rock'n'roll of Roxy Music. He emerged exhilarated—his throat raw from actually screaming with excitement—if a touch envious.

"That was a turning point," he says. "It was like, Fuck, the bar's been raised."

Everyone was trying to outdo one another, not least, in their teasing battle of one-upmanship, Elton and the now UK-chart-dominating Marc Bolan. For the T. Rex singer's birthday the previous September, Elton had cheekily sent a gift of a life-sized blow-up photographic image of himself. Returning the gesture, but going further, in March, for Elton's twenty-fifth, Bolan had given him the silver disc for his "Jeepster" British number two hit and, similarly, an enlarged reproduction of his own image. "Of course, his was much bigger than mine," Elton notes. Indeed it was—nearly thirty feet tall and delivered to the Wentworth bungalow in a moving van. It had to be left out in the garden.

On a similarly grand scale, Marc Bolan had recently completed a movie, *Born to Boogie,* directed by Ringo Starr and released via Apple Films. Elton appeared with him in two scenes shot in the basement studio of Apple's offices in Savile Row—doing his best vamping Little Richard impersonation as Marc screamed "Tutti Frutti" and Starr thumped the drums beside him, and playing on "Children of the Revolution" with Bolan's head sticking out of a hole in a mock grand piano where the strings should have been. But, viewing himself in exaggerated dimensions on-screen at the film's London premiere in December, Elton couldn't help but wince. "I look like a fucking gorilla," he said. "So ugly."

His self-consciousness would regularly return to unsettle him, and it was with mixed feelings he returned to Pinner County Grammar School just before Christmas, following an invitation to play a concert at his alma mater. He fretted in the days leading up to it: "What will they think of my act? Because it was a bit wild."

He certainly didn't dress down for the occasion, rolling up in his Ferrari in a fox fur cape adorned with a diamond brooch, a purple suit, and matching glasses. Many of the teachers he'd known at the school he'd left only eight years before were still employed there. If they all looked much the same, the metamorphosis of Reg was astonishing.

The school kids turned feral upon Elton's arrival and older pupils were forced to link arms to form a human chain to protect him as he pushed through the halls to the student lounge. Once safely there, he requested only a cup of tea and presented them with a color TV set for the common room. The concert was, of course, a roaring success. Blowing away his clouds of self-doubt, there was perhaps no greater validation.

"When I drove away," he later remembered, "I thought, *You've made it. You've arrived*. It was a nice feeling."

As 1973 DAWNED, Elton was in the mood for adventure. Even before the album recorded the previous summer at the château had been released, he had to start work on its successor. The château was temporarily unavailable as a result of legal wrangles over its ownership, and so he decided to continue to explore the concept of recording on location by looking farther afield. Following in the fresh footprints of the Rolling Stones, who'd just recorded *Goats Head Soup* at reggae producer Byron Lee's Dynamic Sounds Studio in Kingston, Jamaica, Gus Dudgeon flew out to check out the facility and see if it was suitable for the making of Elton's next album.

En route, the producer's luggage was lost by the airline, and so he found himself wandering through the sweltering streets in the clothes he'd been wearing back in England: thick leather trousers, big padded woolen jacket. "I didn't dare go in any shops," he remembered, " 'cause I was quite convinced somebody was gonna cut my head off or yell, 'Get out of here, honky . . .' "

Dudgeon arrived at Dynamic Sounds and was given a playback, through the studio's booming sound system, of some of the reggae tracks recorded there. He was mightily impressed. "The biggest bass I've ever heard in my life," he marveled. "It was fantastic. I thought, *Well, this is a pretty cool place.* So I went back and said, 'Yeah, it's great, let's go there.'"

Landing in Kingston on January 23, the day after the high-profile boxing match at the city's National Stadium in which George Foreman had taken only two rounds to beat Joe Frazier and become the world heavyweight champion, the party arrived in a swarming city bristling with excitement and danger. As they drove through the streets, Elton was captivated by the sight of tumbledown record store shacks at the side of the road, but he couldn't get his head around the scenes of third-world poverty passing just beyond the window of the car.

Quickly overwhelmed by the sensory assault of Jamaica, he bunkered himself into his room at the Pink Flamingo hotel. Adding to the discomfiting, threatening air of the city was his discovery that Astrid Lundstrom, the girlfriend of Rolling Stones bassist Bill Wyman, had been raped at knifepoint by an intruder in the very same room only three weeks before. Terrified to leave the hotel, Elton rented a Fender Rhodes electric piano, sat down with a pile of Bernie's recently completed lyrics, and, in three days, wrote twenty-one songs.

His weed-loving band, meanwhile, staying in the north coastal resort of Ocho Rios, were off sampling the herbal pleasures Jamaica had to offer. It was here in Jamaica that Elton first tried marijuana, if in a more unusual form. "I wasn't smoking at the time," he says. "So I did liquid ganja, which was like Newcastle Brown Ale. It was fucking brilliant. I'd recommend it highly."

One night, there was cause for celebration: the release on January 26 of Elton's sixth album—named, after his retort to Groucho Marx, *Don't Shoot Me I'm Only the Piano Player.* To toast the album's arrival into the world, he and the band threw a small party in the dining room of the Pink Flamingo. Elton went to bed earlier than the others, leaving them to their carousing, only to suddenly burst back into the dining room, naked under a sheet. While drop-ping off to sleep, he'd discovered a huge centipede crawling across his body and fled his room in wimpish terror.

When the sessions began at Dynamic Sounds, everyone—including Dudgeon, who'd perhaps not examined the setup closely enough on his initial visit—was shocked to discover that the studio was in fact run-down and woefully inadequate. Having been used to playing Steinway grand pianos, Elton sat down at the studio's bat-tered Yamaha upright and tried to bash away at a rocking, up-tempo new song he'd just completed called "Saturday Night's Alright for Fighting."

"Elton was hitting the piano and cockroaches were flying out of it," Bernie remembers.

Worse, there was a distinct lack of urgency among the studio staff, which was entirely at odds with the band's normally highly productive work rate. "I mean, Jamaica's a really lovely place," says Elton. "But, God knows . . . the Stones must've brought all their equipment there. We just came into this studio and it was like, Oh my God. And, y'know, everything was on Caribbean time. 'Well, we need a Leslie speaker.' 'Oh . . . oh yeah . . . two or three days is okay?'"

Davey Johnstone, for his part, knew they were in trouble when Nigel Olsson was setting up his drum kit and he heard one engineer tell another, "Carlton, get the mike." "We went, Oh fuck," John-stone says. "We used twenty mikes on the drums even in those days, y'know. It was like, Oh, we're in deep shit here."

Even the toilet at the studio was troubling. "It was just crusted in yellow," Dudgeon recalled. "I've never seen a more disgusting lava-tory in my life. We used to go in and hover over it. You didn't dare sit on the bloody thing."

The fact that everyone in the band was ludicrously stoned helped to take the edge off. Trying out the sad, slow New Orleans jazz of another new song, "Sweet Painted Lady," Johnstone suddenly came up with an idea for a complementary part he thought he could play on his banjo. He popped open its case, pulling the instrument out by the neck, only for the body of it to fall away, having been wrecked by airport baggage handlers. Everyone dissolved into giggles. "Elton falls off his piano, Nigel falls out of the drums," Johnstone remembers. "We're completely out of it. I was kind of staring at this poor banjo that's completely fucking trashed."

Together they plowed on, in far from ideal circumstances. The fact that Dynamic Sounds was situated in a compound circled with barbed wire to deter would-be thieves made for an ugly creative environment that was uninspiring in itself. But Elton and the band's visit also coincided with a strike by workers at Dynamic Sounds' on-site record plant, ensuring that their journey to work every day became extremely unnerving. Some of the strikers banged angrily on the sides of the band's Volkswagen van. Others wielded blowpipes, forcefully puffing through the vehicle's open windows what turned out to be crushed fiberglass. Everyone's skin broke out in nasty red rashes.

They persevered for a few days, making a determined effort to capture "Saturday Night's Alright for Fighting" before eventually nailing what felt like a great take of the song. But when Elton and the others entered the control room to hear what they'd just recorded, it sounded horribly tinny, like a swarm of angry wasps or, in Dudgeon's words, "thirty million very small, blaring, distorted transistor radios."

It was hopeless; they were forced to give up. But even trying to leave the island turned into a nightmare. A dispute broke out with the studio owners over who was to settle the hotel bills. As a result, in a standoff, all of the band's equipment and rental cars were impounded behind the gates of the recording facility.

Back in Ocho Rios, the band sat around the pool and tried to work their way, as Dudgeon remembered, "through five sacks full of dope . . . and never actually succeeded. It was the first time I actually left some dope behind."

Escaping to the airport in a taxi, Elton was alarmed when his driver swerved into a sudden diversion through a sugarcane field. The cabbie was only taking a highly unorthodox shortcut, but in his hyper-paranoid state, Elton thought he was being taken away to be killed.

. . .

Don't Shoot Me I'm Only the Piano Player was an absolute commercial triumph—becoming Elton's first transatlantic number one album—but a creative muddle, probably as a result of its agitated creation. Interestingly, then, even though he had been exhausted while writing and recording it, *Don't Shoot Me* boasted more up-tempo songs than any of his previous LPs, as if the singer had been trying to use his own music to summon up energy from somewhere within him.

Nevertheless, a lot of it was fairly uninspired stuff—"Teacher I Need You" sounded like a 1950s jukebox 45 refracted through glam rock, "Midnight Creeper" was an unspectacular imitation of the Rolling Stones. "Crocodile Rock," with its falsetto "la-la-la-la-la" hook, owed much to Pat Boone's "Speedy Gonzales" and would later prompt an out-of-court settlement with that song's publisher.

In effect, the album was a hastily recorded homage to the rock'n'roll records that had inspired Elton as a youth. The cover even harked back to the fifties, with its image of a greaser and his jive-skirted date standing at a cinema box office beneath a backlit electric sign for the imaginary main feature, "DON'T SHOOT ME I'M ONLY THE PIANO PLAYER" STARRING ELTON JOHN. To their right, a poster for the Marx Brothers' *Go West* hinted at the title's inspiration.

Elton himself thought the album was "ultra-pop" but "disposable" and, expecting it to be ripped apart by the critics, was surprised when it was widely praised. In *Rolling Stone*, Stephen Holden declared that "the heart of the album is a sequence of American movie fantasies whose chief aim is to delight . . . engaging entertainment and a nice step forward in phase two of Elton John's career."

The real beauties on *Don't Shoot Me* were to be found where the tempo slowed. "I'm Gonna Be a Teenage Idol" found its inspiration in the tale of Marc Bolan's reinvention from cross-legged acoustic-guitar-playing starchild to teen-scream pop star. The dreamy "High Flying Bird" was a heartbroken ballad par excellence, which hinted that the narrator had lost his partner through suicide or possibly murder. Best of all was "Daniel," an achingly sentimental and compellingly mysterious song, written from one brother to another, that in March '73 became Elton's follow-up single to "Crocodile Rock."

Bernie had written the lyric for "Daniel" the summer before at the Château d'Hérouville, having read an article in *Time* magazine about a Vietnam vet confined to a wheelchair after being injured in the Tet offensive. Returning to America, he'd been hailed as a hero by everyone around him in his small Texas town. Troubled by the attention, the soldier longed instead to slip away unnoticed to a quiet life on his farm. Taupin could clearly relate to this desire for a peaceful rural existence away from fuss and hubbub.

The lyricist transformed the story into a song about a pained soul who wants to disappear, as watched by his recounting sibling, conflating the narrative with Bernie's own memory of his brother's move to Spain to study there in 1968. Crucially, though, obscuring the meaning of the song, when Elton came to write the melody, he scrubbed out a final verse that he felt made the song overlong but that in fact explained the story. As a result, "Daniel" was interpreted by listeners as being about a family dispute, or even as a gay love song. "It was really a brother's reflection on his elder brother leaving to find peace of mind somewhere else," says Bernie. "If you know what the story is, then you go back and reference it against the lyric, perhaps it makes a little bit more sense."

The release of "Daniel" was to cause a temporary rift between Elton and DJM. To Dick James's ears, the slow-paced track didn't sound like a hit, particularly coming off the back of "Crocodile Rock," but Elton put his foot down. When James refused to advertise the record's release in the music press, the singer stubbornly said he'd pay for the promo himself. "I can't believe it," Elton protested at the time. "He says the single isn't commercial and it's coming out at the wrong time. He says it will harm the sales of the album. But I want it out. We've reached a compromise where if it's a hit, he'll pay for the advertising. But not before."

With the quarrel having gone public, Dick James was forced to defend himself in an interview in the music trade press. "This is a very one-sided viewpoint," he fumed. "It's untrue to say I don't like 'Daniel.' It's a beautiful, fantastic number, one of the best Elton and

Bernie have written. Steve Brown, Stephen James and myself all came to the same conclusion independently about not releasing 'Daniel.' We are releasing 'Daniel' as a single solely because of the pressure from Elton."

Upon its release, "Daniel" made number four in the UK and number two in the States. Elton had been proved right. From here on in, his relationship with DJM would be characterized by a series of skirmishes and outright battles.

EVERY SINGLE OR album he put out now seemed destined to fly into the Top Five. If Elton seemed super-confident, even invincible, then he would sometimes make funny, self-deprecating remarks in interviews about his appearance, saying he couldn't possibly compete with the likes of David Bowie or Mick Jagger when it came to their slinky stagewear. "I haven't got the figure for it," he admitted. "I'd look like Donald Dumpling from Dover. So I try and make people grin a bit."

At the same time, further souring their fairly remote association, he took a dig at Bowie. "I know David has always wanted to be Judy Garland," he declared. "Well, I'm the Connie Francis, then, of rock'n'roll."

The year before, "Judy" and "Connie" had met for tea one afternoon in Los Angeles, in a summit intended to reach some kind of détente between the two. It didn't go well. "We had tea and cakes," Bowie remembered, in his slightly passive-aggressive account of their head-to-head. "We asked each other how we found America. After a polite half hour, I made my apologies, declining another cuppa. We didn't exactly become pals, not really having that much in common, especially musically."

Elton was clearly an anomaly when it came to the accepted look and sound of the cool 1973 pop star. He was comedic when you were supposed to be enigmatic, and he was, as was now becoming increasingly evident, balding. "I think he was very confused about his identity," says Annie Reavey, the costume designer Elton drafted in as his pop star status began to rocket. "The easiest way to cover up that confusion was to become almost like a cartoon character."

As unlikely as it might once have seemed, Elton was now attracting a devoted army of teenage fans. "If they scream at me," he quipped at the time, "it's probably in horror." His spring tour of '73 in the UK was filled with chaotic scenes. These were the days before professional security firms were brought in by promoters to protect stars from their more ardent and determined fans, with most venues usually staffed by local bouncers often ill equipped to cope. Sometimes, particularly if Elton was performing on a low stage, it made for alarming encounters with his adoring female admirers.

"To be onstage and see some sixteen-stone girl hurtling towards you is a frightening sight," he only half joked at the time. "I don't know what it takes for a girl to get it into her head that she must touch me. When they grab hold of you, it takes about six guys to get them off the stage. There were times when I thought the fans would rip us apart."

In Glasgow, he was trapped inside the Green's Playhouse for over an hour after the show when the shrieking devotees outside refused to disperse. In Newcastle, ten policemen were sent to the City Hall to protect him, though the promoter still broke an ankle in the melee as Elton tried to force himself through the crush of fans to make his getaway. In London, one girl tried to jump in the band's car just as it was pulling away. Nigel Olsson remembers, "I was trying to . . . in the nicest possible way, say, 'No, you can't come with us.' I had to kind of push her out. The fan deal got out of hand. They were nuts."

Over two nights at the 1,850-capacity Edmonton Sundown Theatre in north London, as girls fainted in the front rows, Elton chose to rise to the occasion, appearing onstage in a quilted cloak of many colors over a green satin suit, then throwing himself into the shows and drinking in the madness surrounding him. A week later, running a news story with a headline bearing a slightly incredulous exclamation point, *Melody Maker* declared, NOW ELTON'S A TEEN IDOL!

What had once made him seem an improbable pop star was what was now making him unique.

"I did feel like a bit of an outsider," he says. "But y'know what? It helped me. There was only one Elton."

. . .

OFFSTAGE, IT WAS record-obsessed Reg who followed Elton's successes with the delight of the super-keen pop watcher. He carefully made sure the releases didn't clash with other singles or albums that might impede their progress on the charts. Shrewdly, he had delayed the arrival in the shops of *Don't Shoot Me I'm Only the Piano Player* until January 1973 to avoid the big pre-Christmas possible contenders of Neil Young's *Journey Through the Past* and Carole King's *Rhymes & Reasons* (while getting a two-month jump on Led Zeppelin's *Houses of the Holy*). "When mine came out, there was nothing else," he stressed with some satisfaction.

Every Tuesday morning, when the trade magazines were published, he would sit with his nose in *Billboard* and *Record World* and *Cashbox,* studying the hotly tipped hits and the chart rises and falls. He had instant opinions about everyone and their latest singles: Gilbert O'Sullivan's "Get Down" ("Great, right?"), the Faces' "Cindy Incidentally" ("Good"), Roxy Music's "Pyjamarama" ("A good record that won't make it in the States"), Donny Osmond's "The Twelfth of Never" ("Dreck"), the Carpenters' "Sing" ("Double dreck").

All of this baffled Bernie. "I had no interest in what was going on with our records in the charts," he says. "Back then I just was not even aware of it. It never crossed my mind to pick up *Billboard* and see what our album was doing. Elton would tell me. He was totally the opposite, infatuated by that whole thing."

Whereas the bands of the 1960s, not least the Beatles and the Rolling Stones, had been mercilessly ripped off in bad deals and through shady or naive advice, Elton and John Reid were completely on it when it came to business. As Stephen James had predicted, as time passed, Reid had pulled away from Dick James to better Elton's contracts. In August 1972, he'd left his job at DJM as Elton's salaried manager and set up his own company, John Reid Enterprises, with an office in Soho.

His first act had been to boldly review the DJM deals, bringing in the New York lawyer John Eastman—brother-in-law of Paul McCartney, following his marriage in his Beatles days to Eastman's sister Linda. The attorney advised Reid that the publishing deal with DJM USA, in which the split between the company and the songwriters was 70-30, could reasonably be deemed unfair. Dick James, who had of course invested not only money but also confidence in Elton in his struggling years, was hurt. No further action was taken by Elton and John Reid, not least because they needed James for the time being, while the IRS was assessing the singer's U.S. tax status. But it was a warning shot across the bow.

Even with this arguably reduced royalty rate in America, Elton was still rolling in money. Investing further in art, he bought two etchings by Rembrandt and six paintings by the British pop artist David Hockney, the latter batch as gifts for Reid. The singer was known to ostentatiously waltz into Tower Records on Sunset Strip and sometimes spend as much as six thousand dollars on records and tapes in one quick splurge. For Elton, this was less a vulgar extravagance than a desire to live only for today. "I'm not decadent," he insisted. "My attitude to money is that tomorrow I could be knocked down by a number nine bus or something, so I might as well spend it."

Money meant freedom and money meant power, and the two combined in early 1973 with the launch of Elton's own label, the Rocket Record Company. Although his contract with DJM prohibited him from recording for Rocket himself—at least for the time being—it was of course a fanboy's dream to own such an enterprise.

The notion had first been floated during a drunken night at the château the year before. With the vin rouge flowing, Davey Johnstone had admitted that he wanted to make his own album but couldn't find a deal. It was Elton who first slurringly suggested they should "start our own fucking label!" Everyone said, "Yeah!" The next morning, all with aching heads, the conversation was brought back up again with the words "Were we serious?"

They were, and a plan was put into action. The board of the new label would comprise Elton, Bernie, John Reid, Gus Dudgeon, and Steve Brown. Elton bluntly and enthusiastically set out the ethos of Rocket in an interview with *Disc:* "What we are offering is undivided love and devotion, a fucking good royalty for the artist and a company that works its bollocks off."

Of course, forming their own label had proved disastrous for the Beatles, with the money-sucking hole that was Apple Records. Elton and Reid were shrewder—Rocket was funded through a deal with MCA Records, and the recording artists, even if enjoying a generous royalty rate, would receive modest advances against sales. Still, there were early signs of nepotism and an Apple-like blinkered A&R policy. Two of Rocket's first album releases were Davey Johnstone's *Smiling Face* and *If It Was So Simple* by folk rockers Longdancer, featuring Nigel Olsson's singer/guitarist brother, Kai.

The birth of Rocket seemed to warrant not just one, but three parties. The first on March 25, pantingly described by *Melody Maker* as "the biggest name-dropping rave-up of recent times," was a booze-soaked bender thrown on a boat, the *John D,* moored on the Thames. Among the guests were Ringo Starr, Harry Nilsson, Rod Stewart and the Faces, Cat Stevens, and Paul Simon, who were entertained, in typical 1970s fashion, by a female stripper.

The second bash was less star-filled, if a touch stranger. On May 3, Elton chartered a train, filled it with Rocket employees and journalists, and took it the seventy miles from London's Paddington Station to the picturesque Cotswolds town of Moreton-in-Marsh. En route, the drinking began, and one carriage even housed a disco. Upon their arrival, while a comparatively dressed-down Elton in a plaid shirt and white Oxford bags signed autographs for fans and then awkwardly attempted to run away from them like a newborn foal in platform boots, a brass band led the two hundred fifty guests to a local hall where a medieval banquet and gallons of champagne were laid on. Afterward, Longdancer and another Rocket signing, Mike Silver, played short sets before Elton and the band joined them for a triumphant, well-oiled jam session.

Rocket was launched in Los Angeles in some style at Universal Studios on a back lot used to film westerns. A mock cowboy gunfight opened the proceedings. Elton was brazenly attired in white satin shorts, knee socks, a green-and-blue-striped jacket, heart-shaped glasses, and a floppy hat under which his hair was dyed orange and pink. He bashed out "Crocodile Rock" and Jerry Lee Lewis's "Whole Lotta Shakin' Goin' On" for the trendy Hollywood set, joined on backing vocals by Dusty Springfield and his old pal from "Patti LaBelle and her Blue Bellies," Nona Hendryx.

There were multiple parties for Rocket, but by contrast, at least initially, there were few hits. The one notable exception was the UK number-thirteen-charting "Amoureuse," an atmospheric ballad by the new label's most significant signing, Kiki Dee. The twenty-six-year-old, born Pauline Matthews in West Yorkshire, had already been something of a teenage wow who'd recorded for Fontana in the UK and in the States as the first British artist signing to Motown, without yielding any real commercial success. Through Motown, she'd met John Reid and, in turn, Elton.

By the early seventies, Kiki's early promise remained unfulfilled. Moreover, Elton saw in her someone who was shy and likely bruised by her experiences of relative failure—something he could of course relate to, given his own past. "She's got a great voice," he enthused at the time. "She needs her confidence built back up again."

"I suppose I was quite insecure," says Dee. "But when I was on-stage and when I sang I felt confident. I think a lot of performers are like that. I saw that Elton had a shy side as well."

When Rocket was just a wine-induced plot the year before, Elton and John Reid had courted Dee by inviting her around to the Water Gardens flat, on the same night that their guests included Neil Young and Elton's mother. At one point, attempting to fetch some champagne glasses from the kitchen, Dee fumbled with the sliding door on a cupboard and embarrassed herself. "All the glasses fell on the floor and broke," she remembers. "Elton came in and burst out laughing."

Only eleven days separated Kiki and Elton in age, and so, through their shared diffidence and sometimes fumbling awkwardness, they came to develop an almost brother-sister bond. Elton co-produced, with Clive Franks, Kiki's first Rocket album, *Loving and Free*. "I got signed at sixteen," she points out, "so for me it was the first time that I was working with people of my own age, really. I'd always been the kid before, with all these grown-ups. So suddenly Elton and the band and John became my family."

Kiki was invited to sing backup on Elton's spring '73 tour of Italy—a jaunt that further emphasized the bedlam around him. In Genoa, two hundred ticketless and frenzied fans attacked the carriage of the train carrying the band into the city ahead of the show at the ten-thousand-capacity Palasport di Genova indoor arena. On the street in Rome, there was a scuffle between the ever protective John Reid and a paparazzo attempting to snap candid shots of Elton. One fellow photographer caught the ugly tussle on film: the manager blurringly launching himself at the defiant snapper as the concerned singer looked on. It wouldn't be the last time Reid's pugnacious Scottish temperament was to get him into trouble.

As FRUSTRATING AS the failed Jamaican trip had been, it nevertheless produced close to two dozen still unrecorded songs for the next album. And so, when Elton and the others returned to the Château d'Hérouville in May, the subsequent sessions were utterly energized. "He was on some kind of amazing long-term roll," said Gus Dudgeon, "which just didn't stop."

To Bernie's mind, being back at the château after the horrors of Jamaica was paradise. As Davey Johnstone remembers, the heavy-puffing atmosphere of Kingston was transported back to northern France. "Tons of hash," he says. "Rolling joints like there was no tomorrow. I think it reflects in the music. There's not a lot of uptightness to it, y'know."

At odds with this laid-back vibe, however, was "Saturday Night's Alright for Fighting," the most aggressive track Elton and Bernie had written to date, which was successfully completed at the studio. More reminiscent of the Stones or the Who than the balladeering piano man many still thought Elton to be, it was driven by Johnstone's gnarly guitar riff. Taupin took its lyrical inspiration from his teenage nights at the Aston Arms in the small Lincolnshire town of Market Rasen watching almighty ruckuses break out among the drunks.

The recording process of the song was as atypical as its sound and found Elton stepping away from his piano—which was later overdubbed—to stand up and sing at the microphone and aggressively marshal the band through the take. Nigel Olsson remembers Elton stomping around the live room shouting, "Come on, you bastards!"

In a concentrated three-week period, they laid down track after track after track. It was becoming clear that this next album would be a double. Bernie and Elton began throwing around ideas for titles: *Vodka and Tonic; Silent Movies Talking Pictures* (strangely deemed too camp by the singer); and—jokily, since the perma-stoned guitarist was forever experimenting and piling on the overdubs— *How Many Guitar Sounds Can Davey Johnstone Get on This?*

"Saturday Night's Alright for Fighting" was released in July as a single ahead of the still-untitled double album, and issued in a picture sleeve that spelled out the song's title in a dagger tattoo design and featured Elton in the guise of an antisocial thug swigging from a bottle of wine. Some radio stations instantly banned the record, understandably deeming it an incitement to violence. "I wouldn't want to be blamed for provoking anybody into a fight," says Bernie. "But at the same time it says a lot about the power of the song."

It hit number seven in the UK, though strangely only number twelve in America. But again, Elton had confounded expectations. Interviewed in the dressing room at *Top of the Pops,* he spoke about how he was "becoming fed up with the singer-songwriter records. They drive me mad. I've always fought against the Elton John Syndrome."

Elton believed that the public's perception of him was one of a safely noncontroversial piano-playing balladeer, and he was defiantly determined to kick against that image.

But even if 1973 so far had seen him seize full control of his career, his thoughts were once again turning to giving it all up before the public lost interest in him. He had designs on concentrating on Rocket full-time, on becoming solely a music businessman.

Elton had achieved a level of fame previously inconceivable to him. Yet now, his greatest desire was to "gradually fade myself out."

Realistically, it wasn't going to happen. It was too soon to begin his descent. The double album was given a title: *Goodbye Yellow Brick Road.*

He was just about to ascend to the next flight level.

A vision in rhinestone-encrusted glasses and feathers. Outlandish Elton in '73.

8 ALL ABOARD THE STARSHIP

THE 136-FOOT-LONG JET was an Air Force One for the rock star elite. As the very first Boeing 720 to roll off the production line back in 1960, it had been flown for thirteen years by United Airlines before being sold to Ward Sylvester of Contemporary Entertainment, manager of TV caperers the Monkees and teen idol Bobby Sherman. From here, after a major interior refit, the now private plane was renamed the *Starship*.

July 1973 saw it chartered by Led Zeppelin, after a turbulent and anxious flight for the band down the coast from San Francisco to Los Angeles in a tiny Dassault Falcon eight-seater forced their manager Peter Grant to think bigger. That summer it became for the British megagroup what their tour manager called "a floating gin palace"—the notorious scene of sexual shenanigans with groupies as generous lines of cocaine were snorted through rolled-up hundred-dollar bills.

Stepping through the *Starship*'s forward boarding door, you entered a front lounge with galley kitchen and passed through a club room with revolving leather armchairs before walking into the Grand Salon with its maroon shag carpet. Here a thirty-foot couch ran along the inside fuselage facing a bar in which an electric organ had been installed for musicianly in-flight entertainment. To offset the ravages of boozy touring life, packs of vitamin pills were laid out on the counter. These could be washed down by beer or the potent cocktail of your choice.

At the rear of the plane lay what was nicknamed the Hippie Room, filled with beanbags and a low-level sofa in its own unique airborne crash pad arrangement. Behind it there was a bedroom featuring a shower cubicle and queen-sized water mattress covered with a throw of white fake fur.

As soon as he set eyes on it in August 1973, Elton fell in love with the *Starship* and its trashy approximation of high class. Among its state-of-the-art luxury features was a video player, to go with its well-stocked film library of everything from Marx Brothers films to hardcore pornography.

"I remember showing my parents *Deep Throat* on the *Starship* while they were having their lunch," Elton says mischievously, conjuring up a mind-boggling image of a highly unusual family meal scenario at thirty thousand feet.

However, as he didn't possess an entourage on the scale of Led Zeppelin's (or their extraordinary appetites), often when Elton and the band were in midflight, they felt they were rattling around inside the plane, with too few of them really to fill the rarefied environment. Sometimes there were only eight people in a jet that could more than comfortably hold forty.

Still, for major league musicians, the *Starship* revolutionized high-level touring. No longer did they have to endure the all too familiar, energy-depleting run of hotel–sound check–gig–hotel–sound check–gig–hotel. Instead, a band could base themselves in the major U.S. metropolises—New York, Los Angeles, Chicago, Houston—and commute back and forth to shows in the smaller cities.

Such an operation was befitting Elton's biggest U.S. tour to date. From the middle of August to the end of October, he would play forty-four dates at arena and stadium level. In keeping with this upward scaling, he decided that his show was now going to be "Liberaceized." More elaborate capes and suits were ordered, but it was in the specs department that he decided to go super-large. The singer had been commissioning the L.A. eyeglass designers Optique Boutique to conjure up ever wilder designs, and for this tour, the company's Dennis Roberts outdid himself with one massive pair costing five thousand dollars that spelled out Elton's name in flashing lights.

"I had a battery pack," Elton recalls, "which was like a fucking milk crate. I'd sort of stagger on the stage like Quasimodo and then, singing . . . my nose would be squashed by the weight of the glasses."

Sometimes the enormity of the shows took him by surprise and was more than he could physically handle. In Kansas City, at the Arrowhead Stadium, he leaped off the twelve-foot-high stage only to suddenly realize that he couldn't get back up onto it. A little shamefacedly, he had to sprint around to the backstage area before he could make his triumphant reappearance.

All roads, however, were leading to the Hollywood Bowl on September 7. It was a show designed to go over the top of the very top itself.

No EXPENSE IT seems was spared in the high-profile buildup to Elton's appearance at the 17,500-capacity 1920s amphitheater set deep in the Hollywood Hills. It was only three years since he had first set foot in Los Angeles with his mind reeling. Now on Sunset Strip a mammoth billboard advertising the show, featuring an illustrated image of the singer as a thirties song-and-dance man in top hat and tails, smiled down on passersby.

On the evening of the gig, a Friday, the same cartoon image, stretched to wide-screen, stared out from the back of the shell-like stage at the Hollywood Bowl: Elton as Fred Astaire, flanked by chorus girls. Outside, scalpers were selling tickets for anything up to $500. Inside, as the sun fell, the audience slipped into their seats.

Come stage time, none other than Linda Lovelace, the star of Elton's beloved *Deep Throat,* stepped up to the microphone to open the show. "Ladies and gentlemen, I'd like to welcome you to the Hollywood Bowl," she began with breathy, giggly excitement. "On this spectacular night, we hope to revive some of the glamour that has all but disappeared from show business. We're very lucky in having this evening with us many distinguished guests from all parts of the world, none of whom would dare to miss this show tonight."

Then, down a sparkling stairway came a parade of look-alikes, resembling the cover of *Sgt. Pepper* brought to life: the Queen, Elvis Presley, Frankenstein, the Pope, the Beatles, Batman and Robin, Groucho Marx, Mae West . . .

"Lastly," Lovelace went on, "the gentleman you've all been waiting for and the costar of my next movie. The biggest, most colossal, gigantic, fantastic Elton John!"

He made his entrance at the top of the stairs in white fur chaps and matching wide-brimmed bolero hat. As he descended the steps, the 20th Century Fox theme boomed and trumpeted through the PA. The lids of five mock grand pianos, painted red, orange, silver, blue, and pink, were raised, spelling out E-L-T-O-N. From inside them were released four hundred white doves, flying out from the stage and into the night. More or less. Some of the birds, frightened by the bright lights and noise, refused to leave the comfort of their opened piano cages. Sidestage, John Reid was going nuts, shouting, "I want them out *now*!" Bernie found himself sitting inside the body of one of the dummy instruments trying to fling reluctant white doves into the air.

Elton slammed into "Elderberry Wine" from *Don't Shoot Me I'm Only the Piano Player* before moving through a sixteen-song set comprising his biggest hits and still unheard numbers from the upcoming *Goodbye Yellow Brick Road*. By "Saturday Night's Alright for Fighting," as one lost dove winged around the stage in a panic, he was up on his feet, cajoling the crowd, before leaping atop his pink-satin-covered piano and throwing himself around in Jagger-esque dance moves.

As much as Elton was now visibly in his element, Bernie wasn't entirely convinced by his partner's dress-up antics. "Bernie fucking *loathed* it all," Elton admits. "I think it did hurt the music. People thought it was more style than substance . . . which I disagreed with, obviously, because the music was there. But I understood where they were coming from."

"There were certain areas where I was less than enamored by his wardrobe," Bernie confesses. "Elton's larger-than-life persona has been probably detrimental to him as a musician. Because when you become a star of that magnitude, eighty percent of what people want to know about you, or hear about you, is what you're wearing, how you're living, how many cars you have and how much money you have."

But there was no stopping the pantomime. Similarly eccentric scenes filled his first show at Madison Square Garden in New York two weeks later, where he appeared once again in his daring white rodeo cowboy getup. At the close of the show, for "Your Song," the audience expressed their approval in a way Elton had never experienced before, as they lit matches and thousands of delicate flames flickered in the darkness.

He was now, to use the phrase John Lennon coined during the heady early days of the Beatles, at the toppermost of the poppermost. If Elton privately doubted he could remain at this level for any great length of time, he wasn't alone. After the Madison Square show, one music business insider was heard to mutter, "I don't know how he can keep it up. But for the moment we're all people who gain from it."

Unsurprisingly, his punishing schedule was again causing his temper to flare unpredictably. One night in a restaurant, as Dee Murray remembered, for no apparent reason Elton stood up and started yelling at the band, "You're all nothing but a load of bastards," before walking out. He returned a minute later and continued to heckle the bewildered members of the group before flouncing off for good.

After a show at the Nassau Coliseum in New York, Elton threw an almighty strop that was to embarrass him for years to come. He stamped onto the *Starship,* ahead of takeoff for the short flight to Boston, parking himself in a chair in the front lounge of the plane. From the Grand Salon came the sound of someone playing "Crocodile Rock" on the bar's built-in organ. Elton was gently encouraged by those around him to go back and join the party and check out the guest keyboardist.

"I was in a shit mood," he says. "I'm sitting up at the front of the plane sulking and everyone's saying, 'We've got a surprise for you.' 'Fuck off! I don't want a fucking surprise.' In the end, they were crying and they said, 'You've got to come back . . . it's Stevie Wonder.'" Elton, suddenly coming to his senses, realized he was being "an asshole."

There was more in the way of unwanted drama later in the tour, at Baltimore Civic Center Arena on September 30. From the stage, Elton could see security personnel harassing fans and refusing to allow them to get up and dance. Then, one girl ran to the front of the stage to take a photograph and a beefy guard grabbed her and threw her aside. Furious, Elton stopped the show, jumped off the stage, and started goading the guards through the microphone. "You should be at home minding your babies," he shouted, to the sound of cheers. Pissed off by this very public put-down, the security people deserted their posts. Freed from their control, around five hundred audience members dangerously stormed the stage, threatening its collapse.

Down south one night in Atlanta, Georgia, as the tour drew to a close, the exhilaratingly demented Iggy Pop and the Stooges, an Elton fave, were playing a late-night show in the city at a club called Richard's. Partway through their reliably ferocious set, someone in a gorilla costume leaped onto the stage and started grooving along, to the fist-pumping delight of the manic crowd.

A stoned Pop was disturbed by the interloper, though, somehow getting it into his head that he was a speed-freak biker in cunning disguise come to attack the band. He was tempted to knock him out with a punch. Then the stage invader removed his gorilla mask to reveal himself. It was Elton. With surprising strength, he hoisted Iggy up into his arms and the part superstar, part gorilla stomped his cares away to the sound of proto punk rock.

MEANWHILE THE PROCESSION of look-alikes that had opened the momentous Hollywood Bowl show was reproduced, with a different cast, on the *Goodbye Yellow Brick Road* double album. In Bernie's mind, key parts of it were images of old Hollywood reflected in modern songs. "It's all of these characters collapsing into one," he says. "They're falling off the silver screen."

It was an album populated by the stars and archetypes Bernie and Elton had viewed from their seats in cinema stalls throughout their childhoods. At the Embassy in North Harrow back in the fifties, young Reg had seen Roy Rogers make a personal appearance with his faithful horse, Trigger. Now, on the new album, this heroic Trucolor cowboy was remembered in a song that took his name and painted him in a far more romantic light than Bernie's previous depictions of the harsh Old West. A timeworn nine-to-five working narrator, numbed by adulthood, gets home, closes his curtains, and relives youthful thrills, watching old Roy Rogers movies on TV as his wife and child sleep in another room. In "Sweet Painted Lady," the harlot-with-a-heart protagonist mirrored the makeup-caked saloon hookers of cinematic westerns. Elsewhere, "The Ballad of Danny Bailey (1909–34)" was an elegy to a gunned-down gangster who very much resembled the mobster models of Jimmy Cagney or Edward G. Robinson.

In an album of many standouts, "Candle in the Wind" was to become as enduring as the legendary status of its tragic subject. Bernie, like millions of others the world over, had been captivated by the glamour and fragility of Marilyn Monroe. For the lyricist's twenty-first birthday in May '71, Elton had bought him one of Monroe's dresses, housed in an illuminated Perspex display case. The evocative title of the song quoted a line that record executive Clive Davis had used to describe Janis Joplin (although the lyricist says he was also aware of the 1960 dystopian play of the same name by Russian writer Aleksandr Solzhenitsyn). Bernie took the phrase and built from it a memorial to Monroe from "the young man in the twenty-second row" seeing the film star as someone "more than sexual," who had been acutely vulnerable and exploited by the movie business and the media.

Later the song's ubiquity and heavily emotional tone made Taupin feel that the lyric of "Candle in the Wind" had been one-dimensionally interpreted as being written by someone utterly in awe of the dead star. "To be quite honest I was not *that* enamored with Marilyn," he insists. "What I was enamored with was the idea of fame and youth and somebody being cut short in the prime of their life. The song could've been about James Dean, it could've been about Montgomery Clift, it could've been about Jim Morrison . . . how we glamorize death. How we immortalize people."

For his part, Elton, while understanding the power of the track, "thought we were gonna get groans from people." Instead, "Candle in the Wind" was to become possibly the most famous song in Elton and Bernie's catalog.

Throughout *Goodbye Yellow Brick Road,* there was a recurring theme of sympathy for the troubled outsider. In "All the Girls Love Alice," the promiscuous sixteen-year-old central character gets lost in the murk of the gay scene and ends up dead in a subway. The nihilistic boozer of "Social Disease," wasted from morning to night, at first seems to be happy in his alcoholic haze, until he reveals that he feels his days are aimless and hopeless.

All of this was a desire on Bernie's part to add grit to his and Elton's songs, partly in the wake of the throwaway pop of *Don't Shoot Me I'm Only the Piano Player*. "I wanted a little angst in what we were doing," he says. "I didn't want us to be just thought of as this pure pop machine."

Elton, musically, was also darkening the tone, particularly with the double album's two-part, eleven-minute opener, "Funeral for a Friend / Love Lies Bleeding." The first half, a mournful symphony for synthesizer played by David Hentschel, was written by Elton when he was in a fog of depression and imagining music for his own wake: "I got very down one day. I'm hung up on things like that. I like tearful, plodding music." The second part is far angrier, a thundering up-tempo song of heartbreak with hints of almost suicidal torment.

In fact, the death count on *Goodbye Yellow Brick Road* was high—Danny Bailey, Alice, Marilyn, and in "Funeral for a Friend," even the singer himself. Only later would Elton realize quite how bleak the record was lyrically, when a DJ in Philadelphia brought it to his attention, saying, "Hey, your new album . . . Bernie is so bitter these days."

"I listened to it again," Elton reflected at the time, "and it's true. It's a very depressive album, although I'd never thought of it like that before."

At the same time, there was enough in the way of pop sensibility on *Goodbye Yellow Brick Road* to ensure that the hits from the album kept coming. In "Bennie and the Jets," Gus Dudgeon used crowd noise sound effects—lifted in the introduction from the recording of Elton's '72 Royal Festival Show and in the outro from the audience recorded at a Jimi Hendrix gig, mixed in with the band hooting and clapping off-time in the studio at the château—to create a faux live recording. This elaborate sound design backdropped

Elton's most soul-oriented creation yet, slipping between full voice and falsetto over a staccato groove in a hypnotic paean to what Bernie called a "robotized, futuristic rock'n'roll band" fronted by a "butch girl" in electric boots and mohair suit.

Best of all was the title track of *Goodbye Yellow Brick Road,* an affecting ballad that managed to balance itself between jaded sentimentality and soaring optimism while sounding like something Lennon and McCartney might have written in 1967, updated with the production values of 1973. Its lyric was the perfect summation of the tale Taupin had previously explored in "Mona Lisas and Mad Hatters" and "Honky Cat"— the country-born innocent drawn to the alluring flame of city life. In "Goodbye Yellow Brick Road," he has become the plaything of a high society figure, and he is defiantly escaping the gilded cage to return to his farm and plow.

For Bernie, it was a song that had its roots in his first experiences of coming to London back in '67: "It was about me being the country kid coming to town and being a little out of my depth. It was a sort of Dick Whittington tale—going to the city, making it big, but knowing that reality lay back where he came from. It just ended up being a song that seemed to echo those feelings of homesickness that I experienced in my first few months down in London. I was torn between the potential glamour of the bright lights and my country roots."

One of three unarguably classic songs on the double album, "Goodbye Yellow Brick Road" sat alongside "Candle in the Wind" and "Bennie and the Jets" as proof of the now gold standard quality of Elton and Bernie's compositions. At the same time, with its edgy characters and moments of censor-baiting profanity (one "shit," a "bitch," and a couple of "jerk-offs"), the expansive album certainly wasn't just light fare for the pop kids. Like most double LPs, it was experimental and sometimes messy, but it also displayed an impressive array of musical styles and much in the way of light and shade. In short, it was Elton and Bernie's greatest accomplishment up to that point.

As such, it needed a suitably iconic cover. When it came time to hastily conjure up the artwork, DJM sleeve designer David Larkham remembered an advertisement image he'd seen in the portfolio of illustrator Ian Beck: "A guy was gazing wistfully at a poster on a wall and the idea . . . sort of epiphany . . . just gelled." The concept developed into a vivid graphic of Elton on a run-down city pavement stepping, with platform boots the color of Judy Garland's ruby slippers, into a poster of Oz.

It depicted someone magically passing from a drab environment into a brighter otherworld. As a visual metaphor, it perfectly captured in one colorful image everything Elton had experienced in the past four years.

HOLLYWOOD WAS HERE, there, and everywhere and even followed him home. One Sunday afternoon Elton was sitting by the swimming pool at his Wentworth bungalow with a friend, the Scottish TV comedian Stanley Baxter. That week, Bryan Forbes and Nanette Newman had none other than Katharine Hepburn as a guest at their nearby home. The highly spirited star of *The Philadelphia Story* and *The African Queen,* then sixty-six, liked to swim, and she asked the couple about the availability of nearby pools. Elton casually mentioned that the actress could come by and use his anytime she liked.

"I never had gates at my property," he remembers. "Suddenly we see this bicycle riding up the lawn and Stanley Baxter's face . . . *'Oh, fuuuck . . .'* 'Cause that was his idol. There was a dead frog in my pool and I've got a phobia about frogs, so I wouldn't go in it. And she got this huge fucking leaf, dove in, got to the bottom, and threw it out.

"I went, 'How could you *do* that?' And she went, 'Character!' She'd walk in the house and go, 'Your furniture's all wrong. You need that over there. This there.' An incredible woman."

All of this was becoming strangely normal to Elton—a sign that he was finally adjusting to his own stardom. Back over in Los Angeles, the cover of *Goodbye Yellow Brick Road* was being revealed as an enormous billboard teasingly painted day by day, piece by piece, on Sunset Strip. As publicity gimmicks went, it was good. But the record company felt they could go one better.

Journalists in New York and Los Angeles were invited to what was promised to be a cutting-edge technological, bicoastal video press conference via satellite. Bernie on the East Coast said a few words of introduction in New York, followed by Gus Dudgeon in L.A. Then Elton appeared on screens in both locations, broadcasting from his room at the Holiday Inn somewhere in the middle of America, and began to take questions from the assembled writers.

"It was supposedly coming by satellite," Dudgeon remembered. "In actual fact he was sitting in a room about twenty feet away that we made look like a Holiday Inn. They were like, 'Wow, this is great!' Then we started putting up interference on the screen. I'm saying, 'Well, I'm very sorry, ladies and gentlemen, I think we're losing contact with Elton now.' It's going, *crrrr,* y'know, blizzard across his face."

Once the conference was over, there was much excited babble among the journalists as they made their way over to the buffet table. Then, Elton, dressed down and unnoticed at first, stepped among them and started helping himself to the sandwiches. One writer suddenly spotted the star and said, "Wait a minute, fuck, that's him standing there."

"It was a classic piece of hype," said Dudgeon. "It worked a treat. And of course we got fantastic press out of it."

A subsequent playback of *Goodbye Yellow Brick Road* in a screening suite at Universal Studios in L.A. didn't go quite as smoothly. To ensure that journalists heard the album in the highest possible quality, an expensive sound system was brought into the room, with a slide show of images from the album's artwork set to accompany the music. As the lights dimmed and the opening overture of "Funeral for a Friend" filled the air, it was clear that there was something wrong with the sound.

John Reid was incensed. When the first side of the album concluded with "Bennie and the Jets" and the lights went up, he jumped out of his seat and harangued the sound engineer. "Can't you get the fucking thing together?" he snapped. The stressed-out tech fired back, "It's not us, it's the fucking tape." Reid smacked him in the mouth, drawing blood. There was a rush forward by people trying to hold the manager back, but he managed to throw a few more punches at the engineer before being pulled away. As he left, he shouted back at the techs, "Bloody cunts!"

Challenged about the incident in a subsequent issue of *Rolling Stone,* Reid was unapologetic and only a touch repentant: "I don't make excuses. I'm not particularly proud of it. But any time anything like this has happened, it's been in defense of Elton or Bernie, not for personal reasons."

In the end, *Goodbye Yellow Brick Road* received mixed reviews from the critics. Roy Carr in the *New Musical Express* oddly considered the album to be "like an old sweater . . . crafted for maximum enjoyment and quite indispensable," while declaring it "exquisite and by far the finest mass appeal album to have emanated from Downtown Oz." Stephen Davis in *Rolling Stone* was unconvinced: "A massive double-record exposition of unabashed fantasy, myth, wet dreams and cornball acts . . . too fat to float, artistically doomed by pretention but redeemed commercially by a couple of brilliant tracks."

No bad review could sink *Goodbye Yellow Brick Road,* though. In the second week of November, in the States, it hit number one, for the first of an unbroken eight-week run. In December, it reached number one in the UK. In both markets, it was Elton's second chart-topping album of 1973.

SITTING AT A black grand piano in the living room of the Wentworth bungalow—his hair dyed a Ziggyish orange, his accent suddenly affecting curiously cut-glass, upper-class English tones—Elton, talking to Bryan Forbes, insisted that in some ways, the astonishing fame he'd achieved was something a part of him had always anticipated.

"I knew I'd be famous one day," he said, in the mannered speaking voice that with his disheveled bohemian image gave him the air of disgraced royalty. "I mean, I was always convinced. I knew I'd probably have to wait till I was fifty-three. But I just knew. It was the only thing that kept me going . . . this ambition."

The scene was an interview shot for Forbes's documentary *Elton John and Bernie Taupin Say Goodbye Norma Jean and Other Things,* which took the director a full year to cut from eighteen hours of footage before being screened by ITV in Britain and ABC TV in the States. Given exclusive access to the French recording sessions for *Goodbye Yellow Brick Road* and the Hollywood Bowl show, the TV special offered unique insight—thanks in large part to the director's and artist's personal friendship—into Elton's extraordinary circumstances and state of mind in 1973.

"At twenty-six, he walks confidently on five-inch heels where others fear to tread," Forbes stated in his verbose introductory voiceover, which had the knowing tone of the insider. "Sometimes as bright and unyielding as the diamonds he wears on his fingers. Sometimes plunged deep into self-critical gloom. Extravagant and generous, seeking fame one moment, determined to reject it the next. The life and soul of the party. The party destroyer. The genuine article. The superstar who does his own hoovering."

Cutting between the glitziness and intensity of Elton's live shows and footage of him kicking a ball around his garden with his dogs, the film was designed to depict him as a runaway musical sensation with a fairly normal home life. Ultimately, though, the documentary couldn't help but reveal his insecurities, whether through his own admissions or the words of others.

In the film, Elton appeared skinny—if not quite on the virtually emaciated level of Jagger or Bowie at the time—but said he felt fat. If he ate even one slice of white bread, he joked, "I'm instantly the size of the Crystal Palace."

"He's had darker moods since he's made it into the pop world than he ever did before," confessed his mother, before adding what might later have seemed a disclaimer when it came to his private life. "He's always been a very quiet boy, though . . . never been a boy to have the gay life or anything."

Dick James, meanwhile, encapsulated in two sentences the Reg-to-Elton transfiguration he'd witnessed firsthand. "I think he's a paradox in himself to a great extent," he said. "He's an introvert that projects a tremendous extrovert performance and image."

For Christmas, this quiet boy turned tremendous extrovert brought Hollywood back to Britain, a country sorely lacking in glamour during the grim winter of 1973. Prime Minister Edward Heath was locked in a steely battle with the National Union of Mineworkers as the country was slowly being crippled by high inflation rates and the government's capping of public sector wage rises.

Boldly, the miners began a work-to-rule policy that was painfully depleting the nation's coal stocks. In a drive to counter the industrial action, on December 13, Heath announced that a three-day work-week to conserve energy in the UK would come into force at the end of the year. Nonetheless, the shortages would result in power cuts and blackouts throughout the country.

Before their arrival, then, there was possibly no better time to light up the capital. Five days before Christmas, Elton began a five-gig stint at Hammersmith Odeon in west London that echoed the Beatles' festive residency there back in 1964. He even made his own contribution to the canon of yuletide records with a jaunty Phil Spectorish romp replete with clanging tubular bells titled "Step into Christmas," though it was set to be eclipsed in Britain by Slade's cheerful thumper "Merry Xmas Everybody."

The Hammersmith Odeon shows were a series of daft and loose performances. Debuting with the lineup for the first time as a full-time member was Ray Cooper, a chiseled, intense percussionist who would throw his tambourine high in the air and even contributed a bizarre duck call solo to the middle of "Honky Cat." Getting fully into the spirit, Elton played an instrumental piano rendition of "Rudolph the Red-Nosed Reindeer," recalling the pub-playing days of the teenage Reggie back at the Northwood Hills.

At a key point, styrofoam snow tumbled down onto the stage, threatening to throw the whole show into amateur pantomime chaos. The fake blizzard was copious and far too thick. It covered everyone and everything and jammed up the piano keys, much to the cackling delight of the band.

"I'm available for weddings, Christmas parties, everything," Elton the styrofoam snowman laughed, at the close of what had been a momentous year. "Ten pounds an hour."

Elton venturing further and further out there with the ludicrously extravagant costumes while on tour in Australia in 1974.

9 HIGH IN THE SNOWY MOUNTAINS

HE WAS WANDERING past a table at the back of the studio when he noticed there was a line of white powder on top of it. Elton was still so inexperienced when it came to drugs, he really wasn't sure it was what he suspected it might be. He asked John Reid, "What on earth is that?" Reid told him it was cocaine. Elton figured he might as well take a little sniff.

He had started drinking more because it loosened him up, made him feel safer, more secure. Everyone else was taking drugs, and to his mind, he was the outsider. He didn't smoke, so he couldn't share with them even a puff on a joint. He was sick of missing out on all the action.

That first line of coke broke down all of his remaining barriers. It made him chatty chatty chatty. He could really start communicating now.

It felt slightly dangerous, too, and he was sick of being a goody-goody.

More important, Elton thought the fact that he could now snort away with the others made him finally accepted by them. All of a sudden, he was in with the in crowd. He was part of the Class A crew. He'd finally arrived.

"I did get into drugs 'cause I wanted to join the gang," he admits. "My band were doing drugs so far ahead. I was so naive."

It was January 1974 and Elton and the others were high—and getting higher still—in the Colorado Rockies at the remote studio location of the Caribou Ranch. Back in the first week of September '73, when he'd been playing nearby at the Coliseum in Denver, he'd gone up to the ranch to check out the studio, which its owner, Jim Guercio, producer of the band Chicago, had opened the year before. Elton liked some of the records that had already been made there: the heavy blues and alien talk-box vocal sounds of Joe Walsh's "Rocky Mountain Way" (from his vividly titled 1973 album *The Smoker You Drink, the Player You Get*), the head-nod groove of Rick Derringer's "Rock and Roll, Hoochie Koo."

Caribou was tough to get to, which was one of its main attractions. From Denver, you drove the thirty-five miles to Boulder in the foothills of the Rockies. Then you took the Boulder Canyon road, slowly ascending almost three thousand feet on the winding route to Nederland. Nine miles on, you passed through the gates of the ranch, set within four thousand acres of mountain land, motoring along another two and a half miles of driveway before you finally reached its doors.

The setup was rustic but lush, with a series of cabins dotted around the building that housed the studio. But life on the ranch, particularly in winter, often caused an extreme climate shock to visiting bands, when the snow was two feet deep and sixty-mile-an-hour winds were whipping it around. Recreation for the hardy might involve scooting around on a convoy of snowmobiles.

There was much in the way of comfort, however, to offset the weather conditions. The residential lodges were furnished with antiques and brass four-poster beds, and movies could be piped directly to TV sets in the cabins. The studio itself was hunting lodge cum seventies chic: mounted deer heads, leather armchairs, thick brown carpets, dark pine walls. Built on a former Native American burial ground, the ranch, like the Château d'Hérouville, was believed to be filled with ghosts. One of its cabins, in particular, Running Bear, was said to be "haunted as hell."

Cut off from everything, Caribou was the perfect place for rock stars to hide away and get down to serious business, whether that be intensive recording or intensive snorting, or often a combination of the two. As such, the sessions for the next Elton album were his and the band's most hedonistic yet.

"A very, very apt word is hedonistic," confirms Bernie. "It was in the winter and we always used to say there was more snow inside than outside."

EVEN AFTER THE outpouring of songs for *Goodbye Yellow Brick Road,* for Elton and Bernie, it seemed as if there was still plenty of creative flow left. The follow-up album, which would come to be titled *Caribou,* was written and recorded at the ranch in a lightning eight days. Much of this accelerated activity, though, was down to the sheer pressure to get the record done and dusted before impending tours of Japan, Australia, and New Zealand.

Up at the ranch, Elton looked in the mirror and saw a bloated zombie staring back. In the past few months, he'd put on forty-five pounds through drinking over half a bottle of whisky a day. At twenty-seven, his hair was rapidly thinning, and he worried that his body was on the verge of collapse. He felt like death warmed over.

Cocaine helped to snuff the hangovers and push him through the process, but still, the making of *Caribou* was excruciating. His mood swings, likely worsened by his newfound narcotic dabbling, were more extreme than ever. As he had been during the recording of *Don't Shoot Me I'm Only the Piano Player,* he was in such a weird mental state that the project lost three days in between songwriting and recording while the singer pulled himself together. Once work resumed, the backing tracks were cut in only two and a half days.

Caribou was an album made on autopilot. Its creators may have been shattered, but at the same time they knew they could knock another record out. "It's a very uneven album," Elton says, looking back. "It was an album that we had to get out under contract."

Bernie and Elton were at this point, the singer confesses, "quite cocky." Some of their songs were flippant and a touch bizarre, such as "Grimsby," a tongue-in-cheek attempt to romanticize the unspectacular east coast English fishing town, sarcastically talking up its culinary delights of pies and peas and cotton candy. "Stinker" was a bluesy sludge as bad as its title, being the confessions of a tramplike figure who lives in a hole in the ground. Highlighting their misguided, coked-up overconfidence, Elton and Bernie even joked about calling the album *Stinker*.

Worst of all was the intentional lyrical gibberish of "Solar Prestige a Gammon," its verses rendered in a hammy operatic Italian voice before it bounced into a jaunty, jokey Euro pop chorus. In the minds of the writers, there was method behind this madness, as well as madness behind the method. Over the past few years, some of Elton and Bernie's songs had been wildly misinterpreted by over-thinking listeners as possessing hidden religious subtexts—the "nailed to my love" line in "I Need You to Turn To" from *Elton John* was said to be about the crucifixion of Jesus Christ; "Border Song" with its "holy Moses I have been deceived" refrain was seen by some as anti-Semitic.

The pair decided to have a little nose-thumbing fun. "We just thought, We're gonna write this load of old rubbish and just put it out," Elton says. "That was us coasting a bit. When you're at number one, you can do anything you want. The very reason we did it was to say, 'Listen, no one's gonna read anything into this.' But, fucking hell, if there's not the name of five fishes in it . . ."

Amid its dippy wordplay, "Solar Prestige a Gammon" happened to list five species of fish—"lantern," "salmon," "cod," and the intentionally misspelled "sardin" and "turbert." This was decoded by some fans as being a direct reference to Christ's Feeding of the Four Thousand. "We got more letters on that song 'cause of the five fishes," the singer remembers. "It was, Oh this has *gotta* be religious."

It seemed there was no way to suppress the code hunters. With uncanny coincidence, one overzealous fan even managed to unscramble the nonsense title of "Solar Prestige a Gammon" as an anagram of "Elton's Program Is a Game."

For an album written and recorded under duress, *Caribou* still contained some great tracks. "The Bitch Is Back" was a tongue-in-cheek soul-tinged rocker poking fun at Elton's reputation as the king of the wicked put-downs, which referred to his "sniffing pots of glue" before—with some irony, considering his current inebriated state—claiming to be in reality "stone cold sober." "I've Seen the Saucers," in Elton's estimation "not the greatest song in the world," was better than he thought it was—an elegant ballad sung from the imagined viewpoint of a true UFO believer. "Ticking" was an evocative short story in song, the tale of a quiet individual who suddenly snaps and commits a mass shooting in a bar in Queens, New York, killing fourteen people before being gunned down by police.

There was one song on *Caribou,* though, that towered above the others. "Don't Let the Sun Go Down on Me," a slow burner that exploded into a pleading, emotionally charged chorus, was in Elton's mind his homage to the Beach Boys, while in truth it sounded like no one other than himself. On the morning he was writing it, a passing Nigel Olsson, heading to bed after staying up all night, heard him playing the song and offered two simple words of appreciation: "Number one," said the drummer.

However, attempting to record the vocal for "Don't Let the Sun Go Down on Me" at the ranch, eighty-six hundred feet above sea level in thinning air, proved to be a challenge for Elton, provoking one of his now notorious tantrums. "A hard song to sing," he points out, in his defense. "It's a naked vocal for the first half. Your voice is sticking out like a sore thumb. I couldn't get the vocal right. In the end, I went, 'You can send this fucking song to Engelbert Humperdinck! And if he doesn't like it, tell him to send it to Lulu!'"

After finally completing the take, Elton walked into the control room of the studio and said to Gus Dudgeon, "If you put this on the album, I'll sodding well shoot you." He hated the song, hated his vocal on it. A year later, "Don't Let the Sun Go Down on Me" was nominated at the Grammys for Best Pop Vocal Performance—Male.

But not before this imagined tribute to the Beach Boys was completed in Los Angeles with the addition of harmonies by the band's Carl Wilson and Bruce Johnston, along with a dramatic horn arrangement by Del Newman that allowed the track to soar. Recorded in a sulk, "Don't Let the Sun Go Down on Me" was nevertheless—if not, as Olsson predicted, number one—a U.S. number two hit.

Still, it was quite a risky track to put out as a single, being five and a half minutes long. Before releasing it, driving along in his car one day, Elton played a cassette of the song for Rod Stewart. The two friends shared a similar sense of absurd humor—giving each other the drag queen alter ego names of Sharon (Elton) and Phyllis (Rod)—

and were always in sharp, if good-natured competition with each other.

Elton sat at the wheel, waiting for Rod's reaction, feeling antsy throughout the two minutes before the chorus of "Don't Let the Sun Go Down on Me" finally kicked in.

Fucking long single, thought Elton, *and so slow.*

Rod turned to him and drily asked, "Ballad, is it?"

FROM JAPAN, IN February, where he was mobbed everywhere he went, he traveled back to Australia before moving on to New Zealand. His first tour in this part of the world in October '71 had been ill-starred. As this second trip would prove, it was a destination where Elton would appear to be cursed.

It started well enough. Even though he was drained and appeared "sedate" to onlookers, he managed to be chirpy when answering reporters' questions upon his arrival. One journalist wondered how he had changed since the last time he was in Australia. "I'm the *balding* Elton John now," the singer quipped.

There hadn't been much development of the Australian concert circuit in the intervening three and a half years, and so again Elton was booked to play an odd mix of sports stadiums and racetracks. Only this time around, he was selling them out and breaking attendance records.

On the tour, he was carrying with him an eye-watering $200,000 worth of personal baggage, in elaborate trunks that folded out into a series of traveling wardrobes filled with costumes and shoes and hats and glasses. He planned to unveil two new outfits in particular during this jaunt down under. The first was a tight black Lurex zip-up suit strung with dozens of small red, orange, blue, and green balls, while others sprouted from his shoulders on piano wire. The second involved a voluminous arrangement of outsized feathers—in tribute to the 1920s–'30s exotic dancer Josephine Baker—that made him look like a psychedelic peacock.

The shows were slick for the slower songs and utterly forceful for the harder rockers, with Elton nightly attacking "Crocodile Rock" and "Saturday Night's Alright for Fighting" in particular. One elated reviewer in Melbourne called him a "genius in feathers" and said that his "piano-playing is comparable to the venom of Jerry Lee Lewis, with at times the delicate touch of a classical pianist."

It was in New Zealand that the tour hit trouble, ahead of Elton's show at the Western Springs Stadium on February 28, where he was to play to a crowd of thirty-five thousand—a shade over one percent of the country's entire population at the time. The afternoon before, a reception was thrown for him by his antipodean label, Festival Records, at a cream-colored, colonial-style pavilion on the grounds of the Parnell Rose Gardens in the city of Aukland. Outside, the party was greeted by the performance of a traditional Maori haka, or war dance. It was only too fitting a prelude for what was to follow.

Inside, as the guests milled around and knocked back free drinks, the bar quickly ran out of beer. Requesting a whisky, John Reid was told that, sorry, there wasn't any in stock. The manager immediately got into an argument with the event's organizer, Kevin Williams, shouting at him, "You're an incompetent!" Williams offered Reid a glass of champagne instead. Reid threw it into his face.

Ten minutes later, at the bar, Judith Baragwanath, a model and writer for Auckland's *Sunday News,* challenged Reid about his behavior. "How could you do that to anyone?" she demanded. "You rotten little bastard." Reid later claimed that she—or perhaps someone else—then added, "You little poof." In a blind rage, and what he described as "a reflex action," the manager punched her in the left eye. Elton, on the other side of the room, was unaware of the commotion.

Later that same night, at an after-party following American pop star David Cassidy's show at Auckland Town Hall, a colleague of Baragwanath's from the *Sunday News,* the reporter David Wheeler, was allegedly heard muttering that Reid and the others were now "marked men." Reid got wind of this and advised Elton it would be best if they all left. Instead, an enraged Elton decided to accost Wheeler, grabbing him by the collar and hissing in his ear, "You no-good son of an Irish leprechaun. You've threatened my manager?" The journalist protested, "I don't know what you're talking about."

Elton was on the verge of hitting him. But Reid got in there first, smacking Wheeler to the ground before laying a few kicks in for good measure.

They made a hasty exit, speeding off back to their hotel. Once there, they received a call from the head of David Cassidy's security personnel warning them that there was now a carload of angry men out cruising the streets looking for them. No one left the safety of their rooms for the rest of the night.

The next day, the police arrived, looking for John Reid. He was arrested and charged with two counts of assault, and refused bail. Only when his attorneys protested that the manager had to be present at the Auckland show that night was Reid temporarily freed, after shelling out five thousand Australian dollars. Incredibly, given the violence and drama that had preceded it, the gig at Western Springs Stadium, before the largest crowd in New Zealand concert history, was a resounding success.

The following morning, Reid was due back in court, and Elton with him, on a charge of assaulting Wheeler. After a twenty-minute hearing at Auckland Magistrates Court, the singer, tamely dressed in a gray suit, was released when the fracas was deemed the result of a misunderstanding. He was charged fifty Australian dollars to cover prosecution costs, and before he left, he signed autographs for fans waiting in the courthouse.

Reid didn't get off as lightly, not least since it was revealed that Judith Baragwanath had suffered a black eye, as had David Wheeler, though the latter's list of injuries extended to chipped and cracked teeth and bruising. In an effort to try to reduce his punishment, the manager had already promised to pay civil damages to both victims out of court, but nonetheless the judge noted "the continuity of the offenses" while adding that Reid had shown "an ill-mannered, arrogant indifference to people in the way he dealt with them." He was sentenced to twenty-eight days in Auckland's Mount Eden Jail.

In the end, Elton completed the remaining dates in Australia before flying home without his manager and partner.

· · ·

MEANWHILE, OVER IN the States, something entirely unexpected was happening. In Detroit, at the R&B station WJLB, the twenty-year-old late-night DJ Donnie Simpson picked "Bennie and the Jets" out of the tracklist of *Goodbye Yellow Brick Road* and began giving it regular spins on the air. Initially, his program controller, Jay Butler, was nervous about this—WJLB catered mainly to a black audience, who he worried might balk at the idea that the station was suddenly playing a song by Elton John, someone from a very white, very pop background. Butler called a few black record stores in the Detroit area. Their managers told him that *Goodbye Yellow Brick Road* was an album already being bought by many of their customers.

Three days later, "Bennie and the Jets" became the song most requested by callers to WJLB. Jay Butler phoned Elton's promotion man, Pat Pipolo, giving him the surprising news and telling him he was going to talk to Rosalie Trombley, the program director at CKLW in Windsor, Ontario. The Canadian AM station's far-reaching broadcasts could be heard throughout the American Midwest, making it highly influential when it came to the Top Forty in both the black and white markets. Hearing from Butler the reaction to "Bennie and the Jets" in Detroit, Trombley called Pipolo. She advised him to release the track as a single, saying it would be a guaranteed hit not just on the pop chart but also on the R&B chart.

No one at the label, or Elton himself, was sure about this. "Candle in the Wind" was already lined up to be the next release. Elton asked Pipolo: "Are you prepared to put your career on the line?" The promo man replied, "Well, no, not really, but I think we should release it as a single. I think you'll be an R&B artist as well as a pop artist."

Pipolo stuck his neck out and "Bennie and the Jets" was released as an A side on February 4, 1974. Within weeks, it had risen to number one on the *Billboard* chart and, amazing everyone involved, number fifteen on the R&B chart.

"I'm a part black man," jokes Elton. "I'm sure there's a part of me that is black, because I've always loved black music. I mean, come on, you're a white kid from fucking Pinner and you're on the black chart. It was validation from the music people that I loved the most. It was one of the nicest things that happened."

"If you look back at that point in time," says Bernie, " 'Bennie and the Jets' wasn't what was going on radio-wise in general. We set a trend, or broke the mold."

AFTER AUSTRALIA AND New Zealand, Elton was wiped out. There was no way he could face the European tour due to begin in April, so all of its dates were canceled. Instead, he took a very much needed vacation, booking himself into the John Gardiner Tennis Ranch on Camelback Mountain near Paradise Valley, Arizona. Spending close to a month there, and on the tennis courts every day, he lost twenty-eight pounds.

Elton returned to the UK in May, fitter, happier, and completely revitalized. He was itching to get back onstage and so seized the opportunity to play a benefit for Watford Football Club, the team he'd supported since childhood and continued to go to watch play whenever he could. Since the previous November he'd even lent his name as a vice president to the club. At the time, Watford, stuck in the Third Division, was suffering serious money troubles. "I wouldn't like to see them go under," Elton told reporters before the show. "I'll do everything in my power to save them." Although high profile, this benefit concert was almost a token gesture. He started to wonder if he might somehow get involved with the club on a deeper financial level.

On the afternoon of May 5, thirty-one thousand fans (five times the number of people who normally came to Watford matches) crammed into the team's Vicarage Road stadium. Elton arrived onstage in a gold-and-black-striped jacket and matching trousers reflecting both the team's playing colors and their nickname, the Hornets. His eyes shielded behind oversized white shades that looked less like sunglasses than ski goggles, he sat down at his grand piano—which was covered in silks of rainbow hues fringed with yellow, pink, and red feather boas—and let rip. It was clear from the get-go that his energy was back at peak level.

Among the hits, he found time to air for the first time his take on the Beatles' "Lucy in the Sky with Diamonds" and, when dark clouds above produced a passing shower, to lead the crowd in a rendition of "Singin' in the Rain." Then he introduced a special guest, the tufty-haired, white-clad Rod Stewart. Together they launched into a harmonizing version of "Country Comfort" (to which Stewart himself had given a raspy treatment four years earlier on his album *Gasoline Alley*).

Out in the crowd, the fans crushed forward and swayed dangerously as girls got up on their boyfriends' shoulders and waved tartan scarves. As soon as the song was over, two St. John's ambulance men rushed onto the scaffolding stage and urged the people at the front barrier to move back. Rod departed after rousing renditions of Chuck Berry's "Sweet Little Rock 'n' Roller" and Jimi Hendrix's "Angel," leaving Elton to finish with a walloping "Saturday Night's Alright for Fighting." In the director's box, the slightly hysterical wife of an American record executive was running up and down the aisles, loudly exclaiming, "He's my generation's Sinatra!"

More sedate was a show on May 18 at the Royal Festival Hall in London in aid of the Invalid Children's Society, and at the request of Princess Margaret, who watched her pop star friend perform a retrospective set that took in rarely heard songs including "Skyline Pigeon" from *Empty Sky* and "Love Song" from *Tumbleweed Connection*. As a thank-you, and clearly understanding Elton's preposterous tastes, the Princess gifted him a pair of stuffed leopards.

By this point, *Goodbye Yellow Brick Road* had been in the U.S. Top Ten for more than half a year. *Caribou* was due to be released in June. In London, Elton went into the BBC studios of *The Old Grey Whistle Test* and, solo at the piano, prerecorded a showcase of two songs, "Ticking" and "Grimsby," from the upcoming album, to be screened in July, by which time he would be elsewhere.

Upon his release from jail in New Zealand, John Reid had gone directly to the United States and begun to negotiate a new record contract for Elton that was highly ambitious in its demands. The singer, due to join him, this time around decided to travel to America at a slower pace and in luxurious style.

In the last week of June, Elton arrived at Southampton dock to board the SS *France* for a transatlantic voyage. On the quayside, to send the ship on its way, a brass band of schoolchildren tootled and banged their way through "Yellow Submarine."

It was a leisurely five-day crossing. But there was still work to do. By the time he got to New York, Elton wanted to have all of the songs written for the next album. It was planned to be an early days autobiography in the form of a long-playing record—one that found Elton and Bernie drowning in nostalgia for a time that wasn't in fact that long ago but now seemed so far away.

The only way to fly. Elton and Bernie and entourage ahead of takeoff on the '74 American tour.

10 FROM THE END OF THE WORLD TO YOUR TOWN

OUT ON THE ATLANTIC, Elton had time to reflect. Here he found a moment of pause, an oasis of calm amid the madness.

At midday, every day, he'd enter the SS *France*'s Salon Debussy, the luxury liner's First Class music room, with its grand piano, gold-lacquered walls, bronzed panels, and statue of a flute-playing girl by the French sculptor Hubert Yencesse. So popular was the Salon that Elton could secure only a two-hour slot to work there each day, during the lengthy lunchtime of an opera singer traveling onboard who'd blocked out the entire time. One day, Elton arrived only to find the ship's concert pianist sitting on the stool he'd prearranged to occupy. To his embarrassment, he was forced to eject her, and she flounced off to another music room directly above. For two hours, briefly interrupting Elton's tranquillity, the sounds of battling pianos filled the corridors.

From his stately position amid this splendor and elegance in the summer of 1974, Elton transported his thoughts back to his struggling days of the late sixties. Laid out in front of him were the sheets of Bernie's latest lyrics, which delved into the duo's failures, doubts, and heartaches during that frustrating time.

"It did feel a long time ago," Elton says. "Those days were the innocent days. They were the tough days of really, really hard graft . . . really, really trying. The disappointments . . . will they ever end? Will you ever get a lucky break? Those memories stay with you forever."

The idea behind the next album was that the pair would revisit and document their story up to the release of *Empty Sky* in June

1969. The springboard was a lyric Taupin had written that starred both of them in alter-ego roles as Captain Fantastic and the Brown Dirt Cowboy: Elton the child, suppressed by a restrictive father, who grows up to discover his "real" self as a superhero-like figure; Bernie the backwoods westerns obsessive wondering if there might be a place for him in the city; the pair of them meeting, pooling their talents, and beginning "a long and lonely climb."

"It was such an autobiographical song that the others fell into place," says Bernie. "The majority of the songs are pictures seen through both our eyes and experiences." Page after page, their tale unfolded. The music business of their early years was depicted as a quasi-Biblical tower populated by greedy and lustful sinners. In an attempt to survive within it, as the Tin Pan Alley Twins, they peddle songs to be sung in pubs and cabaret summer seasons. Surrounded by Kings Road dandies, the duo are broke and despondent, living a life in black and white while everyone around them seems to exist in vibrant Swinging Sixties color.

Late nights in London are spent gazing through the grimy windows of a cheap café, watching drunks and prostitutes stumble by, backgrounded by the flashing blue lights of police cars. The brain-fried, out-of-his-depth country boy Bernie takes the weekend trains home to the safety of his former rural environment, only to return to Frome Court and Reg and a suburban work week of washing dishes and shaving with dull razor blades while optimistically writing endless songs.

Elsewhere, there was room for confession. One evocative lyric spoke of the days of Elton's engagement to a domineering fiancée, leading him inexorably toward unhappy marriage and piling debt, the partnership exploding in a drunken breakup following wise words from a friend. It was a song that alluded to suicide, whether metaphorical or actual.

The real romance in these songs—heightened for the purposes of lyrical drama—was the platonic one between the writers: penning childish songs about scarecrows and dandelions, laboring on, laughing through their worries for the future.

In those two-hour bursts on the SS *France,* Elton tackled the lyrics chronologically as he composed the chords and melodies. "It was about *us,*" he says, "so I felt involved in the actual meaning of the songs. You're writing something that's about your life. It was personal. It just flowed out of me. I wrote them in running order, so you could see the landscape coming up."

Aboard the liner, there was also much downtime for fun and frivolousness. Accompanying Elton on the trip was his friend Tony King, the general manager of Rocket, who'd previously worked for the Beatles at Apple. Also joining them on the journey to New York was John Lennon's first wife, Cynthia, and their son, Julian, then eleven, en route to visit his dad. Their days on the ship were frittered away in very pleasant circumstances, as Elton recorded in his diary:

> *June 22: At 3:30pm, play squash with Tony. He is just beginning and I am not much better. But we do quite well and attract an audience who quickly pick up a few tips on the lesser art of the game.*

There were rounds of backgammon and laps swum in the cold saltwater indoor swimming pool. Now on a health kick, Elton was trying to observe a no-alcohol, low-carbohydrate diet. In this environment, however, with its lavish banquets of food and beverages, it was tough to uphold. There were drinks with the captain in the Riviera Bar. There was dressing up in suits and bow ties, in an approximation of a perfect English gentleman, for fine dining on caviar and pepper steak in the Chambord Room.

Still, even with his success and riches, Elton, sporting streaks of green in his hair, was made to feel like a low-class upstart by some of his fellow travelers. During dinner one evening, he heard a posh voice loftily announce, "That man over there is Elton John. He is very famous, but I have never heard of him."

Among the singer's group, this prompted much laughter. Together, though, they could outbitch anyone, and they were usually to be found casting a withering eye around them at their snooty fellow passengers.

"You can tell the continental people from the Americans by look-

ing at their clothes," Elton noted in his diary. *"Why do large American ladies squeeze themselves into dresses that show every inch of flab?"*

In truth, even if he looked like a deviant glam rocker, by this point Elton could buy and sell virtually everyone else on the SS *France.* Midvoyage, more incredible news came through from America, which he duly recorded in his journal.

> *I am whisked away for a ship-to-shore telephone call— "Caribou is now platinum. Congratulations. Roger and out."*

RESTED, REFRESHED, AND lighter in body and spirit, Elton docked in New York. There was much to do. Aside from promoting the already runaway *Caribou,* he was set to help launch the U.S. career of Kiki Dee with her second Rocket album, *I've Got the Music in Me.*

Owing to his crammed schedule, Elton had been forced to take a back seat in the making of the LP—recorded at the Jimi Hendrix-founded Electric Lady Studios in Manhattan and produced by Gus Dudgeon and Clive Franks. He had nevertheless made his presence felt in an encouraging and sometimes comedic way. Kiki had found herself intensely nervous when getting ready to record the vocal for the driving, ecstatic title track in the presence of such backing soul talents as Cissy Houston and Joshie Jo Armstead (whose combined supporting-role credits included Elvis Presley, Otis Redding, and Bob Dylan).

"I remember Elton running around the studio with his trousers round his ankles, just to make me laugh," she says. "I got the vocal after that. We always had that kind of relationship where physically he'd jump on me and tickle me."

Kiki was clearly Elton's favorite protégée. In ostentatious displays of his generosity, he took the singer on shopping trips in Manhattan, where he loved to blow thousands of dollars on her. "He used to be a bit overwhelming, if I'm honest," she says. "You'd be in some store in New York, and he'd bring over this beautiful black dress and you'd think, Oh my God. He'd get you putting it on and he'd have bought all these things before you knew it. It was crazy. So sweet. There was a bit of a twinkle in his eye when he was doing it. Being able to do it must have been a huge thrill."

There was no sign of his financial momentum slowing, either, since each record he released sold more than the one before. But if *Caribou* was a hit with the record-buying public, the critics noticed that Elton's quality control had slipped. Al Rudis in the *Chicago Sun-Times* stated, "Nowhere is the magic moment that stands out in shining splendor, that demands, 'Listen to me.'" Tom Nolan in *Rolling Stone* was more pointed, calling Elton "a maestro who has presented a series of attractive aural surfaces. The trouble with surface is that it wears thin."

The reviews for *Caribou* stung Elton. "I thought it would get slagged off because it seemed time for something of mine to get slagged off," he reasoned, a touch bruised, in *Melody Maker*. "I'm just sitting back and taking it. I really think some reviewers are just deaf."

The most brutal condemnation of the album would come from none other than its producer. "*Caribou* is a piece of crap," thundered Gus Dudgeon. "The sound is the worst, the songs are nowhere, the lyrics weren't that good, the singing wasn't all there, the playing wasn't that great, the production is just plain lousy." But Elton's ever-growing army of fans didn't seem to notice or care that *Caribou* was rushed and sloppy. In both the United States and the United Kingdom, it reached number one.

The fact that his stock was now unbelievably high made John Reid's task of negotiating a new record deal for Elton a relative breeze. Still, the fearless, tenacious manager exceeded everyone's expectations.

Since *Don't Shoot Me I'm Only the Piano Player*, Elton's releases had been moved over in the States from Uni Records to the label's parent company, MCA. Now that the sketchily detailed distribution deal Dick James had cut with Russ Regan at Uni in 1970 was due to end, MCA's president, Mike Maitland, was determined to keep Elton on the label. In fact, he knew losing the company's most successful artist would leave him shamefaced. "We would have survived," Maitland confessed. "But it could have crippled us for a while."

Reid was clearly in a winning position, but, bravely, he sought no outside advice in the renegotiations. During the previous couple of years, he later admitted, the dense legalese of recording contracts had provided his "bedtime reading" material.

There was one other significant suitor when it came to signing Elton. Over the past three years, David Geffen had built up his Asylum Records to become a protective stable for such artists as Joni Mitchell, Tom Waits, the Eagles, and, since 1973, Bob Dylan. Now he had his sights firmly set on the premier singer-songwriter of the early seventies. Geffen sidled up to John Reid at a party, telling him, "I've signed Bob Dylan. Next I'm going to sign Elton and then we're all going to take over the world."

Reid was wary, and keen to stick with MCA, knowing that changing horses in the midstream of Elton's fast-flowing career was highly risky. "I'm superstitious about changing labels," he later told a reporter. "I don't think you should do it unless something is seriously wrong."

Before anything could be properly discussed, however, Reid and Maitland had to cut a deal with Dick James in London allowing MCA to retain the rights to distribute Elton's back catalog in North America while DJM kept the copyrights. James agreed to the arrangement; he knew that Elton was moving on. Holding on to the catalog—which MCA would of course do their best to continue to exploit—was James's reward for all of his years of belief and investment.

Reid and Maitland put together a fifty-five-page document that guaranteed Elton a total of $8 million from MCA over the five-year period beginning in 1976 (when the DJM contract would be fulfilled), along with an unprecedented 28 percent royalty rate—almost twice what the highest-earning artist might expect to nail down. It was the most lucrative recording contract the music industry had ever seen. In *Billboard,* Maitland called it simply "the best deal anyone ever got."

To announce this record-breaking agreement between MCA and Elton John, on June 19, 1974, full-page ads appeared not in the music business trade press, as was the norm, but in *The New York Times* and the *Los Angeles Times*. Even Elton, never one for understatement, thought that this move seemed an immodest step too far.

"I couldn't believe the amount of money involved," he said a few years later, noting that it "was the start of the multi-million[-dollar] deal. It made the record business more vulgar and I was partly responsible for that."

It was a complete turnaround from the swindling deals of the sixties. From here on in, seventies artists and their managers would seek out ever more enormous advances for their recording services. But maybe it had gone too far. Rock stars were now as rich as royalty and business tycoons, with money to burn on houses and planes and cars and girls (or boys) and, of course, heaps of white powder.

BRINGING HIS HEALTH kick to an abrupt end, cocaine was to prove the fuel for the mutual appreciation club that was Elton John and John Lennon. Hanging with the former Beatle in Manhattan in that summer of '74 was the biggest hero-meeting thrill yet for Elton. "He's probably the first big star I instantly fell in love with," he admitted at the time. "It usually takes me six or seven meetings with someone, 'cause I'm very withdrawn. But he's so easy to get on with."

Lennon felt much the same about Elton, instantly drawn toward his acerbic English humor and wholly impressed by his skyscraping talents. When he'd first heard "Your Song," Lennon was blown away, publicly stating that Elton was "the first new thing that's happened since we happened." At a time when the erstwhile Beatle was going through a patchy phase, both creatively and commercially, he was astounded by Elton's constant presence on the charts and on the radio. Lennon joked about how even death couldn't possibly increase the amount of airplay Elton received. "You get played enough," John laughed. "If you ever die, I'll throw my radio out the window."

Their first time in the studio together, on the sessions for Lennon's *Walls and Bridges,* Elton felt the pressure. "You're in there with John Lennon," he points out, "you better fucking perform."

Trying to sing along to Lennon's idiosyncratic vocal phrasing for the two tracks he appeared on—"Surprise Surprise (Sweet Bird of Paradox)" and "Whatever Gets You thru the Night"—was hellishly tricky for Elton, and took hours. "People were leaving the room," he reckoned. "Razor blades were being passed out."

It was Lennon's turn to be nervous when he accepted Elton's invitation to the Caribou Ranch in Colorado, where the sessions for the next album were due to commence in July. The plan was to record two of Lennon's songs: the relatively obscure "One Day (at a Time)," a cut from his 1973 album *Mind Games,* and "Lucy in the Sky with Diamonds." Far removed mentally from his Beatles days by this point, Lennon couldn't even remember the chords for "Lucy." Davey Johnstone had to gently remind him.

The normally unflappable Gus Dudgeon was starstruck by Lennon, seeing "his charisma as a glow of light." Still, there were other more pressing concerns when it came down to the business of actually recording—Lennon found himself acutely short of breath when trying to sing in the high-altitude studio environment. "He had to keep rushing to the oxygen tank," Dudgeon remembered.

Lennon stayed on at Caribou for a few idyllic days, riding horses and shopping for cowboy boots in nearby Boulder, before he left Elton and the others to get on with the making of the record. The autobiographical album was now to be called *Captain Fantastic and the Brown Dirt Cowboy,* and the team had learned from the mistakes they'd made on *Caribou.* An entire month was set aside for its recording, making for a comparatively smooth and painless process, as reflected in the music emanating from the speakers, which was shaping up to be possibly Elton's best yet.

Only when recording the vocal for "Someone Saved My Life Tonight"—the raw and moving song that beamed Elton back to the desperate days of Linda Woodrow and Furlong Road—was there any real tension in the studio. At the microphone, he delivered the nearly seven-minute ballad with fitting tenderness. Dudgeon, however, listening in the control room, felt the singer could wring more passion and power out of it, and he kept rewinding the tape and pushing Elton harder and harder.

An embarrassed and irritated Davey Johnstone took the producer aside and said, "Don't you think you should take it easy on the guy? Don't you know what he's singing about? He's talking about attempting suicide."

"That's a fucking hard song to sing," Elton admits. "Gus went, 'Ah.'"

Dudgeon was horrified: "I made him sing the most unbelievably personal things over and over again to get a bloody note right or get a bit of phrasing together."

When Elton listened to the playback of "Someone Saved My Life Tonight," he was overcome with emotion.

"He had to leave the room," Dudgeon remembered. "He just couldn't take it."

WHEN SEPTEMBER ROLLED around, it was time to get back onto the *Starship*. This time, as with the recording of *Captain Fantastic and the Brown Dirt Cowboy,* Elton was far better prepared. He'd even solved the problem of his bleeding, piano-bashing fingers, painting them before the shows with the New-Skin liquid bandage solution used by bowlers, which added a protective film to his long-suffering digits.

It had been six months since the eventful tour of Australia and New Zealand, with only three sporadic dates since—the longest break he'd had from the road in years. But Elton was making up for it with this upcoming U.S. jaunt. He'd be appearing before a total of more than three-quarters of a million people over the next ten weeks.

The tour started with a sweep through the southern states, the band's initial base being a hotel on Bourbon Street in New Orleans. On the first night, in Dallas at the ten-thousand-capacity Convention Center, the show went without a hitch, and Elton left the stage feeling it was perhaps the best gig he'd ever played.

But despite this slicker level of operation, there was often a sense that it was all getting wilder and almost uncontrollable. In Houston, he was given a police escort to the Hofheinz Pavilion that was both dramatic and dangerous, zooming in the wrong direction down one-way streets, causing motorists coming the other way to hastily pull over to the curb. In Mobile, at the Municipal Auditorium, he couldn't hear himself sing and kicked over a monitor. Backstage, he was raging and almost didn't return for the encore, until it was clear that the howling crowd wouldn't let him get away without coming back for more.

In Los Angeles, a total of seventy thousand tickets for four shows at the Forum had sold out in six hours. On the opening night, before an audience that included Ringo Starr, Barbra Streisand, Diana Ross, and Elizabeth Taylor, Elton once again got into an argument with the security guards, who were pushing fans out of the aisles and making them sit back down in their seats. He arrived for the encore carried on the muscular shoulders of his new personal body-guard, Jim Morris, 1973's Mr. America, and cried, "This is your concert . . . come down!" Thousands rushed toward the stage. Afterward, the Forum's manager Jim Appel threatened to have the singer arrested for dangerously provoking the crowd and endangering his staff. The next night, the security detail was doubled.

During the run at the Forum, Elton, always a frustrated disc jockey, took over from regular host Richard Kimball for a two-hour live broadcast on L.A.'s FM station KMET. He was a natural, introducing himself as "EJ the DJ," playing records by John Lennon, Joe Cocker, Little Feat, Aretha Franklin, and of course Kiki Dee. He read out advertisements hawking hair restorer ("If you're going bald like me . . .") and Licorice Pizza ("Gives you a good run for your money") and referred to himself, as if he wasn't himself, as "that little punk . . . that looks like a bank clerk . . . I hate him."

He then talked up his favorite music retail store in the world, Tower Records on Sunset Strip, while at the same time jokingly advertising his latest album. "Because I'm doing this commercial, they're paying me seven million dollars!" he goofed. "They've put a stack of my *Caribou* albums just inside the door. From today to Sunday midnight, they're paying compensation to everyone who falls over them."

. . .

STANDING IN FRONT of the *Starship,* Elton, the band, and the entire entourage lined up for photographer Terry O'Neill. The exterior of the plane had been resprayed in red and a royal blue flecked with white stars to go along with the stenciled words ELTON JOHN BAND TOUR 1974 and the MCA Records logo on the tail.

Elton and Bernie posed in the foreground, dressed in white—the singer in a Panama hat and a faux-military shirt and leaning on an accessorizing walking cane, looking like a benign South American despot; the lyricist in spotless overalls with a patch bearing his name, like a body shop mechanic who'd never actually done a proper day's work. Behind them gathered everyone else: John Reid, Kiki Dee, Ray Cooper, and a couple of dozen others. Their number had certainly swelled since the '73 tour. The message the photograph sent out was clear: We are now massive.

Inside the plane, Elton posed for an O'Neill photo shoot in the rear bedroom, bare-chested and appearing to be naked since his lower half was tucked under the white fur blanket, his eyes peering through large round glasses surrounded by concentric circles dotted with small diamonds, resembling scientific models of orbiting jewel planets. It was the most explicitly sexual image he'd ever projected, tipping toward the homoerotic. But just in case anyone got the wrong idea, a copy of *Penthouse* sat on the bed beside an issue of *Esquire.*

In San Francisco, he managed to stir up more fuss. Constantly plugged in the preceding days as an upcoming guest DJ on KFRC, Elton had to call in sick, laid low with food poisoning after eating a dodgy crab omelet. Embarrassed by the no-show—and with unnecessary melodrama—the station's morning host, Don Rose, announced to listeners, "Elton is ill. I won't say gravely ill. How ill we don't know. There's a doctor examining him in his suite at the Fairmont right at this very moment. We will keep you informed." The news, and the leak of Elton's hotel details, prompted a flood of calls to both the Fairmont and the radio station, from concerned fans worried that first, the concert in Oakland that night was to be canceled, and second, the singer was at death's door. Ever the work-horse, Elton rose from his bed, and the show went on.

All the while, his latest hit, "The Bitch Is Back," pumped out of radios everywhere, even if some DJs were reluctant to read out the song's title in their introductions and more conservative stations banned the record or, ridiculously, bleeped out the word "bitch" every time it appeared, which was often. Of course, ever the provocateur, Elton found this hilarious.

If he felt untouchable in his bubble of super-fame, it was becoming evident to others as well. *Rolling Stone*'s Ben Fong-Torres joined Elton on the road for an upcoming cover story, the writer observing that the people around the star now seemed to be overly protective of him. "Somewhere between him and the outside," Fong-Torres wrote in the subsequent article, "there are forces which don't seem to understand the nature of Elton John, and the nature of his success." No doubt this was meant as a dig at the gatekeeper that was John Reid, and in his interview with Elton, the writer probed deeper into the nature of the relationship between the singer and his manager, particularly the insinuations surrounding the fact that the two shared a house in England.

"He's just my manager," Elton insisted, seemingly unruffled by the topic, before stating that the team who worked with him were almost like a second family to him. "Everything around us is incestuous, and that's probably why there might be a lot of talk about us. I have a close circle of friends who just aren't in the public—sort of like Elvis and his . . . motorbike people."

If Elton had ducked the line of inquiry, he had in turn highlighted a different truth: There was now indeed something distinctly Elvis-like about the operation. The '74 tour was all about excess, a glitzy display of scale. In Vancouver, Elton and the band drove directly into the Pacific Coliseum in a cavalcade of seven silver limos. A local reviewer breathlessly described him as "the absolute best since the Beatles."

There was no higher praise. At Madison Square Garden on Thanksgiving Day, Elton made the connection explicit with the ecstatically received arrival of John Lennon onto his stage. Afterward, Elton, the temporary king of New York, threw a party at the five-star Pierre Hotel on Fifth Avenue. There, Reg finally got his chance to drop his Elton persona for a minute to say to Lennon, "You must get tired of hearing this, but your music changed my life."

Lennon's face lit up. "You're right," he said. "I do hear that a lot. But I never get tired of hearing it."

Later that night, there was an ugly scene that mirrored the fracas in New Zealand, albeit less violently. The blond wife of a radio DJ, for no clear reason, apparently accosted Elton and called him a fag. Once again, Reid erupted, though this time kept his fists to himself. "This is my party," he yelled at the DJ, "and I'm ordering you and your slag wife to get the fuck out right now!"

"Do me a favor!" Elton shouted at the couple as security personnel hustled them out of the building. "Drop fucking dead!"

While the homophobic insult had been mindless, drunken abuse, it touched a nerve with Elton and John Reid, their relationship being very much a furtive one.

THEY RETURNED TO Britain, and the following month, at his second run of Christmas shows at the Hammersmith Odeon back in London, the crowd standing in the stalls raised their eyes to the upper circle to see Elton perform a daredevil act. Suspended on a wire, he was followed by a spotlight through the darkness of the theater as he flew superhero-style from the balcony to the stage. Cheers erupted, the stage lights went up, and as if in a flash, there he was, sitting at the piano stage right.

It was a feat worthy of the great magicians and, of course, a trick, performed with the use of a dummy. The pantomime had once again come to town, although this time the production values had been noticeably upped. The stage and Elton's piano were covered in a festive crimson, with a stairway leading up to the riser where Nigel Olsson and Ray Cooper performed, alongside the Muscle Shoals horn section. The final gig, on Christmas Eve, was broadcast by the BBC, and showed the singer—in a feathery-shouldered silver getup— barely able to control his laughter as he performed a southern soul take on "White Christmas" and fake snow showered the audience.

He had much cause to be very happy. The year 1974 ended with his first singles compilation, *Elton John: Greatest Hits*—a ten-tracker spanning "Your Song" to "Don't Let the Sun Go Down on Me"—sitting at number one in Britain and the States. The album would lodge itself at the top of the charts in both countries for close to three months.

IF EXPERIENCE HAD taught him anything, it was that it was time to stop and gather himself. And so 1975 began with the still unreleased album *Captain Fantastic and the Brown Dirt Cowboy* in the bag, and space to breathe.

Aside from his own soar-away run of singles and albums—and even though it had continued to pursue a slightly wonky signing policy—the Rocket Record Company had proved to be highly successful. Some of the label's decisions were a touch bewildering, though, such as its signing of a thirteen-year-old Welsh balladeer named Maldwyn Pope, discovered by the Radio One DJ John Peel. While clearly talented, the teen prodigy—whom Elton nicknamed Blodwyn Pig (after the hairy British blues rock band)—came across, with his high, unbroken voice amid the orchestrations of his debut 1974 single, "I Don't Know How to Say Goodbye," as an uneasy mix of Nick Drake and Donny Osmond.

Far more lucrative had been Rocket's signing of Neil Sedaka. By the early seventies, the career of the U.S. pop star and songwriter was in the doldrums, having been virtually sunk by the wave of Beatlemania that hit America in the sixties. Elton and John Reid first met Sedaka in 1973, and they were astounded when he told them that he currently had no record deal in the States. When the pair said that he was welcome to join Rocket, Sedaka offered to sign with them for no advance. "We couldn't believe our luck," Elton remembered in the immediate aftermath. "We sort of ran into a corner and laughed and said, 'This guy must be an idiot.'"

But Neil Sedaka was no idiot. Elton had proved that flamboyant piano-playing singer-songwriters made for big business in the States, and Sedaka wanted some of that magic fairy dust to rub off on him. Rocket repositioned Sedaka, always seen as a singles artist, into the albums market. The resulting record, *Sedaka's Back,* shipped half a million in America, with his comeback single, "Laughter in the Rain," hitting number one.

Elton sold Sedaka hard in interviews, making the latter quip that the former—who was taking a decent cut of his record sales—was "the most expensive publicist in the world." Sedaka was ecstatic about the rise in his fortunes that his association with Elton brought about, letting it be known that "in one year I went from making $50,000 to $6 million."

Amassing wealth now from more than one source, Elton bought himself a house in Los Angeles. A Moorish-style mansion at 1400 Tower Grove Road, set amid the eucalyptus and chaparral of Benedict Canyon, it looked out over Beverly Hills and had previously been occupied by Greta Garbo and *Gone with the Wind* producer David O. Selznick. The purchase saw Elton planting a domestic flag in California soil, but it wasn't long before he was questioning the wisdom of his move.

One morning he woke to find a girl fan sitting at the edge of his bed. Confused and slightly panicked, he reached for his glasses and asked her, "Who are *you?*"

"Oh, you don't know me," she airily replied.

The girl, who'd somehow managed to silently intrude into the house, was gently ushered off the property by the singer. *Christ, she could have had a gun,* thought Elton, reminded of the Manson Family murders of Sharon Tate and her friends only six years before and just over a mile away.

Visitors to the Benedict Canyon house said that it had a lonely, almost spooky air. In those first months of 1975, a gloom seemed to descend on Elton, accentuating his natural moodiness. In L.A., in February, he agreed to appear on the inaugural episode of Cher's eponymous TV show for CBS. On set, Elton was grouchy. It took him eight takes to nail a version of "Lucy in the Sky with Diamonds," dressed in a pointy wizard hat with his gold-and-purple-tinted, diamond-framed glasses glinting under the studio lights. Then he was joined by Cher, far more soberly dressed in lilac shirt and brown tank top, for a part-harmonizing, part-shouting "Bennie and the Jets."

"Cher, I'd just like to say that I really enjoyed doing the show," he told the host at the song's conclusion in a prearranged spiel. "I didn't do it just for the hundred dollars. D'you know, you're the sort of person that in fifty years' time will still be going strong . . ."

This was the slightly clunky segue into a skit, set at the "Final Curtain Rest Home for Aged Performers," in which Elton appeared alongside a comically decrepit Cher (fake sagging breasts nearly touching her navel under a lavender satin top) and Bette Midler (ludicrously balloon-assed in tight pink pants). The singer, in a bald skullcap stitched with gray wings of remaining hair, arrived in a motorized green glitter wheelchair, imploring the others in a Monty Pythonesque screech, "Let's turn on the TV set and watch the show we did fifty years ago!," causing them to collapse into giggles.

The camera zoomed into the screen to show a set filled with balloons and a white-top-hatted Elton, looking like a cross between Liberace and Willy Wonka, as he launched with Cher and Midler into a showbizzy medley of songs including "Proud Mary," "Ain't No Mountain High Enough," and "Never Can Say Goodbye."

It was very daft, very 1975, and appeared to have been a riot to film. In truth, Elton and Cher had been arguing during the dummy runs for the cameras. "He said some very unkind things," Cher recalled. "I got very upset and I began to cry. 'Damn it, Elton,' I said. 'Who needed this aggravation?'"

It was typical of his outbursts: He would blow up and then quietly stew, before repenting. The next day he turned up on set with a gift for Cher of a star sapphire on a gold chain.

AROUND THE SAME time, Elton almost managed to fall out with his old friend Rod Stewart. Two years before, Stewart had told him that he'd been approached by the Who to make a cameo appearance in their upcoming movie.

"They're going to do a film of *Tommy*," said Rod.

"Oh, no, not a film now," Elton groaned, feeling that the band's rock opera about a deaf, dumb, and blind kid who becomes a messianic figure—which they had released as an album in 1969 and played a large segment from in their sets ever since—was in danger of being done to death. "Bloody hell, what are they going to do next?" he wondered. "It'll be a cartoon series soon."

Elton advised Rod against committing to the film. "I said, 'I wouldn't do it if I were you,'" he laughs. "Initially there were rumors that the film wasn't going to be that great."

The year after, Elton received a call from the Who's Pete Townshend, asking him to perform the same song in the film he'd offered to Rod, "Pinball Wizard," before informing him that Ken Russell (*Women in Love, The Devils*) was on board to direct. Elton immediately said yes.

"You don't say no to Pete Townshend," he argues, in defense of this volte-face. "I said, 'Absolutely.' The Who have always been one of my favorite bands. You have to look up to your peers and when they ask you to do something like that, you step up to the plate."

At the Who's Ramport Studios in south London in April 1974, Elton rerecorded "Pinball Wizard," using his own band and Gus Dudgeon as producer, while slipping a reference to the group's debut single "I Can't Explain" into the song's extended outro. He reveled in spitting out the lyric, written from the perspective of the Local Lad character who is dazzled and infuriated by the pinballing skills of the sensory-deprived Tommy Walker.

Filming for the sequence took place over three days at the Kings

Elton in Tommy *as the outsized Local Lad, with the Who erupting around him.*

Theatre in the Southsea resort in Portsmouth, a venue more used to staging variety bills for summer vacationers. Backed by the Who, even though they hadn't played on the recording, Elton teetered on four-and-a-half-foot-high Dr. Martens boots, supported by calipers allowing for only very rigid and dangerous movement. He mugged and grimaced his way through the song, playing a petite keyboard attached to a pinball machine, and gestured in mock anger at Roger Daltrey as the titular hero racking up phenomenal scores, before the band inevitably trashed their equipment.

Showing his dedication to the cinematic version of *Tommy,* Elton turned up at all three premieres of the film, in the UK, Australia, and the United States. There, up on the silver screen, for all the world to see, was perhaps coy Reg's greatest transformation of all, into a ten-foot-tall bobble-hatted thug.

"Of course it became an iconic scene in the movie," Elton points out, "with the fucking boots and clinging onto the pinball machine for dear life.

"Rod," he mischievously notes, almost as an afterthought, "has never forgiven me for it."

The leader of the bigger band: (clockwise from bottom left) Elton, Davey Johnstone, Ray Cooper, James Newton Howard, Caleb Quaye, Roger Pope, Kenny Passarelli.

11 DRIFT OF THE FANTASTIC VOYAGE

STANDING IN FRONT of a glass-bodied baby grand piano, *Soul Train* host Don Cornelius turned to the parade of funky-looking audience members standing around it and joked, "Okaaaay, everybody's waiting for my first concerto." Stepping over to its matching transparent stool, he curiously eyed the piano, a relatively alien instrument to appear on a TV show more used to driving drums, syncopated horns, booty-shaking bass, and a procession of gutsy singers. "Now, let me see . . . which way does it go?" the host wondered, parking himself down, facing the wrong way from the piano, playing the class clown and musical dunce. The prank produced a ripple of laughter among the assembly before Cornelius stood back up again to address the camera and the viewers at home.

"No, on the serious side," he said, "this is especially for a very, very gifted young man, who has combined absolute genius as musician-songwriter with a sort of psychedelic outlook on life, that causes everybody that comes near him to have a lot of fun, besides be thoroughly entertained. If you will, gang, a warm welcome for one of the world's greatest . . . Mr. Elton John."

To much applause, Elton climbed onto the platform, in a wide-lapeled brown pin-striped suit, scarlet shirt, and black fedora with noir voodooish feathers tucked into its glittering headband. Elton had obviously given much thought to what he should wear on the prestigious show nicknamed the black *American Bandstand*. But in reality, there was possibly too much of the Harlem pimp about his flashy attire.

"Allrrrright!" Cornelius grinned. "Where'd you get that suit, brother?"

"Sears and Roebuck," the singer chuckled, name-checking the department store chain that was in truth way below his expensive tastes, and eliciting good-natured guffaws from those around him.

It was May 17, 1975, and Elton was only the third white artist invited onto the show, after Motown's Funk Brothers studio band guitarist Dennis Coffey in '72 and the long-haired Canadian groover Gino Vannelli three months before. Still, there was something about this reticent Englishman that singled him out as absolutely the whitest performer ever to appear on *Soul Train*. Nonetheless, if a touch self-effacing, Elton was visibly at home on the set of a show he watched every week when he was in America.

Before he performed, he took some questions from the audience. "My name is Jolanna Toussaint," said one girl in a blue dress. "I'd like to know . . . of all the songs you recorded, which one is your favorite?"

"That's a difficult one," Elton deliberated. "Um . . . I sorta like the ones I've written the most recently. I like 'Don't Let the Sun Go Down on Me.'" [*Claps and "yeah"s from the audience.*] "And I like 'Bennie and the Jets.'" [*More "yeah"s.*]

Diana Bruner, one of the resident *Soul Train* dancers, wanted to know, "Did you start singing from childhood?"

"No, I've only been singing for about five or six years," Elton fibbed, when in truth it had been almost ten years since he'd fronted the first Bluesology single. "I used to be a pianist in a band." Lending himself some indisputable soul cool, he added, "When I first started professionally I used to back Patti LaBelle and Major Lance and people like that. [*"All right!" shouted someone in the crowd.*] I'm just learning to sing, y'know. I'm having a good time."

Elton laughed and cheekily stuck out his tongue, and then Cornelius asked him to introduce his latest single.

"It's a tribute to the music of Philadelphia and also to a lady called Billie Jean King who used to play tennis for the Philadelphia Freedoms team," he told the host. "We thought it'd be nice to write a song about the tennis team and the music of Philadelphia, 'cause it's given so many people a lot of pleasure."

Taking to the piano with the heart-stirring string intro of "Phila-delphia Freedom" swirling around him, Elton began to sing over the backing track of his latest, never-more-soulful 45. His microphone bounced before his nose as the flimsy stage shook under the feet of the surrounding dancers.

This landmark TV appearance of the pumping R&B track, fea-turing a sweeping orchestral arrangement by the Philly Soul master Gene Page, was ultimate proof that Elton could expertly turn his hand to an array of musical genres. His soul band touring days had indeed proved highly instructive; this music was in his very bones.

"Philadelphia Freedom" was also unique in the sense that Elton had given Bernie the song's title and asked him to come up with a lyric for a tailor-made single. In the past year, Elton had become a tennis fanatic, and close friends with King, who'd even come up onstage to sing with him at the Spectrum in Philadelphia the previ-ous December. At first, Taupin struggled with his partner's request, stumped by the challenge to write something about either tennis or the Pennsylvanian city. In the end, he came up with what he de-scribed as "an esoteric song about being free." Later, the uplifting sound and spirit of "Philadelphia Freedom" was to render it a mod-ern patriotic U.S. anthem.

Once again getting the jump on David Bowie—who'd later per-form "Golden Years" and "Fame" on the show—Elton beat his rival onto *Soul Train* by seven months. But the elaborate sound of "Philadelphia Freedom" was to cause a ruckus with the producers of another key television program back home in Britain, *Top of the Pops*. For years, a bizarre Musicians' Union ruling had forced artists to rerecord their hits especially for TV, typically within the tight space of a half-day studio session, before they were allowed to mime to them on-screen. Some performers dutifully complied with the de-mand; others went into the studio, did nothing except put their feet up for four hours, and then lip-synced to a minimally remixed ver-sion of the original recording.

But the idea of having to unpick and redo "Philadelphia Free-dom," likely backed by the notoriously bad *Top of the Pops* orches-tra, was abhorrent to Elton, and so, given his star power, he refused. Canceling his upcoming appearance on the show, and standing up for both himself and the notion of quality control, he put out a flinty statement that read: "The Elton John Band and their producer Gus Dudgeon are in the habit of spending a great deal of time and love perfecting each number they record. It is completely impossible to reproduce such labor at short notice."

Aside from this strop, there was a deep irony to the fact that "Philadelphia Freedom" was the first and last single to be released under the collective name of the Elton John Band. Two months after it appeared, in a surprising and shocking move, Elton fired his loyal and long-standing rhythm section of Nigel Olsson and Dee Murray. "I just felt we'd gone as far as we could go," he says. "Something had to change musically. It was a really hard thing for me to do."

Like someone stuck in an unhappy marriage, Elton had been brooding over the problem for months, feeling a knot of anxiety in his stomach, along with a tantalizing ripple of excitement that came with the possibility of freeing himself up to work with new musicians. He'd never sacked anyone before in his life. Worse, in a move he would come to intensely regret, he did it over the phone, breaking the news to each musician individually. Olsson was in Los Angeles, Murray was on holiday in the Caribbean. Neither took the news well, but the latter in particular felt deeply hurt and for a time wouldn't even speak to Elton.

"We were never made to feel inferior at all, until later," said Olsson, revealing how the ever ascending star and the players beside him had floated further and further apart as the 1970s had progressed. In the end, the drummer admitted, it had become exhausting working on the Elton John production line: "Towards the latter days, y'know, it was just . . . churning it out."

FOR ELTON, HIS albums came in cycles, each with a beginning and ending point. *Empty Sky* in '69 to *Madman Across the Water* in '71 was broadly his orchestrated balladeer period. *Honky Château* in '72 to *Goodbye Yellow Brick Road* in '73 found him recording with his own live band and genre hopping through New Orleans funk, thumping glam, dance craze rock'n'roll, and impressively authentic-sounding soul. The move to Caribou Studios in '74 had resulted in a more polished sound, and now he wanted to explore that direction further. But if *Captain Fantastic and the Brown Dirt Cowboy* was in its creator's head the final album of this current cycle, it was a very fine way indeed for it to close.

Of all the Elton John albums, *Captain Fantastic* was the most Beatlesque—from Bernie's lyrical ability to imbue the everyday with a certain romance or view it through a surrealistic prism, to Elton's unmannered and brilliant harmony-backed vocals, to Gus Dudgeon's warm and subtly modernist production, whether feeding the piano through an electronic harmonizer or coaxing the band to add layers of artful overdubs.

Some of the songs were episodic and moved in Lennon and McCartneyish fashion through various inventive passages—such as the title track's gear shifting from sparse country verses to rolling funky bridges to the rock propulsion of the choruses, complete with synthesized jet noises that seared from left to right across the speakers. "Tower of Babel" was by turns stark and then gently groovy, as it portrayed the lyric's morality-free scenes of music biz hustlers, letches, and druggies. "Bitter Fingers" found the jobbing songwriter of days gone by at the piano, picking out arpeggios, before boiling over in vexed anger in a deceptively Eurovision-like chorus. The nearly eleven-minute melding of "We All Fall in Love Sometimes" and "Curtains," recorded by the band in a single take, was effectively a short film featuring the young songwriters Elton and Bernie in flashback, with their "naive notions that were childish, simple tunes that tried to hide it."

Other tracks sustained one mood throughout, but were no less vivid. Gene Page and his Philly Soul strings returned to document Taupin's memories of his London-to-Lincolnshire weekend escape acts in "Tell Me When the Whistle Blows." There was desperation and fury in the disco-tinged poverty rock of "(Gotta Get a) Meal Ticket." The breezy easy-listening atmosphere of "Writing" was filled with the ennui and quiet desperation of the aspiring songsmith.

Captain Fantastic wasn't an album written with hits in mind, but nevertheless it produced one. "Someone Saved My Life Tonight," Elton's close-to-suicide confession, as conveyed by Bernie, who'd pulled his friend's head out of the gas oven that day back in '68 in

Furlong Road, was one of their greatest ballads yet. In it, Linda Woodrow, with perhaps unfair grotesquerie, was painted as a "princess perched in her electric chair," and Long John Baldry was "Sugar Bear," the individual responsible for the "sweet freedom whispered in my ear." Even for the listener who didn't know the full story, "Someone Saved My Life Tonight" was clearly a highly emotional and touching song, which spoke directly to anyone trapped in a dead-end or abusive relationship. In July, it scaled the U.S. chart to number four.

The Beatleisms on *Captain Fantastic* didn't stop with its music. For its cover, Taupin and DJM's David Larkham commissioned the pop artist Alan Aldridge to create a colorful illustrated fantasia that stretched across the record's gatefold sleeve. On the front cover, Elton the silver-mask-wearing superhero sits astride a tipped-over grand piano amid a menagerie of strange, unearthly creatures. On the back, in a continuation of the otherworldly scene, a smiling Bernie reclines in a bubble with his songwriting book while a white dove surreally bearing the face of his wife, Maxine, sits on his knee. Above the lyricist's head, the band members, with a significance that in reflection surely wasn't lost on anyone, fly off into the sky in space-age spheres.

The grand design of *Captain Fantastic* extended to a poster, lyrics booklet, and scrapbook (containing old press cuttings, diary entries, and memorabilia) all tucked away within its sleeve, which made the album a highly desirable artifact for fans, although a pricey one. Upon its release in Britain on May 19, 1975, it retailed at £3.25 ($21 today), the most expensive single album released in the country up to that point. In the press, DJM's Stephen James defended accusations that he was fleecing record buyers by saying, "The new album had a very costly packaging, and two sixteen-page booklets and a poster. When you add up the real cost of those, they're actually getting them cheap."

Taken as a whole, from its music to its artwork, *Captain Fantastic and the Brown Dirt Cowboy* was Elton's creative high-water mark of the 1970s. Gus Dudgeon certainly thought so, declaring, "There's not one song on it that's less than incredible. Elton sings better than he's ever sung. From every conceivable point of view, it's better. Therefore, it adds up to being the best."

Before the release, though, Elton worried that the record wasn't commercial-sounding. He thought it would flop. In the end, he was proven spectacularly wrong. *Captain Fantastic* made American rock music history by being the first album ever to debut at number one, and it stayed there for seven weeks.

"It was a pinnacle for me," Elton later reflected. "It was a time when you couldn't switch on a radio in America without hearing one of my songs."

But while he sometimes allowed himself to enjoy this towering accomplishment, at the same time he fretted that he was now wildly overexposed and that the public might be in danger of getting sick of the sight and sound of him.

"People do get cheesed off," he said. "I was getting cheesed off hearing myself as well."

ELTON CHOSE THE Netherlands as the location to assemble the new band, on a vast film studio soundstage just outside of Amsterdam. Filling the shoes of Dee Murray as bassist was a twenty-six-year-old American named Kenny Passarelli, a native of Colorado and a regular on sessions at Caribou Studios, who came on the recommendation of Joe Walsh. Helping to reproduce the layers of keyboards featured on *Captain Fantastic* was the twenty-four-year-old Los Angeles–born James Newton Howard.

Elsewhere, perhaps gallingly for Nigel Olsson, the new drummer was effectively the original drummer, Roger Pope, who'd played on *Empty Sky* and tracks on *Tumbleweed Connection* and *Madman Across the Water* and who'd toured the States opening for Elton as part of the Kiki Dee Band. He wasn't the only familiar face to return: Caleb Quaye was drafted in as guitarist to supplement Davey Johnstone, along with Jeff "Skunk" Baxter of Steely Dan and the Doobie Brothers. Having first begun touring back in 1970 without a guitarist, Elton now had three.

It was typical of the maximalist mood of the mid-1970s. In the past, for Elton, less was more. Now, it seemed, more was more. "The old band . . . used to rattle on," he reckoned. "I've always wanted to be part of a good driving rock'n'roll band."

Each day, this expansive troupe was bused from the Amsterdam Hilton to the soundstage for rigorous ten-hour rehearsals in preparation for Elton's biggest UK show to date, on June 21 in front of seventy-two thousand people at London's Wembley Stadium. The mood within the band was high on their collective musicianship and high on everything else. "The rehearsals were a giant party, man," says Passarelli.

Other rock stars came to hang out—the entertainingly unpredictable Keith Moon, and Ringo Starr, the latter one day sitting in with the band behind the drum kit, delighting them when they found themselves playing "Lucy in the Sky with Diamonds" with an actual Beatle. Starr was at a loose end in his career and wondered aloud whether there was any chance he could join the touring group. There was much agonizing within the ranks, but in the end, with Pope confirmed, Starr was gently let down.

Over those ten days in Holland there was much work and little sleep, thanks to cocaine and alcohol in plentiful supply. The bar bill for the band and crew at the Hilton ran into the thousands. "It was a hell of a great time," Passarelli remembers. "We partied like it was 1999. All the road crew were going, 'Oh my God, how are we gonna pay our bar bill?' And Elton just wrote the check for the entire thing."

The Wembley gig was designed to be the greatest display yet of Elton's monumental success in his homeland. As such, a full day's lineup of supporting artists was announced, including the Eagles and the Beach Boys. The latter group, who might reasonably have been considered hopelessly passé by the mid-seventies, were in fact at the time coasting a wave of nostalgia for the sixties, and so triumphed on the hot summer's day with a hit-stuffed set that ended with encores of "Surfin' U.S.A." and "Fun, Fun, Fun."

The Beach Boys proved an almost impossible act to follow, even for Elton. He opened strongly, with "Funeral for a Friend / Love Lies Bleeding" running into "Rocket Man," "Candle in the Wind," "Philadelphia Freedom" and onward to a first-half-ending, double-featured Beatles tribute of "Lucy in the Sky with Diamonds" and "I Saw Her Standing There."

But then, moving into the second half, Elton made a slightly ominous announcement. "We have a new album out called *Captain Fantastic and the Brown Dirt Cowboy*," he reminded the massive audience. "I'm sorry it's £3.25, but I'll tell you about that later. We're going to do the whole of the album, and usually it bores everyone to tears if you play things people don't know. But we're going to take the chance anyway. This is the whole of the *Captain Fantastic* album. Here we go . . ."

Whether down to miscalculation or hubris, it was a terrible decision. As magnificent a studio album as it was, *Captain Fantastic* had only been out for just over a month and wasn't exactly crowd-pleasing fare for the beery hordes who'd just been punching the air to the Beach Boys. Perhaps anticipating this problem, the introduction to the opening title track had been reconfigured as a country hoedown, losing its laid-back charm, before settling back into the down-tempo pace of the recorded version.

Only a few numbers into this portion of the set, the audience began to exit the stadium by the thousands. Onstage, Elton could see what was happening, but was powerless to stop it. To halt the performance of the new album midway through would be an ignominious acknowledgment of failure, and so he and the band drove on. Encores of "Pinball Wizard" and "Saturday Night's Alright for Fighting" came too late, by which time the audience was embarrassingly sparse.

Afterward, there was a post-show party attended by Paul and Linda McCartney, Ringo Starr, Harry Nilsson, and Billie Jean King. But Elton knew he had misjudged and blown the show. The next week, a damning headline in *Melody Maker* crowed, BEACH BOYS' CUP RUNNETH OVER; ELTON LEFT TO PICK UP THE EMPTIES.

More than just a poorly received gig, it was a sign that Elton's fantastic voyage was beginning to drift off course.

Hungover at the Caribou Ranch, Colorado, July 1975.

12 BURNING OUT HIS FUSE

THE FIRST THING HE DID to annoy the Rolling Stones was land in a helicopter directly behind their stage, and before almost forty thousand of their fans, at the Hughes Stadium in Fort Collins, Colorado. It was the afternoon of Saturday, July 19, and Elton had been asked to make a guest appearance with the band on the thirty-fourth show of their Tour of the Americas '75.

The prospect of appearing onstage with the Stones—whom he'd loved since his late teens—was obviously hugely appealing to Elton, and anyway the gig was only a short flight away from Caribou, where he was recording, so he could easily rotor in. But then, as he sometimes tended to forget when measuring himself against his former heroes turned contemporaries, in terms of record sales, he was the bigger star in the States by this point. The Stones perceived his grand helicopter landing as a showboating stunt and an attempt to upstage them.

Everything went downhill from there. In a pre-show confab, Elton confessed to Mick Jagger and Keith Richards that the only Stones number he really knew how to play was "Honky Tonk Women," which turned out to be their opening song. And so it was agreed that he would join them from the start of their set.

Under drizzling clouds, Elton, in a beige cowboy hat and blue bomber jacket bearing the white logo of the Los Angeles Dodgers baseball team, nervously chewed gum and knocked back scotch as he followed Mick Jagger—his face over-made-up and his body gaunt beneath a shocking pink jacket—up the stairs to the stage. The group's introduction music, Aaron Copland's "Fanfare for the Common Man," blared out toward the bleachers.

They kicked into "Honky Tonk Women," Elton pounding away on a grand piano. Once the song was over, Elton left the stage. But as he remembers it, later on in the set a member of the Rolling Stones' road crew walked up to him and told him that Billy Preston, the band's keyboard player for the tour, had asked if he could come back on and jam along for a few more tunes. Elton returned to the stage, thinking he could play in the shadows, but the Stones made it clear he really wasn't welcome. Mick was now in the mood to mock their guest, pointedly introducing him with the words "On the piano so far we've had Reg from Watford."

Looking on, Kenny Passarelli sensed that Elton being on his stage suddenly threatened Jagger. "Forty thousand people are staring at the guy playing keyboards," he says. "I think Mick didn't want that diversion."

"We should have kicked him off the stage but we didn't," Jagger said later, putting his reluctance down to good old-fashioned English manners.

Post-show, the Stones were due to fly back to Caribou with Elton following his invitation to an after-hours barbecue. But the mood backstage was frosty and it became obvious that the invitation would not be accepted. "All I know," says Passarelli, "is that at one point we were told all the Caribou people had to leave because Mick and Keith were upset that Elton had worn out his welcome."

The singer left in the helicopter in a black mood, which had worsened by the time everyone was in the limo and heading back up the winding road to the ranch. At Caribou, Elton became more upset, then worryingly distressed. Passarelli and Davey Johnstone talked him down from his panic.

The singer finally went to bed, Passarelli set off for a nightclub in Nederland, and Johnstone dropped acid. By the time the bassist arrived back at Caribou the next morning, he found the guitarist sitting in a wheelchair, staring out at the surrounding fields, hallucinating visions of Native American battles going on all around him. "He said, 'Look, Kenny! Look over there!'" says Passarelli. "And I was going, 'Oh, no . . .'"

Elton got up and somehow managed to coax the guitarist, in his altered state, to do some work with him. "He was tripping," marvels Elton. "He had the guitar and I was telling him what to play at seven o'clock in the morning in bright sunshine." Together the pair wrote "Grow Some Funk of Your Own," a full-on rock song with a not coincidentally Jagger/Richards–like swagger. If Elton couldn't join the Stones, he would try to beat them.

It was a scenario typical of the highly intense and drugged-out making of the album that would become *Rock of the Westies*. "Everybody was pretty jacked up," admits Bernie. "That period was pretty much the apex of our abuse."

"Musically, I just wanted to make the band a little bit more raucous," says Elton. "I wanted it heavier." This direction was initially to cause a rift with Gus Dudgeon, particularly since they'd all just come off the layered and considered *Captain Fantastic and the Brown Dirt Cowboy*. For the creation of its successor, the team's cocaine use skyrocketed, which could be heard in the teeth-grinding performances of its songs, rehearsed for a week and then cut live.

"*Rock of the Westies* turned out to be cryptic and almost punkish by our standards," Bernie says. "Nobody really knew what the fuck anything was about, but I quite liked that. Songs bled into other songs. The riffs were sort of archaic and kind of fun."

The expanded band—minus guitarist Jeff "Skunk" Baxter, who'd stayed only for the disastrous Wembley show before returning to the Doobie Brothers as a full-time member—really dug their nails into the songs, as was evident on the six-minute cokey funk-rock jam of "Medley (Yell Help, Wednesday Night, Ugly)." Returning to Bernie's space-age themes, "Dan Dare (Pilot of the Future)" was a faster and grittier take on "Bennie and the Jets" with a Leon Russell swing and a nonsense lyric that included the single-entendre line "Holy cow . . . my eyes never saw a rocket that was quite that size."

Rock of the Westies was high on grooves, if low on melodies. "Street Kids" and "Hard Luck Story" were hyperactive band workouts that must have sounded great blasting out through Caribou's studio speakers. But in the cold light of day and the inevitable comedown, they blew away like the haze from chain-smoked cigarettes. "Feed Me" took a decent stab at smooth Steely Dan–style jazz-rock, but by the closing "Billy Bones and the White Bird" with its ever more insistent "Check it out! Check it out!" hook line, the over-stimulation of the players was obvious, even if their shared enthusiasm didn't similarly affect the listener.

Elton fancied "Dan Dare (Pilot of the Future)" for the first single, though "Grow Some Funk of Your Own" was similarly considered for release to radio. There were perhaps two more obvious contenders, though. "Island Girl" was an up-tempo ode to a Jamaican amazon cum femme fatale turning tricks in the streets of New York for johns unsuspecting of quite what they were letting themselves in for. Tellingly, given the high-octane circumstances of the album's recording, there was only one ballad in the tracklist. "I Feel Like a Bullet (in the Gun of Robert Ford)" name-checked Jesse James's assassin in an oblique Taupin lyric written from the viewpoint of someone with a strong urge to kill a dying relationship. It was the first indication, albeit gently obscured, that all was not well with Bernie and Maxine.

For his part, Kenny Passarelli felt that during the recording of *Rock of the Westies,* Elton was also "going through a bunch of changes." Desperate to stay thin in the rock star spotlight, the singer had taken to subsisting on a not entirely nutritious diet consisting almost solely of avocados and Diet Dr Pepper. In the cover shot of the album, taken by Terry O'Neill during a visit to the ranch, he gazes at the lens through hexagonal shades, his image markedly toned down—unshaven in a blue Harris Tweed deerstalker cap and striped rugby shirt. If at first glance the image made Elton appear open and relaxed, a closer look revealed him to be drawn and washed out.

In contrast, in their back cover lineup picture and individual inner sleeve portraits, the band are the very picture of what it was to be a rock musician in 1975: bare-chested in unbuttoned waistcoats and denim shirts, groin-crushing jeans, alligator boots, and leather chaps.

THE LEADER OF this gang of cocaine cowboys returned to California in August. On the ninth, from the Santa Monica Civic Auditorium,

Elton cohosted, along with Diana Ross, the debut ceremony of the Rock Music Awards, broadcast live by CBS. The concept, cooked up by producer Don Kirshner, was to rival the more pop-oriented Grammys, focusing instead on the harder and more progressive sounds of the likes of Led Zeppelin and the Who.

Elton and Diana Ross arrived onstage from inside a billow of dry ice, balancing on the back of a rickety motorized golf cart contraption bearing a cheap-looking metallic backdrop. The former, in a silver suit, and the latter, in a canary yellow fur coat, walked up to a podium that magically rose from the floor.

"Good evening, everybody in TV land," said Elton. "I'm Captain Fantastic."

"And I'm General Delivery," said Diana. "Better known as Big Bird."

"So I can tell her to 'cluck off' during the program," wisecracked Elton. He then added, "Stay tuned. It gets worse."

Over the course of the show, awards were handed out to Joni Mitchell, Linda Ronstadt, the Eagles, Bad Company, Bob Dylan, and the Who for *Tommy*. Elton's jokes got better, such as when he made a cheeky reference to *Jaws* being the new film starring Linda Lovelace. He even picked up a gong for himself when he was named Rock Personality of the Year. Not everyone was won over by Elton's performance, however, and John Leonard, the cultural critic of *The New York Times*, belittled him in print as "the Bob Hope of the counter-culture."

Sixteen days later, to mark the fifth anniversary of his life-changing Troubadour shows, Elton returned to the club for six charity gigs over three nights supporting the UCLA Eye Institute (a research facility to prevent blindness) founded by MCA's originator, Jules Stein. On the evening of the opening gala performance, the scene outside was very different from Elton's debut there a half decade before. Santa Monica Boulevard was closed to traffic, and a procession of stars rolled up to the door in limousines: Tony Curtis, Mae West, Hugh Hefner, Cher, Ringo Starr.

Elton turned up onstage bearded, much as he had been at the original shows. Surveying the older Hollywood crowd, he carped in a Lennonesque way, "Here's one you can all tap your wheelchairs to." It was his opportunity to introduce the new band to an American audience. The verdict, particularly within the confines of the club, was that they were polished and punchy, but way too loud.

In L.A., BACK in his Benedict Canyon mansion, Elton began to withdraw into himself once again. He would suddenly become terribly and stubbornly depressed, lying in bed for two whole days, wallowing and wondering if all this work was worth anything, as darker and darker thoughts ran through his mind. If John Reid tried to coax him out of his black hole, Elton would spurn his help. Sometimes his friends tried to cheer him up. They'd temporarily pull him out of his nosedive, then he'd plummet back down. Even though he was in a relationship with Reid and surrounded by people who loved him, sometimes Elton still felt deeply alone. "Depressions are very strange," he admitted in 1975. "They can come on in the most unlikely places and for no apparent reason."

There was little time to mope, however. The U.S. tour supporting the soon-to-be-released *Rock of the Westies* began on September 29 at the San Diego Sports Arena and was scheduled to run for just one month, if a rigorous one. Cutting back on the visuals, the new show concentrated instead on the music and stretched to three hours, not including a half-hour interval while everyone, band and audience, caught their breath. The gigs spanned Elton's entire catalog so far, ten albums, returning now little-heard songs such as "I Need You to Turn To" and "Levon" to the set. Elton being Elton, he paraded around in a white jumpsuit and another piano-key-patterned one in blue. But overall, the staging was comparatively understated.

In a way, this band was too conspicuously cool for Elton to rely on the theatrics. If the idea was that reining in the visual histrionics would shine a light on his songcraft and charisma, it worked. One local reviewer who witnessed the show at the Convention Center in Las Vegas on October 2 noted, "No one cared if the sets were too long, or too noisy. It was a night with a legend along the lines of the Beatles, Judy Garland, or Nat King Cole."

Being three hours long, it was a performance that required some chemically aided stamina. At points on the tour, certain members of the band would arrange to meet two cocaine dealers who flew in from Miami with a suitcase full of narcotics. Thousands of dollars changed hands and the tour rolled on, until the next supply was required. As a top-up, just before they went onstage, the musicians were handed little vials of coke by a member of the road crew with the words "Here you go, boys. Do a good show."

A handy coke break came twelve songs into the set when the lights dimmed and the dry ice pumped out to set the atmosphere for the synthesized overture of "Funeral for a Friend." Under the cloak of stage darkness, the players who were partial could snort a line or two off the top of their amps before dynamically smashing back in with "Love Lies Bleeding."

It was a turbocharged and heady time, and adding to this, October 20–26 was declared to be Elton John Week in Los Angeles, set to culminate with two massive outdoor shows at Dodger Stadium. In his most lavish gesture yet, Elton decided to splash out more than a hundred thousand dollars chartering a Pan Am plane as the *Rock of the Westies Express* and flying a hundred thirty people over from England for the occasion, including his extended family, friends, and Rocket employees.

During the flight, everyone was fed steak Diane, filled with champagne, and handed an entertainment pack of jokes and puzzles and sugary sticks of Blackpool rock. Upon arrival in Los Angeles, as everyone filed out of the jet and made their way down the wheeling access ladder, Elton was there to greet them, reserving the biggest cuddle for his squealing mum, Sheila. A convoy of Rolls-Royces and Cadillacs was there to collect the entire gathering and ferry them to their rooms at the Beverly Hills Holiday Inn.

The next day the party was divided into two for some sightseeing larks. A film crew from London Weekend Television followed Sheila and Fred and Elton's Auntie Peg as they were given the tour at Universal Studios, shrieking on fake-collapsing bridges and rubbernecking past sets used in *The Sting* and *Earthquake*. The other half were meanwhile cruising out onto the Pacific aboard John Reid's recently purchased yacht, the wryly named *Madman* (as painted on its side in the florid lettering featured on the cover of *Madman Across the Water*).

Interviewed by LWT's Russell Harty at the Benedict Canyon house, Elton looked exhausted and seemed ambivalent when the subject of Reid's yacht was brought up. "I'm a bit frightened of the sea," he offered, "and after seeing *Jaws* I'll probably never go near a beach again. I'd rather play tennis than go out on the boat. I mean, after five minutes, I say, 'Well, what else does it do? So it floats? Ducks float.' I'm very restless. That's why people say I work too hard."

On October 21, six thousand fans stopped the traffic on Hollywood Boulevard in anticipation of witnessing the singer unveil his star on the Walk of Fame—the first time in 1,662 ceremonies that the street had to be closed because of the volume of spectators. Many impatiently yelled, "We want Elton!" Others waved customized T-shirts bearing the words YOU'RE BETTER OFF DEAD IF YOU HAVEN'T HEARD ELTON.

To discover that his name was to be permanently embedded only a few steps from those of Groucho Marx, Greta Garbo, and Jean Harlow was obviously an enormous deal for Elton. He dressed to impress for the ritual that would cement his showbiz immortality, arriving in a lime-green suit and bowler hat, riding a golf cart customized with a faux windshield of two large stars studded with lightbulbs.

"I'm very, very honored, being British, to have my star on Hollywood Boulevard," he said into the microphone as he stood at a lectern. Then, hunkering down onto the sidewalk, he peeled the cover off the waiting slab with the words "I now declare this supermarket open. Oh, I'm sorry, wrong place, uh. This is more nerveracking than doing a concert, I tell ya . . ."

FROM THIS VERTIGINOUS height, there was only farther to fall. Wrecked by cocaine and overwork, in reality, Elton was in the grip of an acute emotional crisis.

Two days before the first show at Dodger Stadium, his family members and some of the band were sitting around the pool at the Benedict Canyon house when a visibly distraught Elton emerged from his room and made a very dramatic appearance.

Seeing stars: Elton makes his mark on the Hollywood Walk of Fame, Los Angeles, October 21, 1975.

He had just swallowed sixty Valium tablets.

"I'm gonna be dead in an hour," he announced. "I've taken sleeping pills."

He stumbled past everyone and threw himself into the swimming pool.

As suicide attempts went, this was far more serious than the cry-for-help gas oven incident back in Furlong Road.

"It's craziness," he says, flatly. "My life was crazy. It's . . . not being able to get your feelings across and not being willing to deal with them in a mature way. Instead you deal with it in an immature way. And the pressure, I mean . . . fuck."

After he was dragged out of the pool, medics quickly arrived, pumped the singer's stomach, and sped him to the hospital. For the rest of the night, Elton slipped in and out of consciousness.

Standing by the pool, numb, Sheila turned to Caleb Quaye, Elton's oldest friend, and said, "Oh, Caleb, can't you talk to him?" Quaye couldn't look Elton's mother in the eye, feeling complicit in her son's drug taking.

Then, with an impeccable sense of bathos, the tormented singer's seventy-five-year-old grandmother, Ivy, sighed and sadly said, "I suppose we've all got to go home now."

IF, AS JOHN UPDIKE famously wrote, "celebrity is a mask that eats into the face," then Elton was the mask now threatening to eat into the face of Reg Dwight. He had gone too far too fast. It was way too much for him to handle.

Or maybe it wasn't. On the day following his suicide bid, there were long conversations as to whether the Dodger Stadium shows would, or should, go ahead. Incredibly, the singer was deemed by his doctors to be fit to perform.

This flirtation with death only seemed to empower Elton. Before the sound check at the stadium, he charged around the field playing soccer with the band, tackling Kenny Passarelli so hard the bassist thought he'd suffered a broken nose. "I got the ball from him and the next thing I knew I was on the ground," says Passarelli. "He elbowed me. He was the most competitive guy. It was unbelievable. He didn't want to lose at anything."

It seems, for Elton, there was much in the way of defiance and denial involved. To see him onstage at the piano during the sound check, in his striped T-shirt and sweatpants, apparently brimming with energy, no outsider could possibly have guessed at the inner turmoil he had been suffering only two days before.

There was much riding on these shows, and for Elton, failure was not an option. No other artist had been allowed to perform at the stadium after a concert by the Beatles there in 1966 had resulted in near riots. In their wake, Dodger bosses had nixed the idea of future concerts. These two gigs, before a total of 110,000 people over two days, had been the result of six months of negotiations between the baseball team's owners and Elton's U.S. agent, Howard Rose.

The tickets sold out immediately. Some fans applying for them had simply addressed their envelopes to "Elton John, Los Angeles," and somehow the mail had been delivered.

Rock shows had come a long way since the sixties and the prototypical high-level touring days of the Beatles. In addition, lessons had been learned from the horrendous crowd control problems of Woodstock, the Isle of Wight, and the murderous Altamont. No expense was spared at Dodger Stadium when it came to solving the typical difficulties of large-scale concerts—bad sound, poor catering, woeful toilet facilities.

On the Saturday morning of the first show, October 25, the gates were opened two and a half hours early to accommodate around ten thousand fans who'd turned up at dawn to secure a place close to the front of the stage. As the stadium filled up, beach balls were punched around the crowd and people took turns being tossed high in the air by others holding tightly stretched blankets.

Backstage, none other than a lager-sipping, gray-haired but still dapper Cary Grant hung out with Elton and Billie Jean King. Out front, as a peculiar warm-up act, the celebrity California car dealer Calvin Coolidge "Cal" Worthington, renowned for appearing alongside an array of wild animals in his manic TV spots, brought a lion onstage. The bewildered creature and the crowd eyed one another uncertainly. Following this, there were muted responses to the opening musical acts, Emmylou Harris and Joe Walsh. This was an audience keenly waiting for the main attraction.

Late afternoon, in bright sunlight, roadies pulled aside the white curtains at the front of the stage and Elton—in white bell-bottoms, bowler hat, and spangled aqua T-shirt—opened solo with "Your Song." The thousands who'd been lying down on the field stood up and cheers rose into the air as the star's piano slid on a hydraulic platform from the rear to the front of the stage.

Up in the stands, being filmed by the LWT camera crew, Sheila waved a scarf and sang along with Fred, gushing, "He's sensational, isn't he?" As the song closed, she began to cry. She appeared overcome with joy, only later admitting to painfully mixed emotions. Watching her troubled son onstage, she felt he "looked terrible . . . I was so worried."

From the wings, Bernie swigged a beer and watched the audience's overwhelming reaction, seeing it as "American exuberance, y'know. Just fists in the air and yelling and taking your top off and swirling it around your head and just, basically, floating on a breeze of ganja."

The band joined Elton for "Burn Down the Mission" before ripping through "Country Comfort," "Levon," "Rocket Man," "Hercules," and even the rarely heard "Empty Sky." There was a short costume change intermission before he returned wearing the outfit that had been especially tailored for him for these shows by the designer Bob Mackie: a Dodgers uniform in their traditional blue and white, customized in hundreds of light-reflecting sequins and the words ELTON 1 stitched on the back. The singer hopped onto the blue-carpeted lid of his grand piano and expertly volleyed a few balls into the crowd with a baseball bat.

From here, the rest of the show was a home run. Elton dropped to his knees to play Davey Johnstone's guitar with his teeth in an aping of David Bowie and Mick Ronson's provocative ritual. He introduced the band members as their names flashed up on the electronic scoreboard. Bernie and Billie Jean King joined the backing singers, all dressed in white gas station attendant uniforms with ESSO patches on their chests. Bizarrely, kilted dancers appeared onstage to lead Elton in a Highland fling. He was joined by the Reverend James Cleveland and his forty-five-piece gospel choir, and for "Don't Let the Sun Go Down on Me," with perfect timing, the sky began to darken.

By the closing encore numbers of the marathon three-and-a-half-hour, thirty-one-song set, the stadium's lights had flared into life and he stormed into "Saturday Night's Alright for Fighting" and "Pinball Wizard" as mad hippies and teen fans frantically danced together in the crowd.

After all the drama of the week, the Dodger shows were a complete blast. When it was all over, the details of the gigs were hopelessly blurry in Elton's mind. "I remember Cary Grant being there," he said afterward. "I remember crying coming offstage."

Elton had viewed *Captain Fantastic* debuting at number one in

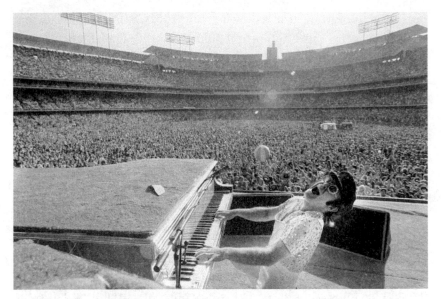

Howling to the sky: Dodger Stadium, L.A.

the U.S. chart as the peak of his success. But for Bernie, it was the triumphs at Dodger Stadium.

"I think we were at the absolute pinnacle of his fame in the seventies," he states. "I mean, he wasn't a very happy chap during that period, or especially at those gigs. But they were great gigs."

All the while, the hits kept stacking up. In the first week of November, "Island Girl" reached number one in America, ending the three-week reign of Neil Sedaka's "Bad Blood," which itself featured Elton on backing vocals. Effectively, he'd knocked himself off the top of the charts. The following week, *Rock of the Westies* became his latest U.S. chart topper in an unbroken seven-album run.

But if business was booming, Elton's personal life was in the process of falling apart. Two days after the Dodger shows, John Reid threw a party in Los Angeles. Elton disappeared partway through and Terry O'Neill found him crying in an alleyway, saying he and Reid had split.

Theirs had always been a turbulent relationship. "My arguments with Elton get so bad that we've ended up knocking one another around," Reid admitted. "I've given him more than one black eye."

For his part, Elton, in a telling use of words, later confessed that Reid had been "more unfaithful than I liked." The singer's recent problems, it seemed, had been exacerbated by his deeply unhappy internecine partnership.

Back in England after their personal—if not commercial—separation, Reid (who had recently expanded his operation to manage the messy business affairs of the fast-rising UK rock band Queen) moved to a house in Montpelier Square, Knightsbridge. Elton, meanwhile, had bought Woodside, a £400,000 Queen Anne–style eight-bedroom redbrick mansion in the countryside near Windsor, west of London. It had been built in the sixteenth century by Henry VIII, officially to house his surgeon, though legend had it that the king in fact kept a mistress there.

Elton's notion to make such a grand upward move had become fixed in his mind after he visited Ringo Starr at Tittenhurst Park, the Georgian country house set amid seventy-two acres that the Beatles drummer had bought from John Lennon when the latter left for New York in 1971. Wandering its grounds, Elton had been struck by "this feeling of complete freedom and privacy."

He had toyed with the idea of permanently relocating to Los Angeles, but his moody months locked away in Benedict Canyon had made him think twice. "I thought seriously about staying in the States," he said at the time, "but . . . I simply couldn't face it. Anyway, I've now made enough money to happily live in Britain . . . whatever the taxman may take from me."

Woodside itself was set within a comparatively modest, if still wildly expansive, thirty-seven acres of land boasting three lakes. The singer sent Sheila and Fred to check out the property while he was readying himself for the *Rock of the Westies* tour. In fact, his stepfather's handyman skills were soon to become useful, as he was put in charge of the mansion's refurbishment. Amid the fallout of an explosive time, once again, Elton was turning to his family for practical support.

In late '75, he moved in and, with his magpie-like attraction to the glint of bright and shiny things, soon filled the rooms with antiques and artworks and vintage pinball machines and an extensive record library to rival the BBC's. Before long, Woodside began to resemble a rock star approximation of Aladdin's Cave. So stuffed were its interiors, the only place left to hang a Rembrandt etching was in the garage.

Happiness returned to Elton in his semirural seclusion. There was much at Woodside to entertain him: a squash court, billiards room, indoor swimming pool, and private cinema. Far removed from his roots, he had now become lord of the manor with a resident staff to serve him hand and foot.

Less than three miles away sat Windsor Castle, the chief English residence of the Queen away from Buckingham Palace. In recent years, Elton's connection with the royals had grown stronger. In early November, he accompanied Princess Margaret to the movie premiere of Neil Simon's *The Sunshine Boys*. He had already given a private performance for the Queen Mother at her royal lodge in Windsor Great Park.

Improvising at the royal piano as he picked his way through "Your Song," he'd changed the line "I'd buy a big house" to "I'd buy Windsor Castle, Your Majesty, where we both could live . . ."

Although the purchase of the firmly off-the-market Windsor Castle was obviously beyond him, Elton's spending power had never been more in evidence than in 1975. He'd continue to surprise the people around him with unexpected gifts—an $800 mandolin for Davey Johnstone, which the guitarist had seen in a New York music store and Elton knew he'd secretly coveted; a Rolls-Royce for his American agent, Howard Rose; a $23,000 raccoon coat for his secretary. For his thirtieth birthday back in January, Elton had given Rod Stewart Rembrandt's sketch for *The Adoration of the Shepherds*.

A *Time* magazine journalist, David DeVoss, accompanying Elton on a shopping trip to Cartier in London, was astonished by the way the star blew the equivalent of $4,300—almost $20,000 today—on a gold bracelet and necklaces, three gold cigarette lighters, a duffel bag, and four briefcases, in a mere fifteen minutes.

That Christmas, all of the employees at John Reid Enterprises received a Cartier watch from the singer. "Well, it's so easy at Cartier," Elton casually told the management company's director, Geoffrey Ellis. "They've got everything I want and they wrap it all up nicely for you."

In making his own plans for Christmas, Elton decided to rent an enclave of houses in St. James, Barbados, and treat his friends and band members to a Caribbean vacation. It was a long overdue and desperately needed respite. John Reid traveled with the party, proving that his and Elton's working partnership—albeit one that still involved plenty of lively arguments—could survive the collapse of their private relationship. There was, it seemed, no need to estrange themselves from each other. After all, business was booming.

Each morning Elton shocked the others to life with a full-volume airing of the disco reworking of "Babyface" by the Wing and a Prayer Fife and Drum Corps. The days were leisurely frittered away swimming in the sea, water-skiing on it, and paragliding above it. Then there was the drinking—heavy, heavy drinking. There were Bloody Marys for breakfast, rum punches at lunch, and piña coladas to smooth out the rest of the day.

It was a final act of largesse in a year full of it. Still, Elton could afford such generosity. In 1975 he had been solely responsible for 2 percent of global record sales. Put simply, one in every fifty albums sold in the world that year was an Elton John record.

Onstage in America in '76: letting rip, knowing it was the "last" tour.

13 AN AUDIENCE WITH THE KING

Two Elton Johns stood before the cameras—one rendered in wax, the other grinning in barely disguised disbelief at the supposed likeness of him to his right. It was March 7, 1976, and the singer had received the dubious honor of being the first rock star since the Beatles to become the subject of his own dummy at Madame Tussaud's wax museum in London. The real Elton looked great, even if he appeared to have dressed that morning in the dark: fur coat slung on over a striped sweater and jogging pants. The replica Elton was all wrong, looking in his shiny three-piece suit like a slightly creepy, visually impaired fiftysomething showbiz impresario.

Still, it was a celebrity landmark of sorts, and in Britain, Elton had kicked off the year by doing the rounds of the mainstream media. Four weeks before, he'd appeared as a guest on *Parkinson*, the biggest talk show in the land. Its genial and laid-back northern host Michael Parkinson asked Elton about fame. "One thing that interests me," the host began, in his unhurried, circumlocutory way, "is how do you cope with all this sort of hero worship, y'know, all the kids who come and see you and no doubt storm the dressing rooms and all this sort of nonsense?"

"You have to live with it," said Elton breezily, before revealing more of his true state of mind. "You become terribly paranoid. But you have to fight it. You can lose touch."

Parkinson then redirected his line of questioning to the immense sums of money the singer was now earning. "I think people have got the wrong idea of me," Elton averred. "They've only got to shake my hand and they think I'm gonna give them a Rolls-Royce Corniche. I'm very, very grateful for the vast amount of money that I'm paid for what I do. But I don't stand with a whip and force people to go into shops and buy my records. I mean, I could release a record tomorrow that will just plummet down the charts.

"In fact," he added, with a smile, "I've got a single out now that isn't doing too well."

The audience laughed. But it was true. Having hemmed and hawed over the choice of the second single to release from *Rock of the Westies,* Elton had hedged his bets for a double A side featuring "Grow Some Funk of Your Own" paired with "I Feel Like a Bullet (in the Gun of Robert Ford)." In the States, it had struggled to number fourteen. In the UK, it had failed to chart entirely.

Back to workaday reality and the ever waiting coal face—and in an effort to shake up the process, having now made three records at Caribou Ranch—Elton traveled to Toronto and Eastern Sound Studio to begin the sessions for his eleventh album. Not in the mood for superstar fuss, Elton fancied walking to work every day for the short distance between his hotel and the studio. It was a nice idea, but it quickly proved impractical when he was chased down the street by a mob of fans. He took to wearing a face-obscuring hockey mask in the streets, but that only made him more oddly conspicuous, and his devotees soon twigged who this weird serial-killer-looking figure actually was.

Following his split with John Reid and his roller-coasting highs and lows of the previous year, Elton was in a strange, self-pitying mood. Any attempt to revive some kind of a love life seemed clumsy and doomed to fail. He took to playing 10cc's achingly plaintive single "I'm Not in Love" over and over: "I'd sob like a baby because someone or other had taken my fancy and it was totally wrong." Frequently he'd turn up late at the studio. When he did arrive, he was more often than not in an inexplicable sulk. "It was a difficult personal time in my life," Elton says, "probably because the drugs began to escalate. But then we went and made *Blue Moves.*"

During that album's creation, heartache was in the air. Bernie was in Barbados and absent from the sessions, his marriage to Maxine on the rocks. When he sent over the lyrics he'd completed for the new record, it was clear that the turbulence in his private life had thrown him into a state of trauma that informed almost everything he'd written.

"It's almost impossible at times," says Bernie, "not to put a great deal of yourself into what you are writing. *Blue Moves* was the first time I wrote about the disillusionment of love and marriage and, y'know, let my pain be released."

"Bernie was a mess at that time," says Elton. "I rejected some of the songs for that album because the breakup with Maxine was going on and, y'know, they were so down I couldn't sing them."

In secret, or so they believed, Maxine Taupin and Kenny Passarelli had begun an affair. "Nobody knew," the bassist insists. "The affair had not come out. But it was subconsciously there. What was happening was that Bernie and Maxine's marriage was falling apart. It was too much money, too young, and too much fame.

"To rethink it with a mature mind, I would have walked away from all of that. But everything was crumbling—Elton and John Reid, Bernie and Maxine. So the lyrics were heavy and it was dark and sad. All these covert dramas going on . . . that becomes part of the energy of the music."

"Covert" was perhaps the key word. In "Between Seventeen and Twenty," a suspicious Taupin wondered aloud whether it might be a "close friend" now sharing a bed with his wife, while at the same time admitting his own infidelities and blaming them on the fact that his rock'n'roll lifestyle had led him astray. Recording the song, Passarelli kept mum and, squirming inside, dutifully played its bass line.

Elsewhere, for once breaking their standard modus operandi of writing apart, the previous summer, Bernie had visited Elton at his L.A. home and heard him playing a mournful piano part for which the singer already had the beginnings of a melody and even a first line, "What have I got to do to make you love me?" As Elton sang it, a title immediately appeared in Taupin's mind: "Sorry Seems to Be the Hardest Word."

It was a unique instance of the pair employing a more traditional writing approach, and it was fitting in the sense that the song seemed to capture on the page the romantic agonies that both were experiencing. An almost unbearably honest cri de coeur, "Sorry Seems to

Be the Hardest Word" was to become the centerpiece of the aptly titled double album *Blue Moves*.

Even if the lyrics were bleak, the party-time recording atmosphere carried over from Caribou to Eastern Sound: mimosas in the morning, followed by lines of coke and frenzied creativity. Still, the cocktail of intoxicants only served to upend Elton's moods. After the band ran once through a funky rocker called "Bite Your Lip (Get Up and Dance!)," the singer stood up from his piano and decisively declared, "That's a wrap. That'll be a hit."

When Gus Dudgeon informed him that it had only been a run-through to get the sounds right, Elton flatly refused to do another take. He was the star, it was his record, and he wouldn't hear another word said about the matter.

Over in England, John Reid's behavior was becoming similarly erratic. One day he arrived back in London from a trip to Los Angeles only to find that because of a mix-up, his chauffeur wasn't at the airport waiting for him. The manager jumped into a cab and arrived at the Mayfair offices of John Reid Enterprises in a raging state. Surprising and terrifying everyone, he sacked his entire staff and ordered them out onto the street.

Across town, the company's director Geoffrey Ellis was in the middle of a dull tax advisory meeting when he was interrupted by a call from Reid telling him what he had just done. Ellis rushed back to the offices to find the receptionist, the only member of the staff remaining, trembling under her desk while still trying to operate the switchboard.

"We can do the royalty statements ourselves, with just our secretaries," Reid told a disbelieving Ellis. "We don't need anyone else." Ellis quietly had a word with the shell-shocked telephonist and the couple of members of staff still bewilderedly lingering on the pavement outside, telling them not to worry, he would sort everything out. Over the next few days, one by one, the workers returned. "No more," Ellis later noted, "was said about the incident."

It really wasn't a time to be sacking everyone who worked on the management team. Elton had a British tour that was about to begin.

Its name, Louder than Concorde, had come from a quip Princess Margaret had made to Elton about the deafening volume of his amplified piano playing.

Minus the touring luxuries that came with traveling around the States, it was designed to be a no-frills affair, on every level. For years, the UK music press had been grousing that Elton had deserted Britain to concentrate on his extensive touring of America. As a long-delayed response, the Louder than Concorde dates were to find him playing theater- and civic-hall-sized shows in small UK towns and cities—Preston, Hanley, Dundee, Taunton—which normally fell off the touring map. Given the relatively short distances to cover, Elton and the band would be traveling not by plane or luxury coach but in cars, albeit a fleet of vintage Daimlers.

It was a month of pints of ale in woody country pubs, stop-off walks on bleak Northumberland moors, ice cream cones in Edinburgh, plates of fish and chips in greasy spoon cafés in Blackpool. It was resolutely un-starlike and as stripped down as the stage set. But at the same time there seemed to be endless photographs taken during the tour of Elton looking bleary-eyed, shattered, or asleep with a drink in his hand backstage while the party raged on around him.

A review of the opening night at the Grand Theatre in Leeds appeared in *Melody Maker* acknowledging the very different tone to the tour: "This was Elton being Elton, with no trimmings. There were no stage props or gimmicks in sight, not a whiff of dry ice, and not even a back projection screen."

It wasn't, however, a tour without incident. At the Kings Hall in Belle Vue, Manchester, in a grim echo of Watford Town Hall back in '72, there was an IRA bomb scare in the middle of the show. All five thousand members of the audience—along with Elton and the band, who weren't allowed to return to their dressing room—were forced to stand in the rain for half an hour while the venue was scoured for suspect packages. Once it was declared safe for them to reenter the arena, the show recommenced with an added edge of electrified defiance.

Nineteen days later, in Newcastle, Kenny Passarelli almost got himself arrested, drunk and dancing on top of the hotel bar. The bassist's father was a police officer back in the States, and so when members of the local constabulary arrived, he somehow wrong-headedly thought this gave him special privileges. He screamed, "Fuck off! My father's a cop too. Leave me alone!" Eventually, he was dragged off to bed, rather than jail, to sleep it off.

For the greater part, the UK leg of the Louder than Concorde tour offered proof that even without his dress-up antics and usual piz-zazz, Elton and his songs and his well-drilled band could still dazzle. Moreover, the unfussy day-to-day circumstances of its operation were a return to something approximating normality and his pre-fame touring. It was a reminder of a life he once knew.

NOTABLY, BERNIE WAS missing from the entourage of the British tour. Year by year, with their downtime spent entirely apart, a distance between the two songwriters had begun to grow. Their brotherly bond had started to unravel. Bernie graphically described Elton at the time as being "Santa Claus one minute, the Devil incarnate the next."

Not that Taupin in 1976 was the model of emotional stability. Down the years, he had slowly acquired a drinking problem that was now becoming serious. "I was very much a lazy bastard hanging backstage drinking all the Jack Daniel's," he says. "I didn't have anything else to do."

Although he was now extraordinarily wealthy, Taupin had struggled to find a role for himself beyond his writing partnership with Elton. In 1971, he had recorded a poorly selling eponymous spoken word album on Elektra Records, on which he read his lyrics and poetry over backing music provided by Caleb Quaye and Davey Johnstone. More successfully, at least in creative terms, the following year he had turned producer for David Ackles's highly dramatic, heavily orchestrated, and critically acclaimed third album, *American Gothic*. In May '76, he had just published a book of his collected lyrics, *The One Who Writes the Words for Elton John*, illustrated by various collaborators including John Lennon, Ringo Starr, Alice Cooper, and Joni Mitchell.

But his was often an oddly aimless existence filled with much empty time. After the disintegration of his marriage, Bernie was sent into what he describes as a "tailspin." Occupying a spartan house on North Doheny Drive in West Hollywood, he lived by night and slept through the day, waking to reach over to his bedside re- frigerator, crack open a beer, drink half of it, and then top it up with vodka.

In the evenings he hung out with the rock star clique who had earned themselves the nickname the Hollywood Vampires, their chosen lair a table on a balcony at the Rainbow Bar and Grill on Sunset Strip. Its loose membership, aside from Bernie and his now close buddy Alice Cooper, numbered Harry Nilsson, Mickey Do- lenz, and Keith Moon. "Bernie wasn't an alcoholic," Cooper stresses. "I was. Bernie could turn it on and off."

Aside from alcohol and his ubiquitous coke habit, Taupin dab- bled in hallucinogenics (LSD, mushrooms) and even on a couple of occasions dangerously flirted with heroin. "I always had the good sense to recognize things that could potentially destroy me," he says with a laugh. "There's nothing fucking heroic about it at all. It's just the stupidity of youth."

These indulgences threw the lyricist into a delicate physical and mental state. "That horrible paranoia that's making you shake," he says. "That awful feeling you get after being up for three days and you can't sleep. Putting towels across the window, y'know. Don't want to see the sun. 'Oh God . . . makes my skin crawl.'"

It slowly began to dawn on this narcotic vampire that it was per- haps time for him to step back into the light.

SOON TO SWELL both Bernie and Elton's bank accounts was the re- lease of *Blue Moves* as the first album of the lucrative MCA deal John Reid had negotiated in '74. Before that could happen, there was a final record owed to DJM. In typical contractual obligation style, it was to be a live album, titled *Here and There*. As much as it was a stopgap release, it highlighted the key differences in Elton's live performances between 1972 and 1974.

The first vinyl side was culled from the '72 Royal Festival Hall performance in London, though notably from the earlier band portion of the set before the sniffy Royal Philharmonic Orchestra members arrived onstage to unsettle him. The token hit inclusion of "Crocodile Rock" aside, it was the sound of the delicate singer-songwriter of "Skyline Pigeon" and "Love Song." The flip side, meanwhile, featured a selection of numbers from the '74 Madison Square Garden show that had guest-starred John Lennon. The visceral excitement of that momentous gig had been successfully captured on vinyl, as evidenced by the wild screams heard over "Funeral for a Friend" as Elton stepped onto the stage, and the squeals of delighted recognition that similarly greeted the opening bars of "Rocket Man" and "Bennie and the Jets."

In the end, *Here and There* served as a contrasting chronicle of the more considered appreciation of '72 Elton in England and the crazed reaction to '74 Elton in the States. It made it clear that British and American audiences expected different things of him.

The year 1976 marked the culmination of the bicentennial celebrations in the United States and so the plans for the American leg of the Louder than Concorde tour—now given the tongue-in-cheek bracketed addendum (But Not Quite as Pretty)—were appropriately far more ambitious. New outfits were designed for the singer: one that gave him the appearance of a glammed-up Uncle Sam in a red-and-white-striped jacket and voluminous top hat; another saved for Madison Square Garden, where he was to be decked out as a bespectacled Statue of Liberty.

America demanded big moves and showmanship and Elton rose to the challenge. But before the tour kicked off, he was to be given a thought-provoking audience with the very man who had set the rock'n'roll agenda.

IT WAS FINALLY going to happen. Two decades after being that tubby nine-year-old kid miming to rock'n'roll records in his bedroom mirror, Elton was going to meet Elvis Presley.

Staggeringly, they were meeting on almost equal terms—Elvis obviously a living legend, but in terms of record sales power, Elton currently the biggest star in America. Appropriately, he took along his mother, Sheila, the person who'd blown his young mind by introducing him to Presley's music in the first place.

It was the last week of June 1976 and Elton and the band were rehearsing in Washington, D.C., for the imminent start of the two-month-long tour. The call came through confirming that yes, Elton was very much welcome to come along to Presley's Sunday show at the Capital Center in Largo, Maryland, only a half hour's drive away. More incredibly, yes, the King would be happy to meet with him before the show.

Arriving there that night, Elton and Sheila were ushered backstage and then—amping up their nerves—left waiting. Finally, they were led into Elvis's inner sanctum. Instantly, they were shocked by Presley's pallid complexion and corpulent figure. No longer merely portly, he had gone to fat: a ballooned phantom in a garish white, gold, and lilac suit. Black hair dye dripped down his forehead.

Elton looked into the eyes of the King and felt there was "nothing there." Sheila was so stunned she couldn't say a word. "It was sad," says Elton. "It was very clumsy. 'Cause what can you say? This is the man who started it all, basically."

The two traded compliments about each other's music. Elton asked Elvis if he could request "Heartbreak Hotel," but it wasn't in the set of songs the band had planned for the night's show. At the end of the brief and awkward summit, in reality it was Reg, not Elton, who asked Elvis for his autograph.

Only minutes before showtime, Elton and his mother were protectively escorted by cops into the arena. As the house lights were killed for the familiar boom of Presley's walk-on music, Strauss's "Also Sprach Zarathustra" (better known as the theme from 2001: A Space Odyssey), they took their seats, stage right, in the second row. A ripple of excitement passed through the audience at the sighting of Elton. One police officer lingered in the aisle, just in case the English star was hassled by any of the other concertgoers.

The past few years had seen Elvis in and out of the hospital, afflicted by various health problems, which were a worrying byproduct of his expanding size and addictions to prescription drugs. His performances were now notoriously erratic. One night he would have his wits about him and there would be flashes of the brilliance of his heyday. The next night, he would slur his way through the songs or forget the words and even the names of the band members as he introduced them.

Tonight, both sides of the unpredictable performer were on display. Grinning and attempting some of his old dance moves, he sounded tired and gaspy in "Fever," but then he managed to summon from somewhere his still extraordinary voice for the nape-tingling operatic crescendo of "America the Beautiful," causing Elton to stand up and applaud madly. Elvis hit the big notes at the end of "Hurt," his latest single, but then he seemed halfhearted and uninterested in "Hound Dog." He ended, as he always did these days, with "Can't Help Falling in Love," draping cheap scarves around the necks of his wide-eyed female devotees in the front row.

Elton was riveted. In both gratifying and disturbing ways, it was an utterly compelling spectacle to witness. "It was someone who was in a complete drug haze giving nylon scarves away to these fans," remembers Elton. "And yet it was still, in a way, magical."

Afterward, Sheila turned to her son and said, "He'll be dead . . . give him six months."

"Well," Elton reflects, "it was a year."

THE PRESLEY SHOW threw up some uncomfortable truths and parallels for Elton. Three nights later, he was set to appear on the same stage at Maryland's Capital Center, and, like his former idol, he, too, was still subjecting himself to a grinding tour schedule while increasingly propping himself up with drugs. He was finding it more and more difficult even to hold a conversation with someone unless he'd had a sizable toot.

"I was nowhere near as bad as he was," he says. "Y'know, I was thin, I was all right, I was functioning very well."

In some ways, Elton was thankful to be grounded by the ego-deflating and sometimes mocking treatment he was given back home by the press in Britain. "In the long run," he reasons, "it's better than being told, 'You're wonderful, you're wonderful, you're wonderful,' all the time. Stars are treated like royalty in America. They surround themselves by yes people and their reality goes out the window."

Nevertheless, Elton's audience with the King in decline had been a warning. Something had to give. He knew that if he didn't make a big change in his life and career, he could easily go the same way.

Having seen firsthand the physically wrecking effects that chemicals and constant touring could have on someone, Elton would announce onstage at the penultimate gig of his seven-night stint at Madison Square Garden that at the age of just twenty-nine, he was quitting. It had been a magnificent and often astonishing era, but he had decided it was over.

For now, however, with the tour still ahead, he chose to keep this decision to himself.

KNOWING IT WAS the last tour, he decided to utterly throw himself into it and have an absolute ball. The keyboard gymnastics were more extreme. He jumped on top of the glittering piano and cat-walked along its theatrically extended length. He dressed up as a clown and hung stuffed cloth bananas and carrots around his neck. From Washington, D.C., to Detroit to Cincinnati, every night was Mardi Gras.

Sometimes, though, the stadium-proportioned crowds were overly drunk and overly rowdy. In Detroit, at the Pontiac, a flying bottle hit Elton, provoking him to rant at the audience. Later the same night, narrowly missing the shoulder of the singer, a pair of hurled binoculars struck Kenny Passarelli in the chest. The bassist thought he'd been shot. From the side of the stage, John Reid urged him to "keep playing . . . keep playing."

Still, even after those tougher shows, once they were back in the sky aboard the *Starship*, everyone was giddy with exhilaration. One night, someone presented Elton with a pair of white roller skates. As the jet hit cruising altitude and the seatbelt signs were extinguished, he gleefully glided up and down the plane, as everyone hooted around him.

As he traveled around the country, Elton attracted other celebrities into his orbit. In Chicago, Hugh Hefner threw a party for him at the Playboy Mansion and someone snapped a shot in which the singer pretended to be transfixed by the sight of the cleavage of one of the bunnies as he signed her wrist sweatband. In Philadelphia, Elizabeth Taylor hopped onto the *Starship* along with the seventeen-year-old Michael Jackson. "Michael was the sweetest kid," says Elton. "I got to know Elizabeth Taylor very well. I could say, 'Ah, you old cow, how you doing?' Everyone treats stars so reverently and they don't want that."

Midway through the sets, Kiki Dee would arrive on the stage to perform "I've Got the Music in Me" before being joined by Elton for the duet that was fast on its way to becoming his biggest hit of the year. "Don't Go Breaking My Heart" had been recorded, almost as an afterthought, during the *Blue Moves* sessions, and released as a stand-alone single.

Conceived as a Marvin Gaye / Tammi Terrell–style soul number, the song had come to Elton one day as he sat in Eastern Sound playing a Wurlitzer electric piano. He'd added a gobbledygook lyric and then played it over the phone to Bernie in Barbados. Bernie quickly scribbled down his playfully romantic pop rhymes and sent them up to Toronto, where Elton recorded a demo version of the tune duetting with himself, singing the female parts in a comic-voiced higher register. Elton and Bernie's lighthearted attitude to this throwaway piece of pop fluff was underlined by the fact that as its writers they chose to credit themselves under the punning pseudonyms of Ann Orson / Carte Blanche (or "an 'orse and cart(e) blanche")—an inside joke that was too obscure for most outsiders to grasp.

Kiki Dee recorded her parts three and a half thousand miles away in London. "I didn't say at the time that we'd done it separately," she points out. "I just kept it low-key. I kind of thought it would be more fun for people to think that we were standing there together in the studio, like on the video."

The highly memorable cut-price promo film for the song was shot in one take in London before Elton departed for the American tour. In it, he and Kiki goofed around at the microphone, the former in a loose-fitting checked suit, the latter in a pink getup that gave her the look of a children's TV presenter. "If I'd known that it would have become such an iconic video," she says, laughing, "I might have been more concerned about what I was wearing. A jumpsuit with tight ankles and little espadrilles. It was a bit Noddy [the petite wooden puppet character created by English children's author Enid Blyton]."

Although Motownish in its intent, in truth, "Don't Go Breaking My Heart" was unabashedly corny, while at the same time being so infuriatingly catchy it proved to be radio gold. It topped the American charts for the whole of August and for six straight weeks back in Britain, as Elton's first-ever UK number one.

A more cred-giving record was the one Elton broke at Madison Square Garden between August 10 and 17, bettering—by one show—the Rolling Stones' six nights at the venue in '75. Raking in $1.25 million and playing to 137,900 people, it was effectively an unofficial East Coast equivalent of L.A.'s Elton John Week the year before. For those seven days, the singer owned New York. After hours he would hang out with Manhattan's hippest of the hippest. "The seas parted for Elton," says Bernie, "and there was Bianca [Jagger] and Andy [Warhol]."

Elton was in no mood for anyone to rain on his parade, and after John Rockwell wrote in *The New York Times* that the opening Madison Square Garden show in his opinion had "offered wallpaper music of the most banal sort," the singer verbally attacked him live on air on WNEW-FM. "If you're listening now, you asshole," Elton spat, "come down here and I'll destroy you. I'll rip you to bits."

It was a public unraveling that showed he was almost at the end of his tether. Before showtime on the second-to-last gig, Elton gathered his band around him in the dressing room at Madison Square Garden. He gave them the shocking news that he was quitting live performance.

Before he could even get the words out, he started crying. He told them, "I just can't do this anymore. I love you all, and this is the greatest, but I have to take some time off." Sweetening the bitter pill, he then said he was giving them all a whole year's salary in advance.

That night, Elton announced to the nearly twenty-thousand-strong audience, to audible gasps, "You won't see me for a while, but I'll be back . . . someday."

IN ANNOUNCING HIS retirement from the stage, Elton preempted the personal revelation that was to result in a steep decline in his record sales in the United States. For years, no journalist had summoned the nerve to ask him outright about his sexuality. In a *Playboy* interview that had appeared at the beginning of the year, the writer Eugenie Ross-Leming pushed him on the subject, asking him what he made of the trend toward androgyny in the rock scene. Did Elton, she wondered, "get off on the bisexuality scene?" He ducked the question. "I really don't know what to say about it," he blankly responded.

The day after the final Madison Square Garden show, Cliff Jahr of *Rolling Stone* spoke to Elton in his suite at the Sherry-Netherland. At one point, Jahr asked the singer, "Can we get personal? Should we turn off the tape?"

"I knew what was coming," Elton recalls. "There were obviously rumors around." Elton said there was no need for Jahr to switch off his recorder. The interviewer then asked, "What about Elton when he comes home at night? Does he have love and affection?"

In a circuitous way, Elton said that he did have "a certain amount of sex" and that he craved to be loved. "I don't know what I want to be, exactly," he stated. "I'm just going through a stage where *any* sign of affection would be welcome on a sexual level. I'd rather fall in love with a woman eventually because I think a woman probably lasts much longer than a man. But I really don't know. I haven't met anybody that I would like to settle down with—of either sex."

"You're bisexual?" asked Jahr.

"There's nothing wrong with going to bed with somebody of your own sex," Elton stressed, if at first not specifically answering the question, before deciding to throw all remaining caution to the wind. "I think everybody's bisexual to a certain degree. I don't think it's just me."

It hadn't been an outright admission of his homosexuality, and during the interview he even lied about having had a relationship with John Reid. But some kind of truth was now out there. "I had no problems about doing it," Elton reflects. "It felt as if the time was right to actually say it. I was just thrilled to get it out."

In reality, Elton was in danger of being "outed" anyway. In September, a month before the issue of *Rolling Stone* appeared with him on the cover beside the words ELTON'S FRANK TALK—THE LONELY LIFE OF A SUPERSTAR, David Bowie had given an interview to *Playboy* in which the enmity between the two stars had spilled out onto the page. Bowie had previously dismissed Elton as a "token queen." Now Bowie—who had himself admitted to his own, as it would turn out, token bisexuality back in 1972—leveled a loaded accusation at Elton. "I consider myself responsible for a whole new school of pretensions," he said. "They know who they are. Don't you, Elton? Just kidding. No, I'm not."

But whereas Bowie's blurred sexuality had a cool-giving effect, a large part of Elton's audience were conservative Middle Americans. Still, even if coming out damaged his record sales in the immediate aftermath, as he views the period through the distance of time, Elton remembers it somewhat differently, valuing above all the personal liberty it won him.

"A few radio stations were a bit upset," he says, "and people burnt my records. But you know what? It was a very small price to pay for the freedom that it gave me."

IN THE UK, the singer's confession didn't cause much of a fuss, with the normally scandal-hungry *News of the World* running a story under the uncharacteristically sympathetic headline ELTON: MY LOVE LIFE ISN'T SO STRANGE. In fact, the admission seemed to endear him all the more to the British public. He noticed that when he was out and about, more people waved at him in the street.

This unburdening seemed to put Elton in a liberated and reckless mood. When he arrived onstage for what he considered to be absolutely his last show, at Edinburgh's Playhouse on September 17 for a long-scheduled and unavoidable solo gig as part of the city's Festival of Popular Music (being filmed for an ABC TV special in the States), he had obviously been hitting the bottle.

His inebriated state, though, didn't seem to affect his performance. In fact, alone at the piano, he attacked the set list's mix of his best-known hits and deeper album cuts with visible relish, while throughout the show he kept topping up his Bloody Mary from a jug. "I don't want the people at home to think I'm an alcoholic," he proclaimed into the microphone. "I want them to *know* I'm an alcoholic."

The longer the show rolled on, the drunker he got. During a wild and frenetic "Saturday Night's Alright for Fighting," he climbed up onto the piano, picked up a tartan scarf, and tied it around his balding cranium, larked around, tossed his microphone to the floor, and handed his piano stool out to the front row. He was flying on vodka, clearly hammered, but having something that looked suspiciously like the time of his life. "All right, lunacy prevails this evening," he laughed.

In marked contrast, his eleventh album, released five weeks later, was a far more serious affair. If Elton's first double, *Goodbye Yellow Brick Road*, had been the soundtrack of his ascension to stardom, *Blue Moves* was the sound of the comedown. Taupin had addressed the death of fame in key songs: "Cage the Songbird" was about the last hours of Edith Piaf; "Idol" spoke of the decay of a fifties rock star (unmistakably Elvis Presley) while pointing out that all celebrities seem to end up drowning in their own despair.

Although *Blue Moves* was musically adventurous in its freewheeling, jazzy stylings, it sometimes made for uneasy listening. Anyone hearing the bleak lyric of "Someone's Final Song," for instance, might have had real cause to worry about Taupin's mental state, since it was about a writer penning his conclusive lyric before presumably killing himself, or as Bernie later elucidated, "blowing their brains out." With no little understatement, the lyricist later observed, "I think I sank too much into depressive excess on that album."

Altogether, it made for an uncommercial package, even down to its cover reproduction of a painting—*The* Guardian *Readers,* by the Irish artist Patrick Proktor, which Elton had bought at an exhibition—featuring largely faceless, topless men sunbathing on blue-rendered parkland grass. If it was somehow timely for the singer in the wake of his *Rolling Stone* interview, then its vaguely homoerotic nature ensured that a competition to give away copies of the album in *The Sun* newspaper was nixed. "They wouldn't do it because they said, 'There's no women in this painting,'" Elton incredulously noted at the time. "I didn't realize before."

As artistically successful as *Blue Moves* was, it made it only to number three in America, ending Elton's unbroken run of seven number one albums. "In a way, it was a relief," he says. "I'm someone who studies the charts and I just thought, *This is not going to go on forever*. I was prepared for it and I knew that after it *had* stopped, it was a matter of just finding your place."

BACK HOME IN England, Elton found something to ground him.

When Stanley Dwight, on his rare weekends off from the RAF, used to take young Reg to see Watford Football Club play, it had sparked a lifelong devotion. Wherever he was in the world, Elton always had to find out the latest Watford score. In New York, in the spring of '75, on the day that the team were playing their final match of the season, the singer had run into a shop, asking to use their phone to call England and find out the result. When he was told that Watford had lost 3–2 to Walsall and been relegated to the Fourth Division, Elton immediately sat down and began weeping. "They must have thought I was mad," he noted, not unreasonably.

The symbolic title of vice president of the club that he'd been given back in 1973—purely because he was the team's most famous fan—suddenly wasn't enough for him. In June of '76 he became the chairman of the heavily indebted team, bringing with him his financial heft. His hugely ambitious aim, he declared, was to bring the team up from the Fourth to the First Division.

More important, perhaps, it gave Elton something to focus on now that his touring life had come to an end. "It wasn't about just throwing money at the club," he insists. "Even though I paid a lot of money, you couldn't have bought that amount of happiness. It gave me another interest outside of music. Because at that point I had no other interest outside of music."

It also brought him sharply back down to earth. No one that

Elton dealt with at Watford FC was even remotely impressed by his fame. In fact, in that no-nonsense British way, they seemed determined to treat him like everyone else. When the team's nineteen-year-old star player Keith Mercer was trying, and failing, to grow a mustache, Elton boasted that he himself could grow one in a week. The singer returned a week later with a full beard. Mercer took one look at the star's furry face and playfully jibed him with the words "When you can grow that on your face, it's a shame you can't do the same on your head."

Elton loved this kind of banter, and he even cheerfully put up with the insulting chants that would be weekly bellowed at him by the supporters of Watford's opposing teams. They'd repeatedly sing, "Elton John . . . is a homosexual!" or "He's bald—he's queer—he takes it up the rear!" To the tune of the Cockney standard "My Old Man (Said Follow the Van)," they'd chorus, "Don't sit down when Elton's around / Or you'll get a penis up your arse!"

To the singer, this behavior was simply "good-natured English abuse." It shook him out of any last remaining traits of starriness. Over the past seven years, he had slowly lost touch with reality. Now here he was on the receiving end of a major jolt of it.

In America, he had been given a glimpse of what might have easily become his future. He knew that it wasn't one he wanted. "I mean," he said, "who wants to be a forty-five-year-old entertainer in Las Vegas like Elvis?"

Together but alone: John Reid and Elton after their personal, but not professional, split.

14 FLOATING INTO SPACE

ELTON WAS AT HOME watching *Top of the Pops* when the Sex Pistols exploded onto the screen. Seeing Johnny Rotten thrillingly howl his way through "Pretty Vacant," he suddenly felt ancient. Understanding better than most the vagaries of musical fashions, he knew something vital had changed that might well render him redundant. Elton looked at the punks and thought, *What a fucking state they're in.* But at the same time he could relate to them, remembering those days during the glam rock era when he'd dyed his hair orange and green and his eyebrows pink.

He'd turned thirty in March 1977 and it had left him feeling old and tired and slightly vulnerable. Entering your thirties, at a time when pop music was still considered not to be a viable long-term career option, seemed like the beginning of the end. Adding weight to the notion that the sun might be setting on his relevance, he was winning music industry prizes that somehow felt like retirement clocks: Favorite Male Artist at the American Music Awards, an Ivor Novello songwriter's award for the now glaringly old-fashioned "Don't Go Breaking My Heart."

Picking up the Best Singer gong at the Capital Radio Awards in London, he really didn't feel he deserved it and said so in his acceptance speech. "I think this award," he declared, "should go to Elvis Costello."

All of his energies were being thrown into Watford FC. In April, he boldly sacked their current manager, Mike Keen, and replaced him with the Lincoln City Football Club's boss, Graham Taylor. Elton's mother saw the positive effect that being involved with the soccer team was having on her son. "He's mixing with ordinary people," Sheila pointed out. "He's never been more happy."

At the same time, only eight months after he'd dramatically quit live performance, he couldn't stay away from the stage. In May, he agreed to give six relatively intimate performances at the three-thousand-seat Rainbow Theatre in London as part of the celebrations for the Queen's Jubilee year, marking her quarter century on the throne. He viewed the shows, billed as the Elton John and Ray Cooper Charity Gala, as an opportunity to dust off songs he hadn't performed in years.

The first half of the set featured him alone at the piano, reeling off "The Greatest Discovery" from *Elton John,* "Where To Now St. Peter?" from *Tumbleweed Connection,* and "Sweet Painted Lady" from *Goodbye Yellow Brick Road,* along with a cover of Marvin Gaye's "I Heard It Through the Grapevine." He was then joined for the second half—from "Funeral for a Friend" through the likes of "Bennie and the Jets" and "Sorry Seems to Be the Hardest Word"—by Cooper on percussion, whirling around from timpani to vibes and throwing himself into his signature arm-flinging tambourine playing routine.

It was, Elton realized, a fresh and nonflashy way for him to approach concerts. Maybe he could further explore this in the future.

The Queen's first cousin, forty-year-old Princess Alexandra, attended the opening night at the Rainbow. According to Geoffrey Ellis of John Reid Enterprises, who was sitting beside her in the front row, the minor royal didn't seem to know how she should act at a pop concert—whether to clap along with the rest of the audience during the songs or appear more regally reserved. Later, at a backstage party, meeting Elton, she seemed equally unsure of exactly what to say to him. She was impressed by the stamina he seemed to summon up for the two-and-a-half-hour show. Did he take some sort of a drug? she wondered. Cocaine, perhaps?

"I couldn't believe it," said Elton, recklessly relaying the anecdote to reporters after the event. "I was so stunned. I'm not sure what I replied."

When the story appeared in the newspapers, Elton was forced to apologize to Princess Alexandra through the pages of the *Daily Tele-*

graph. "I very much hope I haven't embarrassed the princess," he said. "I thought it was very amusing and that's why I repeated it. Of course I don't take cocaine." Later, choosing his words carefully, if revealing more, he explained, "I told her that I don't take cocaine before I go onstage—which is the truth."

This awkward apology showed just how much Elton valued his position as a royally endorsed rock star. A week before the Sex Pistols tried to subvert the Jubilee celebrations by performing on a boat sailing up and down the River Thames, resulting in the arrest of their manager, Malcolm McLaren, Elton was performing on a variety bill at the BBC-televised Royal Windsor Big Top Show for the Queen and Prince Philip. The ideological distance between him and the punk generation was seemingly immense.

Not that he wasn't down with the kids in other ways. On the afternoon of Friday, June 17, he was at home in Woodside, lying on his bed watching a Wimbledon tennis match on TV, when his housekeeper came in to say there was a bunch of students outside, from Shoreditch College in Surrey, who'd buzzed the intercom at the front gates. Their leader, Ken Hall, had informed her that they'd booked the American soul singer Jimmy Helms for their valedictory ball to be held that evening but at the last minute, Helms had canceled. Was there any chance at all that Elton would consider coming along and performing?

Elton immediately passed back a surprising message: Yes, of course I'll do it. On two conditions—that they find him a decent grand piano, and that they not tell the press. "I wasn't doing anything that night, so I thought, *Why not?*" Elton remembered. "I admired their nerve."

The students were stunned. Returning to college, they were deflatingly informed by their tutors that there was no way, even for Elton John, that they would be allowed to wheel one of the institution's two grand pianos, kept in the chapel, into the main hall where the ball was being staged. Thinking on their feet, the students asked if the singer could instead perform in the chapel itself. And so this quickly became the alternative arrangement.

At 6:30, Elton's personal assistant Bob Halley turned up, checked out the piano and the sound system the students had borrowed from the hired disco, and gave the setup the OK. Elton pulled up in his Rolls-Royce at 9:30, and in an effort not to spoil the surprise for the unsuspecting audience, the organizers sneaked him in through the back door of the chapel.

Everyone was taken aback by how casual and friendly he was. Elton sat down at the piano, took out his Barclays Bank checkbook, and began to write out a rough set list on the back of it. As he did a quick sound check, the rumors of his impending appearance began to spread around the college, building to a buzz of anticipation and disbelief.

Still, come showtime, the chapel wasn't even full, many students believing the news to be some kind of practical joke. Then Ken Hall stepped onto the stage to make the introduction. "Ladies and gentlemen," he said, "I give you, for the first time ever at Shoreditch College . . . Elton John."

Resounding cheers went up as he arrived onstage, and students rushed in to pack the 150-capacity chapel to fire regulation breaking point. Onstage, in a green-striped black jacket, blue track pants, and an olive flat cap, Elton rolled through "Crocodile Rock," "Daniel," "Rocket Man," "Your Song," and more, in a nearly two-hour set. "I was astonished," the college's vice principal, Peter Lacey, later recalled, "by how well he could communicate without any props or lights."

Elton encored with "Bennie and the Jets," stopping midway to pick up the lid of the grand piano and pretend that he was about to hurl it to the back of the stage. The music lecturer's face turned scarlet, thinking his precious grand piano was about to be trashed. In the end, the singer respectfully replaced the lid and finished the song to yells and applause.

Afterward, Elton accepted an invitation to have a post-show drink with a bunch of students in one of their rooms. There, he knocked back their beer and Glenfiddich whisky, regaled them with his tale of meeting Elvis Presley, and defaced a poster of himself hanging on the wall with the words "Watch out, old four eyes is back."

Never once was there any mention of his receiving any payment for the performance. His mum was right. He was enjoying hanging out with everyday people.

. . .

THROUGHOUT THE YEAR, though, hits were hard to come by, particularly in the States in the wake of his "bisexual" confession. Nothing else released from *Blue Moves* made much of an impression: "Bite Your Lip (Get Up and Dance!)" limped to number twenty-eight in both the United Kingdom and the United States; the lightsome funk of "Crazy Water" climbed one position higher to number twenty-seven in Britain but wasn't even released in America.

In August, Elton flew to New York and threw a party at the nautically themed One Fifth Avenue restaurant to try to revive interest in the Rocket Record Company, including, in truth, his own fading passion for the project. He and Kiki Dee performed at the event, but it was becoming increasingly evident that the label was drifting rudderless. "No one was at the center of things," said Kiki at the time. "Maybe it wasn't a hungry label."

During the trip, Elton hooked up with Rod Stewart to discuss an idea the former had for a film, which he imagined might star the two of them. To be titled *Jet Lag,* he envisaged it as a buddy movie caper featuring the pair as tax-avoiding rock stars who flew around the world, living on their private planes. It would take the spirited rivalries of their real lives and blow them up to comedic proportions.

Rod humored his friend but thought it was a "totally barking idea." The film was destined never to be made, and, if anything, the notion only served to highlight just how aimless Elton was.

As 1977 WORE on, he began to be increasingly depressed by the sight in the mirror of his fast-disappearing hairline. In autumn, Elton traveled to Paris for the first of a series of hair transplant procedures. At the clinic of Dr. Pierre Pouteaux, he underwent a long and painful five-hour surgery during which, under local anesthetic, squares of healthy hair were cut from the back of his scalp and grafted onto the top of his head.

Comically, if agonizingly, as a dazed Elton emerged from the clinic to step into his waiting car, he managed to bang his head on the edge of its door, dislodging some of the patches of freshly grafted hair. Meekly, he was forced to turn around and go back inside to have them reattached.

News of his hair transplant made the newspapers, but Elton wasn't the slightest bit embarrassed or ashamed to have people know he had subjected himself to the operation. "It's all one hundred percent vanity," he cheerfully confessed. "But I'm thrilled with the result."

Having spent most of the year resolutely dressed down, he was of two minds as to whether to agree to appear as a guest on *The Muppet Show*. "I don't want to do those crazy, flamboyant costumes with all the big feathers and big glasses and stuff," he told their creator, Jim Henson. In the end, he relented and dug some of his most outlandish costumes out of storage. Over three days in October, at Elstree Studios northwest of London, he filmed sketches and songs for the half-hour show, clearly having a fine old time in the process.

In his bejeweled white skullcap and multicolored ostrich plumes, Elton fronted the show's house band, Dr. Teeth and the Electric Mayhem, for "Crocodile Rock," amid a swamp scene where puppet reptiles performed the falsetto "la-la-la" hook line before hungrily dragging him from his piano stool and into the water. During a dressing room skit, the Muppets' backstage gofer Scooter thumped a piano as he let the singer hear a new song he'd "written" that sounded strangely like a pub-time rendition of "Bennie and the Jets."

"Isn't that the worst song you've ever heard, Elton?" asked a mock-appalled Kermit.

"Well . . . I didn't think so when I wrote it," he deadpanned.

In a lemon and sea-green suit and black bowler hat encircled with piano keys, Elton played it straight for "Goodbye Yellow Brick Road," and even the normally manic and flailing drummer Animal managed to pin down the beat. Finally, to cap the lot, in a spangly pink jumpsuit that revealed just how slim he'd become, he sang "Don't Go Breaking My Heart" with Miss Piggy. "Eat your heart out, Kiki!" growled the porcine diva in the direction of the camera.

During the taping, as he later related, Elton had to do eleven takes of "Don't Go Breaking My Heart" because he kept cracking up with laughter. In an off-camera ad-lib, the voice and animator of Miss Piggy, Frank Oz, suddenly declared, "I'm not used to working with amateurs!" before making her flounce off the set. "Those puppets," said Elton, "are human."

The next month, Elton changed his mind about touring. Since coming off the road, Davey Johnstone and James Newton Howard had formed a band, China, who were subsequently signed to Rocket. As they were rehearsing in Los Angeles, a call came through from Elton in England saying he wanted to do some dates with China both opening for him and backing him during his own performances. He flew to L.A. and rehearsed with the band for three weeks, although, confusingly, now with apparent reluctance.

A charity show to debut this new arrangement was booked at London's 12,500-capacity Wembley Empire Pool arena for November 3. On the day of the gig, the singer was in a terrible mood, throwing a strop backstage when some caps he'd ordered weren't delivered. That evening, in a black leather jacket and matching beret, he turned up onstage and immediately fluffed the introduction to "Better Off Dead" owing to an onstage sound problem.

As the show progressed, he looked and sounded tired, and even while cajoling the crowd into a sing-along, he appeared to be merely going through the motions. Thirteen songs in, talking as he gently picked out the opening chords of "Sorry Seems to Be the Hardest Word," he made another of his dramatic announcements.

"Uh, I'd just like to say something," he began. "Um, it's very hard to put it in words, really. But I haven't been touring for a long time, and it's been a painful decision whether to come back on the road or not."

There were cheers and shouts of "Yeah!" from the audience.

"And I'm really enjoying tonight," he continued. "Thank you very much. But . . . I've made a decision tonight. This is going to be the last show. All right?"

There were cries of "No!" from the crowd.

"There's a lot more to me than playing on the road," Elton concluded, "and this is the last one I'm gonna do."

Onstage, Ray Cooper respectfully applauded the singer's surprise declaration, while the rest of the band seemed stunned as they joined him on the song. Backstage, John Reid was pacing up and down and ranting. Elton hadn't warned him of his decision. "I've got to discuss this whole thing with him," a blindsided Reid told a pack of journalists afterward.

Anyone watching the show, however, could see that Elton was burned out. To his mind, everything had grown uncontrollably enormous. He was tired of seeing his fans crushed up against security barriers and thinking, *Well, this might be great for me, but is it great for them?* He was wearied by how upset he would become if he felt he'd underperformed during a show, and how he'd mentally beat himself up afterward. He wanted somehow to start his life and career all over again.

It was another year, another retirement announcement. This one, however, had an air of finality about it.

IF THERE WAS a sense that everything was winding down, the arrival of his second singles compilation, *Elton John's Greatest Hits Volume II*, seemed to mark the end of the second phase of his success. Coming only three years after his first hits compendium, the album chronologically swept up all the 45s from "The Bitch Is Back" to "Grow Some Funk of Your Own." It was a remarkable feat, really, to warrant two "best of" collections within the first eight years of your career, though a scan down the tracklist of this secondary volume only revealed the diminishing returns of his output.

Elton still wanted to make records, but he now wanted to create them in different ways. His thoughts returned to soul music. He decided to forget the idea of playing the piano, or even really being a songwriter, for the time being. Purely as a singer, he wanted to put himself in the hands of a record producer.

OVER THE PREVIOUS decade, Thom Bell had earned himself a reputation as the Phil Spector of Philly Soul, producing a chain of hits for the likes of the Delfonics, the Stylistics, and the Spinners. Elton put into action a plan to work with Bell, and sessions were booked for

Kaye-Smith Studios in Seattle, where the producer was currently living. Before they began, Bell kept asking the singer if he was entirely sure he wanted to relinquish control of the recording process. The singer said he was. "He was tired," Bell remembered, "and he was smart enough to say, 'Listen, man, I'm gonna get someone else to do it for me this time.' "

In the end, inevitably, Elton brought two songs of his own to the table. The first, "Nice and Slow," was based on a lascivious Bernie Taupin lyric. The second, "Shine On Through," found Elton stepping for the first time outside his songwriting partnership with Taupin. The singer had been visiting his friend Gary Osborne, the lyricist who'd co-written "Amoureuse" for Kiki Dee back in '72, at his Hampstead home when he'd played him a piano part and sung a melody for a song idea that Elton said Bernie couldn't come up with any words for. He asked Osborne if he fancied trying to write something for it, and in time the song was fashioned into a slow-grooving gospel ballad.

Apart from these two compositions, Elton relied on Thom Bell to provide the material. The producer drafted his songwriting nephew LeRoy Bell for three other romantically minded songs, "Mama Can't Buy You Love," "Are You Ready for Love," and the tantalizingly titled "Three Way Love Affair."

In the Seattle studio, Elton tried to deliver these songs in his soul falsetto voice. Bell bravely told the singer that to his ears, his higher register wasn't strong enough. "Thom Bell taught me a lot," Elton said later. "How to breathe properly and use my voice in a lower register." The sessions seemed to go with a swing, six tracks were recorded, and an ABC TV crew invited into the control room at Kaye-Smith caught a listening party in full flow with the musicians, along with the singer and John Reid, dancing and clapping along to the playbacks.

When Elton returned to England, Bell traveled to Sigma Sound Studios in Philadelphia to add orchestrations. But when he heard them, the singer felt the tracks were overproduced and "saccharine" and, frustrating everyone, canceled the further sessions planned for the new year. For now, the tapes of the Thom Bell sessions were shelved.

. . .

THROUGHOUT 1977, ELTON and Bernie's physical remove from each other—the former largely in Britain, the latter remaining in the United States—had gradually turned into a state of estrangement.

Having experienced a moment of clarity in the midst of his drinking and drugging, Bernie had gone to Mexico for an extended break in an effort to dry out. He'd been followed there by Alice Cooper, himself fresh from a period in a rehab clinic and in a straight, if fragile, condition. Cooper would entertain Taupin with stories of the various oddball characters he'd met in the sanatorium cleaning up his act. "Bernie," he said, "I was in a writer's paradise."

Together, the pair began throwing around ideas for songs to be co-written about this concept, which would result in the 1978 Alice Cooper album *From the Inside*. Meanwhile, back in the UK, Elton found himself writing more and more with Gary Osborne.

"Because of the geographical thing," says Bernie, "we were being musically seduced elsewhere. We were dabbling in creating things with other people."

"I think when it initially happened," Elton says, "we were a little jealous of each other. That's just human, because of the love we have for each other. It's kind of like letting your wife sleep with another man. Y'know, it's like, [*sheepishly*] 'Oh, it's okay.' But you had to get over that.

"The two of us were too close," he reasons. "Even though we had our own lives, it was necessary for us to find our own bases."

And so, ten years after they'd first met, Elton and Bernie split. Incredibly, both say there were no angry scenes during this breakup period. "Never had an argument with him," says Elton. "We're not those kind of people. I could never shout and scream at Bernie 'cause I love him too much."

"No, we never argued about it," Bernie confirms. "It was continental drift. *Blue Moves* was sort of the apex. It was our Mount Everest in a way. We'd gone to the top. I'm sure drugs, alcohol, the geographical thing, it all contributed. The base core of it was that I don't know if we knew what we wanted to do next. Or even if we *could* do it."

. . .

AT THE OUTSET of 1978, Elton entered the Mill Studio, situated in the village of Cookham on the River Thames, west of London, to begin work on his first album without Bernie. Gus Dudgeon in fact owned the facility, but Elton decided to co-produce the record himself along with Clive Franks, although of course Dudgeon would enjoy some remuneration in the process via their renting of the studio. The arrangement suited Gus fine, who felt that he and Elton had exhausted their collaboration. "The challenge had gone," said the producer.

The sessions carried on, in sporadic bursts, as the months went by. Everyone was in high spirits, not least a coked-up Elton who was also drinking as much as two bottles of brandy a day and, now that he had taken up smoking, puffing on joint after joint. His songwriting process with Gary Osborne was very different from the one he'd built with Bernie. The two would generally write in the same room, riffing ideas and coming up with titles and phrases.

It had been nearly two years since Elton had thrown himself so deeply into the creative process. In what would turn out to be an unwitting assessment of the quality of much of the material, though, he said at the time he felt he was suffering from "writer's diarrhea."

Nonetheless the first product of these sessions was in fact a John/Taupin song written, though unrecorded, for *Blue Moves*. "Ego" was a forceful, elaborately arranged rock song that aimed for New Wave but landed closer to the baroque style of Queen, with a lyric that found Elton inhabiting the persona of a demented fame-and-money-hungry superstar figure.

Talking about the track when it was released as a single in March 1978, Elton pulled no punches in exposing who, in his mind, the song was directed at. "It's dedicated to the Jaggers and Bowies of this world—and especially to Mr. McCartney," he crowed. "David Bowie is a pseudointellectual, and I can't bear pseudointellectuals. And McCartney's music has gone so far down the tubes, I can't believe it. They just all annoy me."

Only later did he realize that in "Ego," he might as well have been singing about himself. Fittingly, an ambitious promotional video was commissioned for the song, at great expense, overseen by Michael Lindsay-Hogg, director of the Beatles' *Let It Be* and the Rolling Stones' *Rock and Roll Circus*.

In the video, a glasses-free, contacts-wearing Elton in dark suit and pink tie stands mouthing the song's lyric with punkish aggression in front of neon signs unfortunately bearing the words "Elton" and "Ego" divided by a burning Olympic flame. Intercut were scenes of photographers flocking around an unseen star at a press reception and staged flashbacks of a child actor, John Emberton, resembling the young Reg, traveling on a train and acting in a school production of *Romeo and Juliet*.

As a slightly desperate attempt to remake himself for the post-punk age, it wasn't Elton's finest hour. Premieres of the video held in cinemas in London and Los Angeles didn't stir up any real interest in the endeavor, and "Ego" stalled at number thirty-four in both the British and American charts.

Elton was furious about the failure of the single, and in an interview with *The Sun* newspaper he even questioned the accuracy of the chart compiled by the British Market Research Bureau for the BBC, lambasting it as "highly inaccurate . . . everybody in the business knows it's ridiculous. But far too few people have had the courage to say so. Until something is done about it, I've decided to withdraw my record company's advertising from any publication printing the BMRB chart."

By now, the title "Ego" was beginning to seem all too appropriate. The following week, John Reid, on a trip to Australia, called the offices of Rocket to chew out the label's pluggers for their failure to get the song's video screened on *Top of the Pops*. "It was all done in a fit of anger," said Reid in reflection, once he'd cooled down. "I have apologized for screaming so loudly."

In April, Elton was profiled in *The Sunday Times* in the UK and seemed determined to underline his significance and integrity at a time when both appeared to be slipping away. "Most people have completely the wrong idea of me," he bristled. "I turned down one offer of a million dollars to do a week in Las Vegas. I didn't even think about it. I'm looked upon as one of the artists in this country who has the least credibility and I think I have the most credibility."

. . .

ALL OF THIS seemed to smack of wild insecurity worsened by cocaine-induced paranoia. If outwardly he was displaying much bravado and bluster, within himself he was feeling acutely vulnerable.

One Sunday in August, Elton was at home, in a peculiar frame of mind, filled with strangely morbid thoughts, when he began playing a haunting, compellingly dreamy refrain on the piano. A line kept returning to him over and over: "Life isn't everything."

On the same day, Rocket's seventeen-year-old courier Guy Burchett was killed in a motorcycle accident. Elton learned the awful news on Monday when he went into the office. In his head, he immediately titled the composition "Song for Guy" in tribute to the teenager cut down in his prime.

The coincidence of the tragedy with his own dark ruminations struck Elton as eerie. In reality, the circumstances surrounding the writing of the song said more about the singer's precarious mental state in the summer of 1978. He later wrote in a *Billboard* advertisement for the subsequent single release of "Song for Guy": "I imagined myself floating into space and looking down at my own body. I was imagining myself dying."

Elton and Ray Cooper outside the Summer Palace, Leningrad, USSR, May 1979.

15 SUPER CZAR

EIGHT YEARS AND SEVEN WEEKS after he'd stormed the Troubadour, it was a very different Elton John who tentatively stepped onto the stage at the Plaza hotel in New York for his first live performance in eleven months. He was in an extremely wobbly state. His knee was quaking so badly he was forced to rest his foot on one of the piano's pedals to try to quell the tremors. It didn't work. "It just kept shaking," he confessed afterward.

Elton was the surprise solo guest performer for two hundred fifty delegates who'd flown in from all over America for the October 1978 MCA Records national convention. He kicked off with "Bennie and the Jets," enthusiastically crooning "Ooh yeah" over the song's opening piano stabs, before comically adding, "Notice how I've toned down my act?" He was in fine voice. No one in the audience would have been able to tell how terrified he actually was.

That was until he forgot the words in the third verse of "Sixty Years On," replacing them with an ad-libbed "doo-doo-doo-dah-dah." The record company employees laughed and clapped in support. "Just testing," Elton joked. Still, his uneasiness then made him mumble some of the lines in "Daniel." "We're gonna do a couple of songs from the new album now," he announced, forgetting he was onstage alone. "As I have never sung them in public, I should probably be dreadful."

He wasn't, and the soulful yearning of "Shine On Through," followed later by the delicate ballad "Shooting Star" segueing into "Song for Guy," all walked tall alongside his best-known songs.

A look designed to kill flashy Elton. The cover shoot for A Single Man, *Long Walk, Windsor Great Park.*

"I'm nervous as hell about the album and I'm nervous as hell coming on tonight," he admitted to the industry crowd. "Thanks very much, MCA. We've had our ups and downs . . . and I'm sort of on a downstroke, I think, really. Perhaps I got a little bit too cozy in what I was doing, and too safe. And it's a good thing that we had a two-year layoff, 'cause I'm excited again." His enthusiasm was infectious. Everyone left convinced that his comeback album would be a massive hit.

As if trying to obliterate his former flamboyance, the cover of *A Single Man* featured him dressed in oddly funereal fashion. Resting on a cane in black greatcoat, top hat, and jackboots, he gave the appearance of someone about to attend a Victorian burial, an impression heightened by the fact that he was positioned on the dramatic Long Walk road leading up to Windsor Castle. He stared seriously at the camera, specsless and somber.

Inside the gatefold sleeve, he posed in tweed cap and jacket at the wheel of his vintage Jaguar, looking every inch the country squire off to do a spot of clay pigeon shooting. In finally shaking off his now old-fashioned glam rock past—and having given up trying to keep pace with the New Wave pack—his new look was that of someone belonging to an imagined rock aristocracy.

A Single Man, however, was a patchy effort. The ballads were strong, but there was an abundance of weak-to-middling tracks. The barely veiled gay flirtation tale told in "Big Dipper" (audaciously featuring backup vocals from Watford FC players) wasn't as great an idea as it had probably seemed in the studio. "Return to Paradise" was a song of summer romance rendered in an easy-listening style that would have made Reg cringe if it had been in Long John Baldry's cabaret set back in '67. Later in the running order, "Georgia" was a decent gospel revival rouser in the style of the Band, though the lead single, "Part-Time Love," was a blandly bouncy ode to the apparent joys of infidelity, with even a returning Paul Buckmaster orchestrating on autopilot.

There was something—or someone—missing. If the title *A Single Man* could easily have been construed as barbed, in seeming to refer to his "divorce" from Bernie, Elton insists it wasn't. "No," he avers, before adding a less decisive "not really."

Bernie, for his part, didn't perceive the album's name as a gibe. "I don't think there was anything bitter in that title," he says. "I suppose it could have been conceived [that way], but I know it wasn't. Obviously it could be seen as [meaning] our artistic marriage had dissolved and he was in fact a single man. But the truth of it was he actually wasn't because he was working with other people. He'd just remarried."

A Single Man did decent business, shipping gold in the States in October and turning platinum the following month, Elton's confession about his sexuality two years earlier apparently having faded in the minds of the more conservative American record buyers. In the end, it was "Song for Guy" rather than "Part-Time Love" that provided its standout hit in the UK, with the gently entrancing, largely instrumental bossa nova carrying a wistful quality—lent poignancy by its sad backstory—that found it peaking at number four in Britain, although it made no impression whatsoever in the United States.

Buoyed as he was by his comeback, Elton was still determined not to resume a cosseted superstar lifestyle. He'd even begun to travel alone, amazing himself with the thrill of being able to board a flight, jump into a taxi, and check himself into a hotel entirely unaided. "A few years ago, I would have had it all done for me," he mused. "I thought, *Here you are at the age of thirty-one and at last you can do it on your own, you stupid sod.*"

He was feeling alive with renewal and the invigorating freedom of something approximating normal life. He realized now that he had been locked away for years, like a prize tiger.

THEN, ON NOVEMBER 9, before leaving Woodside to travel to Paris, he collapsed.

He'd been sitting down, talking on the phone. He stood up and his legs gave way. His PA, Bob Halley, called an ambulance.

"I had terrible pains in my chest, arms, and legs," Elton later remembered in horror. "I couldn't breathe. I could hardly move for the pain."

He was dashed to the cardiac wing of the Harley Street Clinic in central London, having suffered a suspected heart attack. Someone leaked the information and this became translated into absolute confirmation of his condition in a news bulletin read out on BBC radio: "Pop star Elton John has been rushed to hospital after suffering a heart attack."

Almost immediately, journalists flocked like hungry crows on the pavement outside the clinic. Inside, Elton was being subjected to a battery of tests. Eventually the diagnosis came through: He'd keeled over from a panic attack brought on by nervous exhaustion.

He really hadn't been looking after his health in recent months. Aside from the high intake of alcohol and other stimulants, his eating habits had become wildly erratic: One minute he'd be dieting, drinking too much coffee, and popping vitamins; the next he'd be wolfing down a tub of ice cream.

"This has really shaken me," he told a reporter as he left the clinic. "When you're used to nonstop tours across the States and so on, you start to think you're superhuman. Then something like this happens and you realize you're not. Sometimes you've got to slow down like everyone else."

ABSOLUTELY THE LAST thing he needed to do was book an extensive tour for 1979, which is exactly what he did. After three months of rest following his collapse, he was itching to get back onstage. "I was wrong," he said, in explaining how he suddenly regretted retiring from live performance. "I didn't know how much I would miss it."

Nonetheless, he had no desire to re-form the band and return to the stadiums. Instead, he revived the two-man operation consisting of himself and Ray Cooper that he felt had worked so successfully at the Rainbow. This was a show that didn't rely on glitziness or volume. In rehearsals, stripping the songs back to their basic constituents, Elton looked back on the decade that was nearly over and recognized just what he and Bernie had achieved together. He rediscovered his back catalog and in the process "realized what great lyrics and songs they were."

In all his years of touring, Elton had sorely neglected Europe, and now he decided to remedy the situation. Two preliminary comeback shows—the first he'd given for paying crowds in the fifteen months since the halfhearted Wembley Empire Pool gig with China in November '77—were booked for the Stockholm Concert Hall in the Swedish capital on February 5 and 6.

Those first gigs were tough for him. Later he admitted that up there onstage he'd suffered another attack of the shakes, and for the first part of the set, without Cooper, he felt "bloody lonely." But he offered a positive post-show assessment to the press: "It was a good start and it's going to get better."

From here the tour moved through Copenhagen, Hamburg, the Hague, Rotterdam, Amsterdam, Mannheim, Munich, Berlin, Cologne, Paris, Antwerp, Dusseldorf, Wiesbaden, Lausanne, Nice, Barcelona, and Madrid in the space of five weeks. For someone who had just suffered an exhaustion-provoked health scare, it was a crazily intensive schedule, and one that said everything about Elton's obsessive drive to perform, perform, perform.

He hit the UK in March and gathered momentum, playing Glasgow, Edinburgh, Newcastle, Preston, and Belfast before arriving in London for six shows at the Theatre Royal, Drury Lane. Every night, he'd play for a generous, if energy-sapping, three hours. After the last, triumphant gig, he threw a fancy dress party at the Legends nightclub. Elton turned up in a curly blond wig and told everyone he'd come as Rod Stewart.

Ten days later, at the gig in Oxford, the balding, thick-mustache-sporting Vladimir Kokonin slipped in among the audience. As the deputy director of Gosconcert, the Russian state's music promoter, he was there mingling with the crowd at the Oxford Theatre on something of an under-the-radar mission.

After watching the extensive, highly entertaining, and—most important—nonprovocative show, the next day Kokonin called his superior back home and gave his approval. A phone call was then made from the offices of Gosconcert in Moscow to the promoter Harvey Goldsmith in England. The organization would be honored to invite Elton John to become the first major Western rock star ever to perform in the USSR.

ELTON HAD FIRST suggested the idea over lunch with Harvey Goldsmith and John Reid. He wanted to play places he'd never been to before and wondered aloud, "What about Russia?" Goldsmith said he'd see what he could do. The promoter wrote a lengthy letter detailing the request, which was passed via the British Foreign Office to the Russian Ministry of Culture. This in turn had resulted in Kokonin's trip to Oxford.

The planned tour was an arrangement that suited both sides. There was a controversy brewing over the fact that Russia had been given the opportunity to stage the 1980 Olympics. In light of this, Elton's visit was planned as a cross-cultural warm-up to the international athletic and sports event. At the same time, it marked a softening of the USSR's hard-line attitudes, both in allowing Elton to perform in the first place and in permitting Western media to glimpse Russian life, or at least an edited version of it. For Elton, it was both a new adventure and a massive publicity coup. The only Western pop star who'd previously performed in Russia—three years before, in 1976—was the wholesome British singer Cliff Richard, hardly the kind of international name to attract worldwide press headlines.

In a way, Elton's invitation to perform behind the Iron Curtain was something of a backhanded compliment—having been completely vetted, he was deemed not to be a subversive figure. There was no way, for instance, that the far more dangerous Rolling Stones would have been afforded the same opportunity. For now, it seemed, Elton's announcement of his "bisexuality" was unknown or overlooked. If he had outwardly declared himself to be gay, then his visit to a country where a homosexual act carried with it the threat of a five-year prison sentence would surely have been nixed.

On May 20, the Elton John party boarded an Aeroflot flight from London to Moscow, the singer traveling with Ray Cooper, John Reid, Bob Halley, Harvey Goldsmith, Geoffrey Ellis, and his mother and stepfather. Western journalists invited onto the tour included David Wigg of the *Daily Mail* and Robert Hilburn, the *Los Angeles Times* writer of Elton's career-starting "turbo review" of the debut Troubadour show. Joining them to film a documentary of the excursion were Ian La Frenais and Dick Clement, better known as the writers of the British sitcom *The Likely Lads* than as directors.

Elton was nervous on the plane. He had no idea what might happen during the upcoming concerts and he was fretting about how he would be received by Russian audiences. At the same time, this was one of his main motivations for making the trip. "I didn't know what to expect," he said. "That makes you play harder."

He arrived in a country still under the control of Leonid Brezhnev, the Russian ruler who had held power since 1964 and who'd trampled the cultural freedoms gently instituted by his comparatively liberal predecessor Nikita Khrushchev. The Soviet Union in 1979 was suffering tight state control under a Politburo whose membership, in Brezhnev's policy of "mature socialism," consisted mostly of septuagenarians. An agricultural crisis had resulted in meat and dairy shortages and long queues outside largely empty shops. Understandably, amid the general populace, alcoholism was rife.

From Moscow, Elton and the others boarded the Red Arrow night train, which would carry them the four hundred miles northwest to Leningrad. "The Russians wouldn't let us fly," said Elton. "We had to go by train. We presumed there was something they didn't want us to see." To compensate, the Gosconcert organizers added to the train an opulently furnished coach normally reserved for high-ranking Soviet officials.

Shadowing them closely on the journey were two women from Gosconcert, along with an inscrutable young man named Sacha who everyone suspected was a member of the KGB. Before the train set off, fans on the platform threw their Elton John albums in through its windows to have them signed and returned. This slightly desperate sight caused Elton and Sheila to weep, suddenly overcome by the emotion of it all.

TICKETS FOR THE show on May 21, the first of four at the 3,800-seat Oktyabrsky Hall in Leningrad, were officially on sale for the equivalent of $9–$31 today—though on the black market they were fetching up to twenty times as much. The official program for the events revealed just how the Soviet officials viewed the star, with the stiffly chosen words "Audiences are specially attracted to the lyrical ballads and folk songs performed by R. Dwight." In the printed running order of the songs, "Rocket Man" had been translated as "Cosmonaut."

Surveying the crowd as he stepped onto the stage and bade them good evening (*"Dobry vecher"*), Elton could see row upon row of middle-aged to elderly officials and their wives. The real, younger fans were positioned toward the rear of the venue or upstairs in the balcony. Dressed in a flat cap and green shirt, his blue velvet trousers tucked into his boots in Cossack fashion, he sat down at the piano and picked out the opening arpeggio refrain of "Your Song" to enthusiastic if self-consciously restrained cheers from the back of the auditorium and polite applause from the front.

It was clear from the first few numbers that the Elton devotees knew all the words to his songs, having learned them from their bootleg records or mass-copied poor-quality tapes that had originated from Soviet soldiers recording West German radio broadcasts while stationed in East Germany. Still, the crowd reception remained muted until the singer launched into his first set-ending version of "I Heard It Through the Grapevine," prompting wilder roars. Elton thanked the audience in Russian, with a polite *"spasibo."* Between songs, girls tentatively approached the stage, proffering bouquets of flowers and even requesting midshow autographs, something that was never done in the West.

The second set managed to achieve real liftoff when, partway through the opening "Funeral for a Friend," panels rose on the stage to reveal Ray Cooper's enormous percussion setup and he began to animatedly thump a pair of timpani. The Russian officials in the crowd appeared uneasy, unsure of exactly how to deal with this audience of now excitable youths. Rock'n'roll had finally arrived in the Soviet Union, albeit in the slightly neutered form of grand piano and acoustic percussion.

Then the erupting moment came with the rambunctious introduction of "Saturday Night's Alright for Fighting," as Elton kicked away his piano stool and stood up to give the Russians their first taste of his full Jerry Lee Lewis routine. Kids rushed the stage. From here, he moved into "Pinball Wizard," ending the song with the impishly improvised addition of "Back in the USSR," even though he didn't really know the lyric. "It just came to me," he said, "and I was singing it before I realized I didn't know any of the words."

It seemed to be all over in a flash and Elton was dizzied by the experience. "I'm knocked out," he told Hilburn afterward. "This has to be my biggest achievement as an artist. I'm at a loss for words."

In the street three floors below his dressing room, thousands of ticketless fans broke through the security barriers and police cordon shouting, "Elton, Elton!" The singer waved at them from his window and threw tulips, his eyes brimming.

FOR THE NEXT show, officials tried to impose two rules on Elton after the scenes they'd witnessed on the opening night. First, they objected to his knocking over his piano stool, on the grounds that he was damaging Russian property (not to mention inciting the crowd to dangerous enthusiasm), and second, he must not sing "Back in the USSR." He complied with the first request and ignored the second. During the gig, whenever the fans stepped into the aisles, Soviet guards pushed them back into their seats. Onstage, Cooper urged them to "Come on!"

After the shows, everyone hung out in the "hard currency" bar of their hotel, where only Western money could be spent. There one night Elton confessed to Geoffrey Ellis that he had struck up a "close friendship" with Sacha, the aloof and good-looking suspected secret police agent. (Later, in Moscow, Elton would be shocked when Sacha brought his wife and children backstage to meet him.) One evening, as a great deal of champagne and vodka was being downed, Elton, with Ray Cooper on drums and live soundman Clive Franks stepping in on bass, entertained everyone in the restaurant with a lively disco-grooved take on "I Heard It Through the Grapevine."

The next morning, Elton awoke with a pounding hangover and missed a planned trip to the Winter Palace, leaving Cooper to attend alone. (Getting wind of the story, one British newspaper ran a headline that dramatically blared ELTON SNUBS RUSSIANS IN WINTER PALACE REVOLT.) Later that day, however, the star managed to rouse himself for a tour of the Summer Palace, where in the treasury of the Hermitage Pavilion he was shown a collection of jewelry and gold artifacts that of course appealed to his expensive tastes.

Arriving in Moscow on May 25 ahead of the first of the quartet of shows at the slightly smaller twenty-five-hundred-capacity Rossiya State Central Concert Hall, Elton was surprised to find that the Russian capital was a far prettier city than he'd imagined. To his eyes, it looked very much like Manchester.

In Moscow, there was a full program of activities set out for him during the days. He visited the still-under-construction Olympic Stadium and attended a soccer match between Dynamo Moscow and an opposing team culled from the ranks of the Red Army. Appearing as a guest on the austere set of a Russian talk show, he was asked innocuous questions about his image ("I wear clothes to express my feelings at the moment, and my moods change") and the influence his visit to the USSR might have on his music ("I think I've gleaned something from the atmosphere to write something").

The shows in Moscow were even more rigidly controlled, though on the final night, May 28, he clearly had nothing to lose. The performance was being broadcast live on the BBC back in Britain using a complex satellite relay system that went via Ukraine, and the pair were in fiery form. Leading into "Pinball Wizard," Cooper hoisted his percussion mallet aloft and banged a huge gong, which brought an ovation. Elton toasted the audience with a tumbler of vodka poured from a bottle he had kept atop his piano throughout the show. Downing the drink in one swig, he threw the empty glass over his left shoulder to smash on the stage.

As the Aeroflot jet taking them home lifted off the ground the next day, Elton and Bob Halley began screaming. The takeoff had revealed that their seats weren't secured to the floor. They had both been tipped backward by the thrust.

Happily and gratefully back on terra firma in London, Elton, invigorated by his Russian experience, faced what he felt was a highly negative interrogation by the British press corps. He was asked if he now supported Communism.

"I'm against bigotry and prejudice and persecution," he responded. "But if that stopped me playing my music, I wouldn't play here because of the [far-right political party] National Front or the campaign against homosexuality. You don't go in with guns blazing, saying, 'I want this and that.' You've got to approach things gently. I'd be very presumptuous to consider myself an ambassador of any sort, but I'm glad to do my bit."

He seemed keen to sing the praises of the USSR. "It was one of the most memorable and happy tours I've been on," he said. "The country is not dark, gray, or drab. It's very beautiful and the people are very warm. The only negative experiences I had were two or three hangovers from vodka."

Elton had clearly made an impression on the Soviet officials, who sanctioned the release of *A Single Man* on the state record label

Melodiya, though they retitled it *Poet* and omitted—for their lyrical content, not their inferior musical qualities—both "Part-Time Love" and "Big Dipper."

The *Daily Mail* had even given him a dynamic new nickname: Super Czar.

In the years to come, however, Elton would look back on photographs of himself taken in Russia and feel he looked prematurely aged and unhappy in them: "I look twenty or thirty years older. You can see how sad I am. I see those pictures and think, *How could I have looked at myself and not seen that there was something desperately wrong?*"

IF ELTON REMAINED emotionally unstable, it was a condition reflected in his next, unarguably poor album.

The singer had first met its producer, Pete Bellotte, in his days at the Top Ten club in Hamburg back in 1966, when he'd been with Bluesology and Bellotte had appeared on the same bill as the rhythm guitarist in Linda Laine and the Sinners. Since '72, Bellotte had been living in Munich and had forged a partnership with the electronic music pioneer Giorgio Moroder that had resulted in a string of innovative disco records including Donna Summer's 1977 hit "I Feel Love." When Elton had picked up a copy of that record, he'd been surprised to find the name of his old friend among the credits.

The two reconnected when Bellotte came backstage after one of the Drury Lane shows to say hello. It was there he first suggested that the pair of them might work together on a disco album. Elton was open to the idea, but only if Bellotte wrote and produced the music and he could appear only as a singer.

That summer of '79, Elton was in the south of France when he received a call from Bellotte saying the backing tracks were ready. Elton flew to Germany and in an eight-hour session at Musicland Studios recorded his vocal contributions to what would become the much-maligned *Victim of Love,* rush-released only two months later in October.

Conceived as a nonstop dance party marrying disco with rock, the thirty-five-minute album was the shortest of Elton's career. It began with an eight-minute version of Chuck Berry's "Johnny B. Goode," which tried to update the rock'n'roll classic for the age of the underlit dance floor. Later in the unrelenting running order, the unconvincing rebel groove of "Born Bad" and the unfortunately titled "Thunder in the Night" further dragged down the proceedings.

Most of Elton's contemporaries had made their disco-influenced records a year before—Rod Stewart ("Da Ya Think I'm Sexy?"), the Rolling Stones ("Miss You")—and even then perhaps a little too late. As a result, *Victim of Love* sounded like the death rattle of an expiring musical fad. The album made the Top Twenty in Australia and Norway but tanked everywhere else.

"It didn't do my career a lot of good," Elton admitted. "I don't regret doing it whatsoever. I wanted to make a record that people could dance to without taking the needle off. I can understand why it wasn't successful. I enjoyed it, [but] it was self-indulgent. I'm not ashamed of it. I'm not going to hide that record in the cupboard."

The critics were brutal. "*Victim of Love* hasn't a breath of life," declared Stephen Holden in *Rolling Stone*. "There's no getting around it," Lester Bangs stated in *The Village Voice*, "Elton's got problems."

ON THE UPSIDE, earlier in the year, in June, almost two years after they were recorded, three tracks from the sessions with Thom Bell had been released as an EP. The extracted single "Mama Can't Buy You Love" had produced Elton's biggest American hit in three years, repositioning him as a Top Ten artist when it reached number nine.

Off the back of this success, Elton returned with Ray Cooper to the States for his first major tour there since 1976, naming it Back in the USSA. As he had done in Europe and Russia, he faced the American audiences without his trademark spectacles. "The big glasses and the weird clothes were a way of hiding my shyness," he explained. "Since I started wearing contact lenses I've had to overcome that. I was forced to look people in the face, and you have to find confidence from somewhere to do that."

The tour started well, with two dates in Tempe, Arizona, and three in Berkeley successfully completed. But then, onstage at the

Universal Amphitheatre in Los Angeles, Elton fainted. A stomach bug had been making the rounds of the crew and it had finally caught up with the singer. He left the stage for ten minutes, was advised to force himself to throw up, and then returned to complete the three-hour show.

In New York, four weeks later, he played eight shows at the Palladium. The Elton-and-Ray double act was a well-oiled routine by this point. But not everyone was won over. Writing in *The New York Times,* Robert Palmer denounced the show as having "a supper club ambience . . . he's just about ready for Las Vegas."

And still the tour rolled ever onward, finishing with two weeks of concerts in Australia, which took him almost to the end of the year. The final gig tally of 1979 was impressive, if perhaps ill advised: Between February and December Elton had played a health-defying 125 shows.

THOSE CLOSEST TO him could see that he was propping himself up with booze and drugs. Only one person was brave enough to confront him about it.

On Boxing Day 1979, five days before the seventies ended, Elton turned up at Watford Football Club's Vicarage Road stadium to watch the team play Luton Town. He had a self-imposed rule that he would never take cocaine during the matches.

"But I could still do half a bottle of scotch," he laughs.

Elton had been up all night and looked terrible. After arriving at the stadium, he had a quick shave. Then the club manager he'd appointed, Graham Taylor, gestured to the singer to follow him into his office.

"I want to see you, Elton," said Taylor, holding a bottle of brandy.

"Here you are, fucking drink this," the manager angrily implored him. "It's what you want, isn't it? For fuck's sake, what's wrong with you? Look at the state of you. Get yourself together."

Elton was terrified by the outburst. Taylor then turned calm and conciliatory.

"He sat me down and said, 'Listen, you seem to want this more than anything else in life,'" remembers Elton. "I could take it from him 'cause I respected him. And he was only saying it out of friend-ship."

It was the eve of a new decade. As far as Elton's self-destructive lifestyle was concerned, there were two distinctly different ways it could go.

The whisky-drinking Donald Duck onstage in Central Park.

QUACK!

THE SONG SOUNDED LIKE A VIVID CONFESSION. In it, the singer depicts himself facedown in a cocaine-smeared mirror, where he's remained for twenty-four hours. He's virtually stupefied, but nevertheless he pledges his devotion to the drug, even though he knows this is a habit that has gone way too far. He snorts another line, which sends a chemical jolt to his run-down brain.

Titled "White Lady White Powder," it was the first track on side two of *21 at 33,* Elton's first new album of the 1980s, and one of the songs that marked the surprise lyrical return of Bernie Taupin. These were words of explicit divulgence written from the memory of Bernie, now clean, sung by someone who was not. Elton had arrived at the fork in the road where he could have decided to follow a route to a healthier lifestyle. Instead he chose to venture further down the path of heavy indulgence.

Theirs was a tentative reunion, and "White Lady White Powder" was one of three new collaborations that made the album, selected from the ten songs Elton and Bernie had completed in the summer of '79 in Grasse on the French Riviera. "The first song that we wrote when we got back together was a thing called 'Two Rooms at the End of the World,'" remembers Bernie.

"That was quite a good song," he adds, "but . . . most of [the new material] was shit."

As if awkwardly trying to revive a failed marriage, Elton insisted that the pair's working relationship remain open. He still demanded the right to see other songwriting partners. "It was necessary for us to go off and write with other people," he insists.

In the three years since *Blue Moves,* Bernie had continued to seem adrift in terms of a career plan. After his 1978 album with Alice Cooper, he'd collaborated on a coffee table book with the photographer Gary Bernstein, *Burning Cold,* contributing romantic stanzas that probably few actually read, since they were accompanied by *Playboy*-style shots of a model named Kay Sutton York. More recently, Bernie had readied a second solo album for release in 1980. This time around, rather than reading out his verses over music as he had done on his eponymous 1971 debut, he stepped up to the microphone to respectably sing on the apparently self-aggrandizingly named *He Who Rides the Tiger.*

Posing on the moody black-and-white cover with bow tie undone, leaning on a pool table like an upmarket shark, Bernie came across as far less cocksure in its Eaglesish songs of life in the California fast lane. One in particular, "Approaching Armageddon," was baldly autobiographical and found him casting his mind back over the last ten years and realizing how his life had irrevocably changed. From here he surveyed a landscape littered with rock casualty friends who'd succumbed to whisky and heroin, and he broached the subject of his failed marriage and its temporarily destructive effect on his writing. "Ten years on I'm wiser," he concluded, "but I'm still a farmer's son."

There had been no bust-up between himself and Elton and so there was no need for them to apologize to each other. Instead, when Bernie arrived in the south of France (along with his new wife, the fashion model Toni Russo), he and his estranged songwriting partner slipped back into their old familiar routine, even if both had been dented by their experiences in different ways.

The record *21 at 33* came out in May 1980, its name derived from a creative accounting that took in all of Elton's albums— including live LPs, compilations, and the belated 1975 U.S. release of *Empty Sky*—to tally it up as his twenty-first record, released in his thirty-third year. Recorded near Nice at Super Bear Studios, owing to technical problems it had to be completed in Los Angeles, where an increasingly unreliable Elton often didn't turn up, leaving Clive Franks to shoulder much of the burden when it came to their co-production credits. Still, there was a mood of nostalgia and reconciliation in the air, and even Dee Murray and Nigel Olsson made respective cameos on bass and drums.

Although not exactly a return to Elton's peak form of the early seventies, it was a step in the right direction. The opener, "Chasing the Crown," burst out of the speakers with a Roxy Music–ish art rock swagger and a Taupin lyric voicing the imagined thoughts of an omnipresent character who has swept through various moments in history, from the building of the Great Wall of China to the Boston Tea Party, in his quest for dominance. It was something of a misleading start, and apart from the deceptively upbeat "White Lady White Powder," much of *21 at 33* relied on ballads ranging from the wishy-washy ("Little Jeannie" and "Dear God," both co-written with Gary Osborne) to the quietly graceful ("Sartorial Eloquence," written with the British singer and gay rights activist Tom Robinson).

By this point, though, the critics seemed to be deaf to even Elton's better efforts. "Ever since 1975 . . . Elton has sounded confused, bitter, exhausted," Ken Tucker wrote in *Rolling Stone*. "We're now into the fifth year of the Elton John crisis, and frankly some of us here on the Elton watch are getting worried."

In the UK, the singer really put his back into the promotion of *21 at 33*, throwing open the doors of his Woodside mansion to the media. At the same time, a gossip column report in the *Daily Express* noted with some glee that his mum, Sheila, had recently moved away to Brighton on the English south coast and wouldn't now be on call to attend to his domestic chores. "Who will water Elton's newly transplanted thatch?" the writer bitchily mock-agonized.

In July, Elton invited BBC Radio One's Andy Peebles into his home. The broadcaster was given a guided tour by its proud owner, who showed off his now gargantuan record collection, which Elton, or an echo of the teenage Reg, explained that he still cleaned and cataloged himself. On a trip to the bathroom, Peebles was surprised to find a Rembrandt etching hanging on its wall.

Elton said he never worried about intruders at the mansion, joking that "the constant Dorothy Squires records blasting out of the loudspeakers tend to drive people away." Later, he revealed that he'd begun rehearsing for an upcoming American tour with Nigel

Olsson and Dee Murray. Ten years on, he had come full circle. His new band was basically his old band.

His mood of reflection lingered when he was interviewed for a BBC TV series titled *Best of British*. With characteristic honesty, he spoke about how he now viewed his 1970s. "Great from a career point of view," he said, "but from a personal point of view . . . terrible. A lot of the time, I was a complete mess. Around 1975, especially, I started acting like a real spoiled brat. There are parts of it I can't even remember."

RETURNING TO THE Troubadour a decade on perhaps seemed a touch overly sentimental, and so, on August 25, 1980, the tenth anniversary to the day of that life-changing event, Elton marked the occasion by playing a set at the Palomino, the country music honky-tonk venue in North Hollywood. In remembrance of a more distant era, he even performed Jim Reeves's "He'll Have to Go," a staple of the sixteen-year-old Reggie's pub piano sets back at the Northwood Hills.

To Elton, this show rang with more resonance than the Hollywood-star-packed fifth-anniversary gig at the Troubadour in his troubled year of 1975. "I guess that's because I always figured that I'd be around for five years," he told Robert Hilburn afterward. "But there were times when I wondered if I'd make it through for ten."

The set list for the upcoming U.S. tour similarly harked back to his heyday, with inclusions of "Tiny Dancer" from *Madman Across the Water*, "All the Girls Love Alice" from *Goodbye Yellow Brick Road*, and the still affecting "Someone Saved My Life Tonight" from *Captain Fantastic and the Brown Dirt Cowboy*. If the shows were something of a victory lap, then it was one he had earned, although the tickets didn't always sell out and some radio station programmers seemed to have forgotten his name. Up there under the lights, the flashiness of old had been reinstated in his stagewear: a Spanish toreador jacket here, a hotel doorman suit festooned with piano keys there.

Even if he didn't have the box-office pull he had once enjoyed, there was one surefire way to attract attention: stage a free concert on a massive scale. In a deal organized with the New York City authorities and with sponsorship from Calvin Klein, it was announced that Elton was to play the Great Lawn in Central Park on Saturday, September 13.

As promotional stunts went, it was peerless, and moreover, it was to benefit the city. Revenue raised from merchandise sold that day—$75,000, as it turned out—was to go to the restoration of key areas of the park, including those that would be trampled by his fans. Forty-eight hours before the show, people were already camping out on the Great Lawn and roping off choice areas for themselves, even as the stage was being constructed.

On the afternoon of the momentous gig, the sun had burned away the early autumnal haze of morning cloud, and viewed from the stage, close to half a million people were packed together as far as the eye could see. Backstage, Elton had been knocking back whisky, and as a result, come three o'clock when he arrived onstage, if looking chunkier than he had a year before, he was in feisty form. The original three-piece band comprising himself, Dee Murray, and Nigel Olsson was augmented by James Newton Howard on keyboards, and guitarists Tim Renwick and Richie Zito, both new faces found during the sessions for *A Single Man* and *21 at 33*.

As the foreboding chords of "Funeral for a Friend" echoed off the skyline surrounding the park, giving way to "Love Lies Bleeding," Elton rocked back and forth at the piano in a sporty lime-green, azure, and black outfit adorned with yellow circular mirrors and completed by a white Stetson, making him look like a cowboy out for a glamorous jog.

To gain a better vantage point, people began to climb the trees that edged the immense area while the singer rolled out the hits: "Goodbye Yellow Brick Road," "Rocket Man," "Philadelphia Freedom," "Sorry Seems to Be the Hardest Word."

At the end of the first set, he reemerged in his piano-patterned suit and peaked cap. Facing the greatest number of people he had ever performed before, Elton was now determined to stun. He attacked "Saturday Night's Alright for Fighting" with throat-shredding passion, and partway through, he booted away the piano stool. It was the move that had served him well since the first time Reggie had stunned the church hall audience with the Corvettes back in Pinner. Over the years it had enlivened and sometimes saved his shows. Today, it provoked mad cheers from the massive crowd. Girls jumped onto the shoulders of their boyfriends and waved Union Jack flags and howled in the direction of the stage.

Hitting the opening chord stab of "Bennie and the Jets," Elton stood up from the piano and turned to the audience to further stir them up. But as the song kicked in, he scanned his eyes around the stage looking angry about some onstage sound problem and started maniacally barking the song's verses and screeching the choruses in his demented Monty Python voice. In his extreme effort to entertain a crowd this vast, he was in danger of overdoing it. When he moved into the piano solo at the end, it was too intense, too long, and rescued only when the band launched back in to close the nearly ten-minute extended rendition.

"We're gonna do a song written by a friend of mine who I haven't seen for a long time," he said, introducing his cover of "Imagine." Elton looked across the park in the direction of the Dakota, adding, "He only lives just over the road. He hasn't made a record for ages but he's doing one at the moment." Grinning and riffing on Lennon's lyric, he sang, "You might say I'm a screamer." Each time he hit the line "Imagine all the people," he turned again to look incredulously back at the audience, an unimaginable number of people to be here watching a man playing a piano.

The scene astounded Pat Pipolo, the MCA promotion man who'd been with Elton since the beginning of his American campaign ten years before. "All you saw was a sea of faces," he remembered. "I just said to myself, *My God, from the Troubadour to this.* Unreal. Just unreal."

When Elton left the stage ahead of the final act, there was a lengthy pause. The ultimate costume change seemed to be taking forever. Behind the stage, aided by his PA, Bob Halley, the singer was struggling into the costume especially designed by Bob Mackie for the Central Park show. But in the heat of the moment, Elton couldn't remember how to juggle his limbs into it: He was trying to force his legs into armholes and arms into leg holes.

At last he returned to the stage, to gasps and wild applause, dressed as Donald Duck. In his blue bib and bird-beaked cap, fat white tail and yellow legs with enormous webbed feet, he could barely walk. He even had trouble sitting down at the piano. He had been drinking all day, and the whisky seemed to take effect as he began to sing "Your Song," dissolving into fits of giggles and punctuating key lines with an enthusiastic "Quack!"

No one, not least the singer himself, could ever have predicted that ten years after its release, the sullen-looking man on the cover of the *Elton John* album would have been performing its signature song for close to half a million people in Central Park while dressed as a cartoon duck.

WHEN IT WAS all over, an after-show bash was held aboard the SS *Peking,* a ship docked at the South Street Seaport on the East River. Elton turned up in a striped blazer and straw boater accessorized with a badge that read BITCH. He hung out with Calvin Klein, Andy Warhol, and, for the first time in years, John Lennon and Yoko Ono.

Wiped out after the Central Park gig, arriving at the postshow party on the SS Peking.

He was understandably exhausted after the show, however, and didn't stay at the party long.

HIS PROFILE DULY raised, in the days and weeks that followed, Elton seemed to accept every media invitation, especially those that put him back on American TV screens. Four nights after Central Park, he was interviewed by Tom Snyder on NBC's *The Tomorrow Show,* appearing in a colorful variation of the doorman outfit patterned with arrows that he reckoned made him look like "a freaked-out parking attendant."

Had it sunk in yet, Snyder wondered, how many people had turned out to watch Elton's show in the park? "There was a party afterwards," the singer explained. "I went there for about three seconds and blinked and then it began to hit home. So many people want to come and say 'Fantastic!' and everything. I just went back to the hotel and stayed on my own and, y'know, got out a dirty book." He erupted with mischievous laughter.

"If you were to start off today to be a rock star," Snyder went on, "could you do again what you've done?"

"A lot of what has happened to me," Elton mused, "was being in the right place at the right time. Just sheer fortune. I got pressured into coming to America the first time where it all happened. I've been lucky. I've been through a lot of things in ten years. I wouldn't change anything. Even the terrible times and the depressing times."

A month later, during a ramshackle and amateurish episode of Phil Donahue's talk show, filmed in Chicago and syndicated nationally, Elton remained in a ruminative frame of mind. "I look back on the last ten years," he said, "and I think, Cor, you're thirty-three, and I've just got the enthusiasm to start touring again and to make records. And I think, after that ten years . . . and a hell of a lot has happened . . . thank God I've got some enthusiasm left. If it all ended tomorrow, I would be quite happy selling records in a record store. As long as I was involved in music."

In Los Angeles, on *The Tonight Show* with Johnny Carson, Elton admitted that after Russia's invasion of Afghanistan in December 1979, there was no way he would consider returning to play in the

Soviet Union. "I was very disappointed when they invaded Afghanistan," he deadpanned, "because I was growing some of my best pot there."

On November 6, he returned to the Forum in L.A. for four consecutive sold-out dates. Backstage one night, Elton was introduced to Sting, lead singer of the Police, the latest British act to break in America. In a photo opportunity, the two posed together, the older star symbolically endorsing this younger challenger. Looking back, Elton would wince when realizing how ludicrous he must have looked at that moment, dressed as he was in a Minnie Mouse costume. "Minnie Mouse was pretty bad," he cringes. "Sting is looking at me as if to say, 'Fucking hell, what's going on here?'"

It was the point when Elton realized that maybe, just maybe, his stagewear had reached the point of ridiculousness. "For me, up until 1976, it was just completely done on instinct," he says. "Then it became a question of 'What do I wear?' I think everything you do at the beginning of a career on impulse is exciting. Then you have those five years at the top, which are done on adrenaline and instinct and you find your place, and then it's not adrenaline and instinct anymore. You lose that innocence, you lose that naïveté, you lose that edge. Then you make mistakes. Those five years, I never thought about anything. And then when you start thinking, that's when things start to go wrong."

HE WAS IN Australia, on the final leg of the 1980 tour, flying from Brisbane to Melbourne. His private plane touched down and John Reid boarded it to tell Elton the shocking news: John Lennon had been murdered in New York.

"I just didn't believe it," he said afterward. "It didn't sink in."

Numb and unsure what to do, he arranged for a special service to be held at St. Patrick's Cathedral in Melbourne. There he sang Psalm 23 ("The Lord is my shepherd / I shall not want . . .")

He knew that Yoko would be deluged with cards and messages of condolence, so instead, he simply sent her and his godson Sean an enormous chocolate cake with a message: "Love from Elton."

Onstage, on December 11 at Melbourne's aptly named Memorial

Drive, he introduced his version of "Imagine" with the words "This week the worst thing in the world happened. This is a song written by an incredible man." After performing the peace anthem, he was overwhelmed with sadness and had to briefly leave the stage.

Bernie was in Los Angeles when he heard about Lennon's death. He couldn't watch the news, couldn't read a paper. Instead, he picked up his pen and wrote a lyric titled "Empty Garden (Hey, Hey Johnny)," imagining the New York venue where Lennon had played his last show. Later, Elton set it to music, though, finding the song too emotional to perform onstage, he did so only rarely—most memorably two years later, with Yoko and Sean in attendance, on the stage at Madison Square Garden, where he felt the loss of Lennon even more.

THERE WAS NO Elton John tour in 1981, although he did stage one private concert as a special request. That year, Prince Andrew was set to turn twenty-one, and Elton was asked to perform at the party, to be held at Windsor Castle. He chose to appear with Ray Cooper in the stripped-down two-man routine. Sound-checking inside the castle's ballroom, Elton surveyed the rows of empty golden chairs awaiting the extended membership of the royal family. He suddenly thought, *Oh, Christ.* He'd never been more nervous about the prospect of any concert in all his years of performing.

Come showtime, Elton was now petrified, arriving onstage to be faced by the intimidating sight of the royals gazing up at him (including Prince Charles and his fiancée, Lady Diana Spencer), along with their four hundred guests. The show, however, went without a hitch. As with that starmaking debut show at the Troubadour, when Elton was under pressure, he often played his best. At the back of the hall, soundman Clive Franks, wearing a black dinner suit rented for the occasion from the High Street tailor Moss Bros., expertly oversaw the proceedings. Partway through the show, Princess Margaret crept up beside Franks to sneak a cigarette.

At the end of the set, Elton and Ray took their bows and a twenties-style jazz band replaced them on the platform. Out on the floor, Diana Spencer asked Elton if he'd like to dance with her. Together they giggled and shuffled and kicked their way through improvised steps vaguely resembling the Charleston. After a buffet dinner in an adjoining room, Princess Anne led the singer back into the ballroom, where a DJ was now spinning records. It was, thought Elton, the quietest disco on earth.

He was dancing with Princess Anne when he heard a cut-glass-accented voice in his ear inquire, "Can we join you?" Elton turned to face the Queen, and just at that moment, the DJ cut into Bill Haley's "Rock Around the Clock." And so it was that Reg found himself bopping with Her Majesty Queen Elizabeth II—dressed in peach, her handbag dangling from her arm, her diamond tiara glittering under the ballroom lights—to one of the records he'd mouthed along to back in his bedroom as a shy, chubby youngster.

Now, IT SEEMED, he'd seen and done it all.

Elton had been extraordinarily famous for almost eleven years. It had left him a touch unhinged, and an uncertain future stretched out before him.

He was still indulging in dangerous habits, even though he was fully aware of the damage they might cause him.

He still didn't know quite who he really was or quite where he was going.

He'd work it all out, eventually.

EPILOGUE

"I REALLY DIDN'T SORT OUT my personal persona until I got sober, to be honest with you, till I was forty-three."

In the dining room of his Holland Park townhouse, Elton is talking about his struggles with his identity and his difficult journey through the 1980s, which resulted, in July 1990, in his undergoing rehab at the Parkside Lutheran Hospital in Chicago.

"My life was just totally built about music," he says, "and the amount of work that I did was astonishing. I'm not complaining 'cause I loved every minute of it. But my whole life really was about work and it wasn't about . . . y'know . . ."

He hesitates, trying to find the right words.

"I was still stuck," he continues. "I had this huge, successful career and then this very unsure private life. I was very immature. There were a lot of complications.

"One thing I'm grateful for [about] the drugs was that in the end they didn't kill me. The only reason is 'cause I still worked while I was doing them. I didn't sit at home. I still made albums, I still went on tour. The work probably suffered for it. It absolutely *did* suffer for it. I'll hold my hand up and say it. But at least I worked."

Elton has joked in the past that no one told him that "the 'me' decade"—the phrase coined by writer Tom Wolfe for the seventies—actually ended in 1979. Instead, he barreled through the subsequent ten years ruled by his cocaine and alcohol addictions while fulfilling a characteristically unrelenting recording and touring schedule.

Through his burgeoning desire to start a family and his growing belief that he could live a "straight" life, the singer surprised the world by becoming engaged to, and in 1984 marrying, the German recording engineer Renate Blauel. Their union would last four years. By 1986, though, Elton's now acute coke and booze habits had begun to result in messy performances both onstage and, with that year's *Leather Jackets* album, in the studio.

"I was so coked out," he admits. "I made that album in Holland. I was just on coke all the time. Some good songs, but I'm ashamed of where I was on that album."

During his live shows of the period, Elton became increasingly agitated about both his playing and the reactions of the crowds. "That's the worst thing about performing when you've done a line," he points out. "You're so paranoid that you're too fast, too slow, [wondering] whether the audience likes it. It's like, *Fucking hell, awww.*

"Even though I was a fucking nightmare in the eighties," he adds, "I still loved my music enough to haul my arse out of bed and go and play it. Sometimes not very well, unfortunately. But how would I know? 'Cause I can't remember half of it."

What, for him, constituted a "line" of cocaine?

"A line for me was an ounce . . . half an ounce. I couldn't do [just] a line. I know what I'm like . . . I have to have everything *now.* So with drugs I'd have to have half an ounce. Two or three days up at a time. I think four days in Australia once."

At points, Elton was in serious danger of losing the plot. In one highly memorable incident, after having stayed up for days on end at the Inn on the Park hotel in London, in a deluded state, he phoned his office to ask if someone could "do something" about how windy it was outside.

Year by year, he gradually began to isolate himself in his drug taking, to the point where he ended up taking cocaine, sometimes as alarmingly frequently as every four minutes, when he was entirely alone. "Towards the end I was in this house . . . and I was upstairs just doing it on my own in my bedroom. It's like, *Urgh.* There would be six months when I was perfectly clean, but there were times when I wasn't. So it was up and down. It was very off-kilter one moment, back on track the next. It was all over the place."

Considering the extent of his drug use, it's incredible, really, that

Elton came out the other end without having done himself permanent physical damage.

"Yeah, it's only a little nose," he laughs. "I don't know how it's still fucking there."

THERE WERE OTHER low points. In 1987, *The Sun* newspaper in the UK seemed to pursue a vendetta against Elton, printing entirely unfounded front-page stories about him. One claimed that he had paid underage rent boys for sex. Another, bizarrely, stated that he'd had the voice boxes of the guard dogs at his home surgically removed because their barking at night was disturbing his sleep. He successfully sued the paper for £1 million in damages.

The following year, in a mood to purge, Elton decided to get rid of the mountains of possessions cluttering his Woodside mansion. Almost two thousand personal items were put up for auction at Sotheby's in London, raising more than $8 million: four entire catalogs' worth of jewelry, glasses, furniture, and ornaments, plus virtually all of his stage costumes. The owners of the Hard Rock Cafe in Los Angeles bought the light-up ELTON specs he'd worn onstage at the Hollywood Bowl for almost $17,000. A rep for the Dr. Martens footwear company purchased his outsized *Tommy* boots for close to $30,000.

Through it all, his presidency of Watford FC helped him maintain some kind of equilibrium. Under his stewardship, the team rose swiftly through the leagues. "It was an incredible, stabilizing thing," he stresses. "Going from the Fourth Division to the First, it was magical. Being around people who cared about me and who were very honest, y'know. 'I don't like your new record.' 'Why are you wearing that?' I didn't find it offensive. I just found them down to earth. Without that, fuck knows what would've happened. I would've gone completely off the rails."

Moreover, his association with the Watford club underlined another truth about Elton—at heart he isn't a loner, and he thrives when he's part of a team. "My whole career's been involved in camaraderie," he says. "When you *are* successful, the actual feeling of it and the sharing of it, it's just so incredible. I don't think I'd have enjoyed myself so much without having the relationship with Bernie. Y'know, if I'd have been writing songs on my own, it would not have been the same. The fact that we are a team has enhanced it."

AFTER 21 *at* 33 in 1980, his and Bernie's writing partnership was fully recemented on 1983's *Too Low for Zero,* with its hits "I'm Still Standing" and "I Guess That's Why They Call It the Blues." Nevertheless, their output continued to be wildly inconsistent in terms of its quality control right up until the turn of the millennium. They are divided when it comes to which album of the post-seventies, pre-2000 era they consider to be their worst. Elton thinks it's undoubtedly 1986's hopelessly weak and ultimately forgettable *Leather Jackets.* "Gus Dudgeon did his best" he says, grinning, "but you can't work with a loony."

"*Leather Jackets* was just awful," Bernie agrees, while rating 1997's *The Big Picture* slightly below it. "I think that is probably the worst album we ever made. Some of the songs on there are actually not bad songs. It's just that the production is abysmally cold and technical.

"I have no regrets, because we're in good company," the lyricist decides, breezily. "We made some horribly crappy records, but then so did a lot of our contemporaries. The Stones, McCartney, even John [Lennon] made some toilet flushers. That's nothing to be ashamed of. If something interests you, try it. If you fall flat on your ass, then you admit it. And we've done that countless times."

In the summer of 2000, Elton and Bernie sat on the balcony of the singer's mountainside house on Mont Boron in Nice and began reminiscing about the thirty-three years that had passed since they met in 1967. Together, they came to a grim realization when it came to the fruits of their collaboration since reestablishing their working relationship with 21 *at* 33.

"We said, 'It's not been fucking good enough,'" Elton remembers. "We made a vow with each other on that balcony. Let's start making albums we can be proud of again. I made albums when I didn't want to make albums, 'cause the record company wanted me to. And I thought, *I can't do that anymore.* I said, 'Let's just start again.'"

The duo's renaissance began with *Songs from the West Coast* in 2001, a return to their warmly produced 1970s sound. Among its standout songs were "I Want Love," "This Train Don't Stop There Anymore," and the affecting "American Triangle," written about the beating, torture, and murder of the twenty-one-year-old gay student Matthew Shepard in Wyoming in 1998.

This sense of revitalized creativity continued through *Peachtree Road* in 2004, the sparse and reflective *The Diving Board* nine years later, and the upbeat and rockier *Wonderful Crazy Night* in 2016. Meanwhile, in 2006, the pair produced a sequel to *Captain Fantastic and the Brown Dirt Cowboy*. But whereas the lyrics on the original album had tackled his and Bernie's years of pre-fame struggle, its successor, titled *The Captain & the Kid,* was concerned with the dizzying effects of their startling success in the seventies.

One song in particular, "Tinderbox," dealt with how Elton and Bernie's relationship had become combustible by 1976. "It's very, very dangerous to live in each other's pockets," says Bernie, "because eventually you rub up together too much and fireworks start. There was a point where everywhere you went, it was Elton John, Elton John . . . You couldn't sneeze without hearing one of our songs. Elton was playing stadiums, our records were coming in at number one. Where do you go from there?

"If you become that obscenely popular," he reasons, "you hit the bridge and you either fall off it or you limp across to the other side. You're never gonna continue with that phenomenal success. Nobody does. It's impossible. But you can survive and reimagine yourself and remain artistically viable. In a way, that is a huge relief."

Looking back, Elton finds it utterly remarkable that his and Bernie's partnership *has* managed to survive. "Even though we live so far apart," he says, "we're so in sync after all this time. There's a natural telepathy between us. We've never, ever screamed or shouted. Which is extraordinary when you look at some of the great partnerships that have fallen afoul of each other because of jealousies and egos. It's never been the case with him and me."

Of all the songs the pair have written, the singer feels that the reflections of their early days in "We All Fall in Love Sometimes" on *Captain Fantastic* best sums up their relationship.

"I find it very difficult to listen to," says Elton, turning emotional. " 'We All Fall in Love Sometimes' is about two people whose love for each other goes beyond . . . I dunno . . . I'm kinda misting up when I say it now. We love each other and we're not close to each other, but I can't imagine my life without him being in it."

IN EFFECT, ELTON and Bernie have become the characters the latter dreamed up for them on *Captain Fantastic and the Brown Dirt Cowboy*. On his ranch near Santa Ynez in California, the Stetson-wearing lyricist lives the life of the modern cowhand: raising cutting horses for riding competitions, attending rodeos, and involving himself in the Professional Bull Riders organization. Unlike in the 1970s, he's very rarely recognized by fans in his day-to-day life. His is an enviable existence involving enormous wealth and relative anonymity.

"Luckily now, my face has become less recognizable, thank God," he says with a laugh. "Up to the point of the *Blue Moves* album, my face was on every album cover very, very prominently and I was very visible at the shows. Back then, it was as if I was a performer, because if I went in record stores or clothes stores or on the street, people actually recognized me. Now, that's dissipated.

"My name obviously still gets recognized. Hand over your credit card and it's like an American Express commercial—you don't know my face but you know my name. And I'm really very happy for that. I could never, never, never be in the position Elton is. I'd kill myself, y'know, because I'm just so, so happy that I can just pretty much go anywhere and do anything and live my life."

As Captain Fantastic, meanwhile, Elton remains the superstar who jets around the world, performing a still incredible number of shows each year (and still heckling heavy-handed security guards from the stage when he feels they're stopping his fans from enjoying themselves: most recently in June 2016 in Leicester, England, where he lambasted the bouncers as "pricks").

In terms of his personal life post–John Reid, in the early eighties Elton was in a relationship with Gary Clarke, an Australian twelve years his junior (and the subject of the 1982 hit "Blue Eyes"), while at the other end of that decade, his boyfriend was the real estate agent Hugh Williams from Atlanta, Georgia, whose example he followed in deciding that he had to enter rehab.

Then, in the autumn of 1993, a mutual friend brought a Canadian advertising executive named David Furnish along to a dinner party Elton was throwing at his Woodside mansion, where the other guests included Richard Gere, Sylvester Stallone, and Princess Diana. Elton and Furnish were immediately attracted to each other. The next day, Elton called David and they met in London for dinner alone, becoming inseparable from that point on.

Furnish seemed to offer the stability that Elton had been craving, resulting in their civil partnership in 2005 and their wedding in 2014, the year that same-sex marriage became legal in the UK. Elton had always wanted to be a dad, which seemed to him somehow incompatible with his life as a gay man. Through surrogacy, the couple are now the fathers of two sons, Zachary and Elijah.

Elton and David's marriage has not been without its controversies—not least in recent years when Furnish took control of his husband's business affairs, causing Elton to jokingly nickname him Yoko. But Elton admits that David has given him some perspective on his past achievements, which, in his drive to push ever onward with his career, the singer is often reluctant to look back on.

"You can't stop and pat yourself on the back," he insists. "[But] David is always saying, 'You've got to do that sometimes.'"

These days, Elton is a far more centered and happy individual. The addictive side of his nature now finds satisfaction in the far less dangerous pursuit of collecting art and photographs. At the same time, his previous experiences and altruistic impulses have down the years seen him, as the self-styled Uncle Elt, throwing his arms around those who have suffered similar troubles, whether it be George Michael or Rufus Wainwright. In this way, he's proved himself to be something of a caregiver for the damaged and famous, as difficult as that has sometimes been for him.

"You get concerned about people," he explains. "When I was doing a load of drugs, George Harrison tried to help me and I just went, 'Woo, fuck off.' You don't want to know. It doesn't mean to say you don't like them as a person. But you might not wanna be near them because they know what you're doing and they're right."

Arguably, as Bernie points out, Elton's greatest achievement other than his musical legacy has been the creation of his nonprofit AIDS Foundation in 1992, which has over the years raised in excess of $200 million spent on care and educational programs.

"Personally, I don't think he's given enough credit for it," says Bernie. "But I don't think that's what he's in it for, so I'm not gonna make a stink about it. In my mind, he's the other Bono. One of the sad things about it is that I still think that AIDS has this stigma about it. It's like, 'Okay, your foundation makes an incredible contribution,' but there's still that little stigma—it's about AIDS, it's not about world relief. Somebody's got to do it, y'know.

"There are kids today that only see him in a certain light—that Elton John as he is today, larger than life, Sir Elton, mega lifestyle. But, I mean, he's an *extraordinary* individual."

IT WAS THE singer's charitable work that led him in 1998 to be knighted by his former dancing partner Queen Elizabeth II. Elsewhere, despite the protestations of his younger self, Elton has indeed ended up doing residencies in Las Vegas, most notably the Red Piano show, in which his performance of "Someone Saved My Life Tonight" was backdropped by a David LaChapelle film that even featured a facsimile of the gas oven back at Furlong Road in which the singer halfheartedly tried to end his life. From time to time, Elton will insist that he plans to cut back on the number of live performances he gives. Now, as then, still impossibly driven, he never really does.

Since *Songs from the West Coast,* he's given up worrying about his chart positions. He admits it was tough. "I've not been interested in singles," he says. "We'd got to a point where we were trying to do stuff because the record company were saying, 'We need a single, we need a single.' And it's hard to let go of that situation when you've been successful for years and used to having hit singles, especially in America. But there comes a point where you have to admit that you're not gonna get played on the radio in America because it's ageist. There's a whole stream of different music come along now. And you have to face up to it."

Ultimately, one thing still propels him forward: his sheer love of music. "It's never died," he says. "It burns as bright in me now as it did when I first started. I still get the same kick going into a record store. I still can go in and come out with an armful of stuff that I don't have and I still get the same excitement. I refuse to get free ones, I'll fucking buy it. And if I like it, I'll buy fifty of them and say to people, 'Listen to this.' "

Elsewhere, in terms of regrets? He's had a few.

"If I could relive it, the first five or six years of my career I would do it exactly the same," he states. "If you had the chance of doing the next ten to fifteen years again, you'd make some alterations. Absolutely. You'd make some visual alterations, you'd make some personal alterations. But, the first five or six years, I don't regret any of it."

LET US LEAVE him now, then: Reginald Kenneth Dwight from Pinner, insecure music addict trapped inside the body of Sir Elton Hercules John, international rock legend, recovered drug addict, gay rights champion, and now husband, father, and pillar of the establishment. At this time of his life, looking back, he sometimes thinks about how he will be remembered.

"An overview of my career is usually . . . glasses . . . homosexuality . . . tantrums," he concludes with a laugh, considering the sheer ridiculousness of it all. "But the music was pretty phenomenal, y'know."

And as Reg would no doubt tell you, the records are all that matter in the end.

ACKNOWLEDGMENTS

FOR THEIR GENEROUS INTERVIEW TIME and for quotes that made their way into this book, thanks to Elton John, Bernie Taupin, Alice Cooper, Kiki Dee, Rick Frio, Davey Johnstone, David Larkham, Nigel Olsson, Kenny Passarelli, Pat Pipolo, Annie Reavey, Russ Regan, "Legs" Larry Smith, and the late Gus Dudgeon. For additional transcripts, thanks to Nick De Grunwald and George Scott.

For still continuing to employ me on the leaky boat that is music journalism and allowing me to disappear (again) to write this book, thanks to Danny Eccleston, Phil Alexander, Andrew Male, Jenny Bulley, Ian Harrison, Mark Wagstaff, Matt Turner, Matt Mason, Ted Kessler, Niall Doherty, Paul Stokes, Chris Catchpole, Sam Inglis, and David Glasper. To my writer pals, let's keep on keepin' on: Sylvia Patterson (the best music journalist in the known universe), Simon Goddard (whose suggested title for this book was both hilarious and unprintable), Dorian Lynskey, John Aizlewood, Craig McLean, Pat Gilbert, Keith Cameron, Mark Blake, Andrew Perry, Alexis Petridis, Andy Fyfe, John Harris, Eamonn Forde, Louise Millar and Amy Raphael.

To all at Penguin Random House in New York who helped to make this happen, including the brilliant Susanna Porter (who instantly "got" this book), Priyanka Krishnan, Greg Kubie, Alexandra Coumbis, Emily Hartley, and Janet Wygal.

To the ever cool customer that is my agent, Kevin Pocklington, at Jenny Brown Associates, especially for reminding me that I'd had this book idea and pushing me to get cracking on it.

Big up to all my nonwriterly mates: the inspirational "Blue" Anth

Brown, Mike Brown, Derek Hood (for reminding me Elton was sitting at the Wurly every time I went up to the loft), Steve Aungle, Steve Wilkins (for his Shoreditch College super-sleuthing), all the Daves—Dave Black, Dave Scott, Dave Tomlinson—Alan Shaw, Robbie and Parm Gunn-Hamilton, Aidan Rose, Syann Gilroy, Nick Walker, Nick Roberts, Jon Mills, Sean Cooney, James Hall, Paul Esposito, Douglas Anderson, Duncan Jordan, Craig Stevens ("Deadline!"), Ben Gregor, and Chris Metzler.

Thanks to my very occasional *Last of the Summer Wine* walking partners Jon Bennett (with me every step of the way) and Craig McNeil ("Mon the Horse!"). For helping me in a more general way, even if it was just listening to me bang on, I thank Matt Everitt, Gordon Thomson, Matt Delargy, Neil Jaworski, Clare Hollister, Ian Beck, and Ross Bennett. Thanks also to Kevin Smalley, Caroline Theakstone, and Joe Medina at Getty Images and to Laura Watts at Rex.

To my family up in Scotland: Heather, Brian, Caroline, Ryan, Lauren, Jimmy, and John, and my uncle Jim Herschell for lending me his Elton LPs when I was a nipper. And to the still saintly-patient Karen for her bathtime reading of the pages of this book (and just basically *everything*) and to the ever gorgeous Amelia, for bringing me food and beer and making "hilarious" "jokes" about my gray hair and "big nose," and for putting up with me saying she's turning into a fourteen-year-old goth/emo . . . which she is, by the way. Love both of you to the moon and back.

DISCOGRAPHY

Albums · *1969–1980*

EMPTY SKY

Empty Sky · Val-hala · Western Ford Gateway · Hymn 2000 · Lady What's Tomorrow · Sails · The Scaffold · Skyline Pigeon · Gulliver · Hay-Chewed · Reprise

US: MCA MCA-2130, JANUARY 1975   UK: DJM DJLPS 403, JUNE 1969

ELTON JOHN

Your Song · I Need You To Turn To · Take Me to the Pilot · No Shoe Strings on
Louise · First Episode at Hienton · Sixty Years On · Border Song · The Greatest
Discovery · The Cage · The King Must Die

US: UNI 73090, AUGUST 1970   UK: DJM DJLPS 406, APRIL 1970

TUMBLEWEED CONNECTION

Ballad of a Well-Known Gun · Come Down in Time · Country Comfort · Son of
Your Father · My Father's Gun · Where To Now St. Peter? · Love Song ·
Amoreena · Talking Old Soldiers · Burn Down the Mission

US: UNI 73096, OCTOBER 1970   UK: DJM DJLPS 410, OCTOBER 1970

FRIENDS—ORIGINAL SOUNDTRACK RECORDING

Friends · Honey Roll · Variation on Friends Theme (The First Kiss) · Seasons ·
Variation on Michelle's Song (A Day in the Country) · Can I Put You On · Mi-
chelle's Song · I Meant to Do My Work Today (A Day in the Country) · Four
Moods · Seasons Reprise

US: PARAMOUNT PAS-6004, MARCH 1971   UK: PARAMOUNT SPFL 269, MARCH 1971

11-17-70 (17-11-70 IN UK)

Take Me to the Pilot · Honky Tonk Women · Sixty Years On · Bad Side of the Moon · Burn Down the Mission (including My Baby Left Me · Get Back)

US: UNI 93105, APRIL 1971   UK: DJM DJLPS 414, APRIL 1971

MADMAN ACROSS THE WATER

Tiny Dancer · Levon · Razor Face · Madman Across the Water · Indian Sunset · Holiday Inn · Rotten Peaches · All the Nasties · Goodbye

US: UNI 93120, NOVEMBER 1971   UK: DJM DJLPH 420, NOVEMBER 1971

HONKY CHÂTEAU

Honky Cat · Mellow · I Think I'm Going to Kill Myself · Susie (Dramas) · Rocket Man (I Think It's Going to Be a Long, Long Time) · Salvation · Slave · Amy · Mona Lisas and Mad Hatters · Hercules

US: UNI 93135, MAY 1972   UK: DJM DJLPH 423, MAY 1972

DON'T SHOOT ME I'M ONLY THE PIANO PLAYER

Daniel · Teacher I Need You · Elderberry Wine · Blues for My Baby and Me · Midnight Creeper · Have Mercy on the Criminal · I'm Going to Be a Teenage Idol · Texan Love Song · Crocodile Rock · High Flying Bird

US: MCA MCA-2100, JANUARY 1973   UK: DJM DJLPH 427, JANUARY 1973

GOODBYE YELLOW BRICK ROAD

Funeral for a Friend/Love Lies Bleeding · Candle in the Wind · Bennie and the Jets · Goodbye Yellow Brick Road · This Song Has No Title · Grey Seal · Jamaica Jerk-Off · I've Seen That Movie Too · Sweet Painted Lady · The Ballad of Danny Bailey (1909–1934) · Dirty Little Girl · All the Girls Love Alice · Your Sister Can't Twist (But She Can Rock 'n Roll) · Saturday Night's Alright for Fighting · Roy Rogers · Social Disease · Harmony

US: MCA MCA2-10003, OCTOBER 1973   UK: DJM DJLPD 1001, OCTOBER 1973

CARIBOU

The Bitch Is Back · Pinky · Grimsby · Dixie Lily · Solar Prestige a Gammon · You're So Static · I've Seen the Saucers · Stinker · Don't Let the Sun Go Down on Me · Ticking

US: MCA MCA-2116, JUNE 1974   UK: DJM DJLPH 439, JUNE 1974

ELTON JOHN: GREATEST HITS

Your Song · Daniel · Honky Cat · Goodbye Yellow Brick Road · Saturday Night's Alright for Fighting · Rocket Man (I Think It's Going to Be a Long, Long Time) · Bennie and the Jets · Don't Let the Sun Go Down on Me · Border Song · Crocodile Rock

US: MCA MCA-2128, NOVEMBER 1974   UK: DJM DJLPH 442, NOVEMBER 1974

CAPTAIN FANTASTIC AND THE BROWN DIRT COWBOY

Captain Fantastic and the Brown Dirt Cowboy · Tower of Babel · Bitter Fingers · Tell Me When the Whistle Blows · Someone Saved My Life Tonight · (Gotta Get a) Meal Ticket · Better Off Dead · Writing · We All Fall in Love Sometimes · Curtains

US: MCA MCA-2142, MAY 1975   UK: DJM 22094, MAY 1975

ROCK OF THE WESTIES

Medley (Yell Help · Wednesday Night · Ugly) · Dan Dare (Pilot of the Future) · Island Girl · Grow Some Funk of Your Own · I Feel Like a Bullet (in the Gun of Robert Ford) · Street Kids · Hard Luck Story · Feed Me · Billy Bones and the White Bird

US: MCA MCA-2163, OCTOBER 1975   UK: DJM DJLPH 464, OCTOBER 1975

HERE AND THERE

Skyline Pigeon · Border Song · Honky Cat · Love Song · Crocodile Rock · Funeral for a Friend/Love Lies Bleeding · Rocket Man (I Think It's Going to Be a Long, Long Time) · Bennie and the Jets · Take Me to the Pilot

US: MCA MCA-2197, APRIL 1976   UK: DJM DJLPH 473, APRIL 1976

BLUE MOVES

Your Starter For . . . · Tonight · One Horse Town · Chameleon · Boogie Pilgrim · Cage the Songbird · Crazy Water · Shoulder Holster · Sorry Seems to Be the Hardest Word · Out of the Blue · Between Seventeen and Twenty · The Wide-Eyed and Laughing · Someone's Final Song · Where's the Shoorah? · If There's a God in Heaven (What's He Waiting For?) · Idol · Theme from a Non-Existent TV Series · Bite Your Lip (Get Up and Dance!)

US: MCA MCA2-11004, OCTOBER 1976   UK: THE ROCKET RECORD COMPANY ROSP 1, OCTOBER 1976

ELTON JOHN: GREATEST HITS VOLUME II

The Bitch Is Back · Lucy in the Sky with Diamonds · Sorry Seems to Be the Hardest Word · Don't Go Breaking My Heart · Someone Saved My Life Tonight · Philadelphia Freedom · Island Girl · Grow Some Funk of Your Own · Levon · Pinball Wizard

US: MCA MCA-1690, SEPTEMBER 1977   UK: DJM DJH 20520, SEPTEMBER 1977

A SINGLE MAN

Shine On Through · Return to Paradise · I Don't Care · Big Dipper · It Ain't Gonna Be Easy · Part Time Love · Georgia · Shooting Star · Madness · Reverie · Song for Guy

US: MCA MCA-3065, OCTOBER 1978   UK: THE ROCKET RECORD COMPANY TRAIN 1, OCTOBER 1978

VICTIM OF LOVE

Johnny B. Goode · Warm Love in a Cold World · Born Bad · Thunder in the Night · Spotlight · Street Boogie · Victim of Love

US: MCA MCA-5104, OCTOBER 1979   UK: THE ROCKET RECORD COMPANY HISPD 125, OCTOBER 1979

21 AT 33

Chasing the Crown · Little Jeannie · Sartorial Eloquence · Two Rooms at the End of the World · White Lady White Powder · Dear God · Never Gonna Fall in Love Again · Take Me Back · Give Me the Love

US: MCA MCA-5121, MAY 1980   UK: THE ROCKET RECORD COMPANY HISPD 126, MAY 1980

Singles · *1968–1981*

I've Been Loving You · Here's to the Next Time

UK: 1968 PHILIPS BF1643, MARCH 1968

Lady Samantha · All Across the Havens

UK: PHILIPS BF1739, JANUARY 1969

It's Me That You Need · Just Like Strange Rain

UK: DJM DJS205, MAY 1969

Border Song · Bad Side of the Moon

US: UNI 55246, APRIL 1970   UK: DJM DJS217, MARCH 1970

Rock and Roll Madonna · Grey Seal

UK: DJM DJS222, JUNE 1970

Your Song · Into the Old Man's Shoes (UK), Take Me to the Pilot (US)

US: UNI 55265, OCTOBER 1970   UK: DJM DJS233, OCTOBER 1970

Friends · Honey Roll

US: UNI 55277, MARCH 1971   UK: DJM DJS244, APRIL 1971

Levon · Goodbye

US: UNI 55314, NOVEMBER 1971

Tiny Dancer · Razor Face

US: UNI 55318, FEBRUARY 1972

Rocket Man · Susie (Dramas) (US), Holiday Inn · Goodbye (UK)

US: UNI 55328, APRIL 1972   UK: DJM DJX501, APRIL 1972

Honky Cat · Slave (US), Lady Samantha · It's Me That You Need (UK)

US: UNI 55343, JULY 1972   UK: DJM DJS269, JULY 1972

Crocodile Rock · Elderberry Wine

US: MCA 40000, NOVEMBER 1972   UK: DJM DJS271, OCTOBER 1972

Daniel · Skyline Pigeon

US: MCA 40046, MARCH 1973   UK: DJM DJS275, MARCH 1973

Saturday Night's Alright for Fighting · Jack Rabbit · Whenever You're Ready (We'll Go Steady Again)

US: MCA 40105, JULY 1973   UK: DJM DJX502, JULY 1973

Goodbye Yellow Brick Road · Screw You (retitled Young Man's Blues in US)

US: MCA 40148, OCTOBER 1973   UK: DJM DJS285, OCTOBER 1973

Step into Christmas · Ho Ho Ho (Who'd Be a Turkey at Christmas?)

US: MCA 65018, NOVEMBER 1973   UK: DJM DJS290, NOVEMBER 1973

Candle in the Wind · Bennie and the Jets

UK: DJM DJS297, FEBRUARY 1974

Bennie and the Jets · Harmony

US: MCA 40198, FEBRUARY 1974

Don't Let the Sun Go Down on Me · Sick City

US: MCA 40259, MAY 1974   UK: DJM DJS302, MAY 1974

The Bitch Is Back · Cold Highway

US: MCA 40297, SEPTEMBER 1974   UK: DJM DJS322, SEPTEMBER 1974

Lucy in the Sky with Diamonds · One Day at a Time

US: MCA 40344, NOVEMBER 1974   UK: DJM DJS340, NOVEMBER 1974

Philadelphia Freedom · I Saw Her Standing There

US: MCA 40364, FEBRUARY 1975   UK: DJM DJS354, FEBRUARY 1975

Someone Saved My Life Tonight · House of Cards

US: MCA 40421, JUNE 1975   UK: DJM DJS385, JUNE 1975

Island Girl · Sugar on the Floor

US: MCA 40461, SEPTEMBER 1975   UK: DJM DJS610, SEPTEMBER 1975

Grow Some Funk of Your Own · I Feel Like a Bullet (in the Gun of Robert Ford)

US: MCA 40505, JANUARY 1976   UK: DJM DJS629, JANUARY 1976

Pinball Wizard · Harmony

UK: DJM DJS652, MARCH 1976

Don't Go Breaking My Heart · Snow Queen

US: MCA / THE ROCKET RECORD COMPANY 40585, JUNE 1976   UK: THE ROCKET RECORD COMPANY ROKN512, JUNE 1976

Sorry Seems to Be the Hardest Word · Shoulder Holster

US: MCA / THE ROCKET RECORD COMPANY 40645, NOVEMBER 1976   UK: THE ROCKET RECORD COMPANY ROKN517, NOVEMBER 1976

Bite Your Lip (Get Up and Dance!) · Chicago

US: MCA / THE ROCKET RECORD COMPANY 40677, JANUARY 1977   UK: THE ROCKET RECORD COM-
PANY ROKN526, JANUARY 1977

Crazy Water · Chameleon

UK: THE ROCKET RECORD COMPANY ROKN 521, FEBRUARY 1977

Ego · Flinstone Boy

US: MCA 40892, MARCH 1978   UK: THE ROCKET RECORD COMPANY ROKN538, MARCH 1978

Part Time Love · I Cry at Night

US: MCA 40973, NOVEMBER 1978   UK: THE ROCKET RECORD COMPANY XPRES1, OCTOBER 1978

Song for Guy · Lovesick

US: MCA 40993, MARCH 1979   UK: THE ROCKET RECORD COMPANY XPRES5, NOVEMBER 1978

Are You Ready for Love · Mama Can't Buy You Love · Three Way Love Affair

US: MCA 13921, APRIL 1979   UK: THE ROCKET RECORD COMPANY XPRES1312, APRIL 1979

Mama Can't Buy You Love · Strangers (UK), Three Way Love Affair (US)

US: MCA 41042, JUNE 1979   UK: THE ROCKET RECORD COMPANY XPRES20, JUNE 1979

Victim of Love · Strangers

US: MCA 41126, SEPTEMBER 1979   UK: THE ROCKET RECORD COMPANY XPRES21,
SEPTEMBER 1979

Johnny B. Goode · Thunder in the Night (UK), Georgia (US)

US: MCA 41159, NOVEMBER 1979   UK: THE ROCKET RECORD COMPANY XPRES24,
NOVEMBER 1979

Little Jeannie · Conquer the Sun

US: MCA 41236, MAY 1980   UK: THE ROCKET RECORD COMPANY XPRES32, MAY 1980

Sartorial Eloquence (retitled Don't You Wanna Play This Game No More in US)
· White Man Danger · Cartier

US: MCA 41293, AUGUST 1980   UK: THE ROCKET RECORD COMPANY XPRES41,
AUGUST 1980

Dear God · Tactics

UK: THE ROCKET RECORD COMPANY XPRES45, NOVEMBER 1980

I Saw Her Standing There · Whatever Gets You thru the Night · Lucy in the Sky with Diamonds

UK: DJM DJS10965, MARCH 1981

BIBLIOGRAPHY

Appleford, Steve. *The Rolling Stones: Rip This Joint—The Stories Behind Every Song* (USA: Avalon Travel Publishing, 2001).

Bernardin, Claude, and Tom Stanton. *Rocket Man: Elton John from A–Z* (Westport, CT: Praeger, 1996).

Black, Susan. *Elton John in His Own Words* (London: Omnibus, 1993).

Bright, Spencer. *Essential Elton* (London: Andre Deutsch, 1998).

Buckley, David. *Elton John: The Biography* (London: Andre Deutsch, 2010).

Bugliosi, Vincent, and Curt Gentry. *Helter Skelter: The True Story of the Manson Murders* (New York: W. W. Norton, 1974).

Cassata, Mary Anne. *The Elton John Scrapbook* (New York: Citadel Press, 2002).

Clarke, Gary. *Elton, My Elton* (London: Smith Gryphon, 1995).

Crimp, Susan, and Patricia Burstein. *The Many Lives of Elton John* (London: Robert Hale, 1992).

Davis, Stephen. *Hammer of the Gods: Led Zeppelin Unauthorised* (New York: William Morrow, 1985).

———. *Old Gods Almost Dead: The 40-year Odyssey of the Rolling Stones* (London: Aurum Press, 2002).

Ellis, Geoffrey. *I Should Have Known Better* (London: Thorogood, 2005).

Flynn, Paul. *Dream Ticket: Elton John Across Four Decades* (Lithonia, GA: HST Management, 2004).

Gambaccini, Paul. *Elton John and Bernie Taupin* (London: Star Books, 1974).

Goodall, Nigel. *Elton John: A Visual Documentary* (London and New York: Omnibus, 1993).

Guinn, Jeff. *Manson: The Life and Times of Charles Manson* (London: Simon and Schuster, 2014).

Guralnick, Peter. *Careless Love: The Unmaking of Elvis Presley* (London: Abacus, 1999).

Hayward, Keith. *Tin Pan Alley: The Rise of Elton John* (London: Soundcheck, 2013).

———. *From Tin Pan Alley to the Yellow Brick Road* (Bedford, UK: Wymer, 2015).

Heylin, Clinton. *No More Sad Refrains: The Life and Times of Sandy Denny* (London: Omnibus, 2011).

Houghton, Mick. *I've Always Kept a Unicorn: The Biography of Sandy Denny* (London: Faber and Faber, 2015).

Humphries, Patrick. *A Little Bit Funny: The Elton John Story* (London: Aurum Press, 1998).

John, Elton. *Love Is the Cure* (London: Hodder and Stoughton, 2012).

———, and Bernie Taupin. *Two Rooms: Elton John and Bernie Taupin in Their Own Words* (London: Boxtree, 1991).

Kanfer, Stefan. *Groucho: The Life and Times of Julius Henry Marx* (New York: Alfred A. Knopf, 2000).

Myers, Paul. *It Ain't Easy: Long John Baldry and the Birth of British Blues* (Canada: Greystone, 2007).

Newman, Gerald, with Joe Bivona. *Elton John* (New York: Signet Books, 1976).

Norman, Philip. *Elton* (London: Hutchinson, 1991).

Nutter, David. *Elton: It's a Little Bit Funny* (London and New York: Penguin, 1977).

O'Neill, Terry. *Two Days That Rocked the World* (London: ACC Editions, 2015).

Pang, May, and Henry Edwards. *Loving John* (London: Corgi, 1983).

Peebles, Andy. *The Elton John Tapes* (London: BBC, 1981).

Quaye, Caleb, with Dale A. Berryhill. *A Voice Louder than Rock & Roll* (USA: Vision Publishing, 2006).

Randall, Lucian, and Chris Welch. *Ginger Geezer: The Life of Vivian Stanshall* (London: Fourth Estate, 2001).

Rosenthal, Elizabeth J. *His Song: The Musical Journey of Elton John* (New York: Billboard Books, 2001).

Shaw, Greg. *Elton John: A Biography in Words and Pictures* (New York: Sire Books, 1976).

Stein, Cathi. *Elton John* (UK: Futura, 1975).

Stewart, Rod. *Rod: The Autobiography* (London: Arrow Books, 2012).

St. Michael, Mick. *Elton John* (London: Bison Group, 1994).

Tatham, Dick, and Tony Jasper. *Elton John* (London: Octopus, 1976).

Taupin, Bernie. *A Cradle of Haloes* (London: Aurum Press, 1988).

———. *The One Who Writes the Words for Elton John* (London: Jonathan Cape, 1976).

Toberman, Barry. *Elton John: A Biography* (London: Weidenfeld and Nicolson, 1988).

Tobler, John. *Elton John: 25 Years in the Charts* (London: Hamlyn, 1995).

Unknown. *Scraps,* insert booklet of *Captain Fantastic and the Brown Dirt Cowboy* album (DJM Records, 1975).

Walker, Michael. *Laurel Canyon* (New York: Faber and Faber, 2006).

PHOTO CREDITS

xv Val Wilmer/Getty Images

xx Steve Morley/Getty Images

2 George Harris/Associated Newspapers/Rex/Shutterstock

18 Michael Ochs Archives/Getty Images

36 Ed Caraeff/Morgan Media/Getty Images

42 Ed Caraeff/Morgan Media/Getty Images

48 Michael Ochs Archives/Getty Images

62 John Olson/Getty Images

80 Michael Putland/Getty Images

97 Michael Ochs Archives/Getty Images

100 Michael Ochs Archives/Getty Images

118 Terry O'Neill/Getty Images

134 Robert Knight Archive/Getty Images

148 Terry O'Neill/Getty Images

165 Michael Ochs Archives/Getty Images

168 Michael Ochs Archives/Getty Images

178 Terry O'Neill/Getty Images

187 Bob Thomas/Getty Images

191 Terry O'Neill/Getty Images

196 Robin Platzer/Getty Images

216 Evening Standard/Getty Images

230 Richard Blanchard/Getty Images

232 Terry O'Neill/Getty Images

246 Chris Morris/Rex/Shutterstock

253 Ron Galella/Getty Images

INDEX

Page numbers in *italics* refer to illustrations.

"A.B.C. Boogie," 7
ABC TV, 130, 211, 225
Ackles, David, 38, 202
African Queen, The (film), 128
"Ain't No Mountain High
  Enough," 164
Aldridge, Alan, 174
Alexander, Arthur, 14
Alexandra, Princess, Honourable
  Lady Ogilvy, 218–19
"All the Girls Love Alice," 126,
  250
"All the Nasties," 76
All Things Must Pass, 54
American Gothic, 202
American Music Awards, 217
"American Triangle," 263
American West, 49–51, 125
"America the Beautiful," 206
"Amoreena," 50
"Amoureuse," 115, 225
AM radio, 57–58
"Amy," 90
Anaheim Convention Center, 60
Andrew, Prince, Duke of York,
  256
Andy Williams Show, The (TV
  show), 60

"Angel," 145
"Angel Tree, The," 28
Animals, 64
Anne, Princess Royal, 257
Apollo 16 launch, 89–90
Apollo theater, xxiii
Apple Films, 103
Apple Records, 113, 151
"Approaching Armageddon," 248
Aquarius (TV show), 65–66
"Are You Ready for Love," 225
Armstead, Joshi Jo, 152
Ashby, Hal, 60
Astral Weeks, xxii
Asylum Records, 154
Atlas, Jacoba, 69
Atwell, Winifred, 5
Auckland *Sunday News,* 141
Auger, Julie, 15
Australian tours, 77–78, 134,
  140–42

"Babyface," 194
Bach, Johann Sebastian, 6, 96
"Back in the USSR," 239–40
"Bad Blood," 191
Bad Company, 183

"Bad Side of the Moon," 40–41,
    56, 59
Baker, Josephine, 140
Baldry, Long John, 15–16, 24, 26,
    28, 64, 87, 174, 233
"Ballad of a Well-Known Gun,"
    49, 61
"Ballad of Danny Bailey
    (1909–34)," 125–26
Baltimore Civic Center Arena,
    123–24
Balzac, Honoré de, 81
Band, the, xvi, xxiv, 49, 50,
    55–56, 82
"Bang a Gong (Get It On)," 70
Bangs, Lester, 243
Baragwanath, Judith, 141–42
Bardot, Brigitte, 14
Barron Knights troupe, 29
Battle of the Bands (Kilburn), 13
Baxter, Jeff "Skunk," 175, 181
Baxter, Stanley, 128
BBC I, 32
BBC Radio One, 249
BBC TV, 77, 145, 161, 219, 250
Beach Boys, 33, 40, 44–45, 89,
    139, 176–77
Beatles, xx, xxiii, 3, 11, 14, 30,
    41, 90, 112–13, 132, 151,
    173, 174, 176–77, 188–89,
    192, 228
Beck, Ian, 128
Beck, Jeff, 3–4
Bee Gees, 32
Bell, LeRoy, 225
Bell, Thom, 224–25, 243
Bellotte, Pete, 242
Bell Records, 34
"Bennie and the Jets," 126,
    128–29, 143–44, 163, 170,
    181, 204, 218, 220, 222,
    231, 252
Bernstein, Gary, 248

Berry, Chuck, 145, 243
Best of British (TV show), 250
"Better Off Dead," 223
"Between Seventeen and Twenty,"
    199
"Big Dipper," 233, 242
Big Picture, The, 262
Billboard, 29, 54, 57, 112, 143,
    154, 229
"Billy Bones and the White Bird,"
    182
"Bitch Is Back, The," 138, 160,
    224
"Bite Your Lip (Get Up and
    Dance!)," 200, 221
"Bitter Fingers," 173
Blauel, Renate, 260
Blue Moves, 198–200, 203, 208,
    212–13, 221, 226, 264
Bluesology, xii, 2, 11–17, 170,
    242
Blyton, Enid, 209
Bolan, June, 63
Bolan, Marc, 63, 70–71, 73, 103,
    108
Bono, 266
Bonzo Dog Doo-Dah Band, 90–91
"Boom Bang-a-Bang," xiv
Boone, Pat, 108
"Border Song," 32, 41, 59–60,
    65, 138
"Born Bad," 243
Born to Boogie (film), 103
Boston Tea Party concert, 55
Bowie, David, xxii, 30, 84, 89,
    103, 110, 131, 171, 190,
    211, 227
Boyd, Joe, 53
Brasil '66, 32
Brezhnev, Leonid, 237
Bridge over Troubled Water, 31
British Market Research Bureau
    (BMRB), 228

Brohn, Ronald, 23
Brown, Steve, xiv, 29–30, 38, 73, 110, 113
Brown, Stu, 10–11, 16
Bruce, Lenny, 39
Bruner, Diana, 170
Buckmaster, Paul, 30, 31, 50, 65, 67, 75–76, 85, 233
Burchett, Guy, 229
Burdon, Eric, 64
Burke, Solomon, 14
"Burn Down the Mission," 41, 43, 49–50, 56–57, 59, 90, 190
Burning Cold (Taupin and Bernstein), 248
Butler, Jay, 143
"Butterflies," 5
Byrds, 39, 45, 55

"Cage the Songbird," 212
Cagney, Jimmy, 125
"Candle in the Wind," 125, 128, 143, 176
"Can I Put You On," 67
"Can't Help Falling in Love," 206
Capital Road Awards, 217
Captain & the Kid, The, 263
Captain Fantastic and the Brown Dirt Cowboy, 149–51, 156–57, 162, 173–75, 177, 181, 190–91, 250, 263–64
Caribou, 135–40, 145, 152–53, 156, 158
Caribou Ranch Studios, 135–37, 156, 172–73, 175, *178*, 179–81, 198
Carnegie Hall, 70
Carpenters, 37, 112
Carr, Roy, 130
Carson, Johnny, 254–55
Cartland, Barbara, 68

Cash, Johnny, 19
Cashbox, 112
Cass, Mama, 60
Cassidy, David, 141–42
CBS TV, 183
Central Park concert, 251–55, *253*
Channel, Bruce, 10
Charles, Prince of Wales, 256
Charles, Ray, 10, 60
Chase, 71
"Chasing the Crown," 249
Château d'Hérouville, 81–84, 90, 93–94, 102, 104–6, 109, 113, 116–17
Chensvold, Stephen, 69
Cher, 163–64, 183
Cher (TV show), 163
Chicago (band), 136
Chicago Sun-Times, 153
"Children of the Revolution," 103
China (band), 223, 235
Chopin, Frédéric, 6, 81
"Cindy Incidentally," 112
CKLW radio station, 143
Clapton, Eric, 55
Clarke, Gary, 264–65
Clement, Dick, 237
Cleveland, James, 190
Clift, Montgomery, 125
Clockwork Orange, A (film), 92
Clooney, Rosemary, 5
Cocker, Joe, 158
Coffey, Dennis, 170
Cohen, Leonard, xii
Coleman, Ray, 85
Coleridge, Samuel Taylor, 19
"Come Back Baby," 12–13
"Come Down in Time," 50
Cooder, Ry, 56
Cook, Roger, 29
Cooper, Alice, 95, 202–3, 226

Cooper, Ray, 132, 159, 161, 168, 218, 223–24, 230, 235, 237, 239–40, 243–44, 256
Copland, Aaron, 180
Cornelius, Don, 169–70
Corvettes, 10–11
Costello, Elvis, 217
"Country Comfort," 41, 51, 56, 58, 145, 190
"Crazy Water," 221
"Crocodile Rock," 102, 108–9, 114, 123, 140, 204, 220, 222
Crosby, Stills, Nash and Young, 45
Crossley, Chris, 25
"Curtains," 173
Curtis, Tony, 183

Daily Express, 249
Daily Mail, 237, 242
Daily Telegraph, 51, 218–19
Daltrey, Roger, 166
"Dan Dare (Pilot of the Future)," 181, 182
"Dandelion Dies in the Wind, A," xiii, 22
"Daniel," 108–10, 220, 231
"Danny Boy," 14
Darrell, Guy, 29
Davis, Clive, 125
Davis, Stephen, 130
Day, Doris, 92
"Day in the Life of a Tree," 89
Dayson, Geoff, 11
Dean, Elton, 24, 26
Dean, James, 125
"Dear God," 249
Dee, Kiki, 115, 152–53, 158–59, 175, 208–9, 221, 225
Deep Throat (film), 120–21
Delfonics, 224
Denny, Sandy, 53–54

Derek and the Dominos, 55
Derringer, Rick, 136
DeVoss, David, 193
Diamond, Neil, 39, 40, 41
"Diamonds Are a Girl's Best Friend," 5
Diana, Princess of Wales, 256–57, 265
Dick James Music, xv
Dillards, 38
Disc magazine, 87, 113
Disneyland, 44
Diving Board, 263
Djangology, 11
DJM, xiv, 17, 21–23, 29–30, 33, 34, 38, 50, 59, 128, 174. See also James, Dick
    Elton's contract and, 26, 71, 203–4
    Elton's publishing and, 112–13
    Reid and, 74, 112–13
    rift with Elton, 109–10, 154
Dodd, Ken, 102
Dodger Stadium concerts, 184–92, 191
Dolenz, Mickey, 203
Donahue, Jerry, 53–54
Donahue, Phil, 254
"Don't Go Breaking My Heart," 208–9, 217, 222–23
"Don't Let the Sun Go Down on Me," 139–40, 162, 170, 190
Don't Shoot Me I'm Only the Piano Player, 93–94, 102, 104–6, 108–9, 112, 123, 137
"Don't Try to Lay No Boogie-Woogie on the King of Rock and Roll," 87
Doobie Brothers, 175, 181
Drake, Nick, 53
Dr. John, 90
Dudgeon, Gus, 30, 58, 68, 82–83, 89, 93, 104–7, 113, 116,

126, 129, 139, 152–53,
156–57, 165, 172–75, 181,
200, 227, 262
Dwight, Ivy (grandmother), 4,
188
Dwight, Roy (cousin), 6
Dwight, Stanley (father), 5–9, 213
Dylan, Bob, xxii, 60, 63, 82, 152,
154, 183
Dylan, Sara, 60
Dynamic Sounds Studio, 104–7

Eagles, 154, 176, 183
Eastern Sound Studio, 198, 200,
208
Eastman, John, 112
Edinburgh Festival of Popular
Music, 211
Ed Sullivan Show, The (TV
show), 44
"Ego," 227–28
"Elderberry Wine," 123
Electric Ladyland, xii
Electric Lady Studios, 152
Elektra Records, 202
11–17–70 (*17–11–70*), 59
Elizabeth, Queen Mother, 101,
193
Elizabeth II, Queen of England,
219, 257, 266
Ellis, Geoffrey, 193, 200, 218,
237, 240
"El Paso," 19
Elton John, 3, 29–34, 50, 54, 58,
64, 67–68, 138, 218, 253
*Elton John and Bernie Taupin Say
Goodbye Norma Jean*
(documentary), 130–31
Elton John Band, 172
Elton John: Greatest Hits, 162
*Elton John's Greatest Hits
Volume II*, 224

Elton John Week (Los Angeles),
185
Emberton, John, 228
Emin, Tracey, xxi
EMI Records, 71–72, 74
"Empty Garden (Hey, Hey
Johnny)," 256
"Empty Sky," 190
Empty Sky, xiv, xvi, 3, 29–30,
33–34, 50, 145, 149, 172,
175, 248
Eurovision Song Contest, xiii–xiv
Everything Stops for Tea, 87
Exciters, 14
Exile on Main Street, 82

Faces, 112, 114
Fairchild, June, 44
Fairport Convention, 53, 71
"Fame," 171
Fame, Georgie, 11, 13
Farebrother, Fred "Derf,"
(stepfather), xi, 9, 10, 25,
28, 62, 93, 185, 189, 192,
237
Farebrother, Sheila Dwight
(mother), xi, 25, 62, 70,
115, 131, 185, 192, 205–6,
217–18, 237–38, 249
Elton comes out to, 73–74
Elton's name change and, 79
Elton's suicide attempt and,
187–89
first marriage and Elton's
childhood, 4–9
marries Farebrother, 93
Federal Bureau of Investigation
(FBI), 96
"Feed Me," 181
Feibelman, Janis, 39
Feibelman, Maxine. *See* Taupin,
Maxine Feibelman

Felton, David, 42
Festival Records, 141
"Fever," 206
Fillmore East, 59–60, 68, 69
"First Episode at Hienton," 31
Fisher, Eddie, 5
Floyd, Eddie, 11
FM radio, 57–58, 76
Fonda, Jane, 81–82
Fong-Torres, Ben, 160
Fontana Records, 12, 16, 115
Forbes, Bryan, 94–95, 128, 130–31
Foreman, George, 105
Fortunes, the, 29
Forum (Los Angeles), 97, 158, 255
Fotheringay concert, 53–54
France, SS (ocean liner), 145–46, 149–51
Francis, Connie, 110
Franklin, Aretha, 60, 158
Franks, Clive, 115, 152, 227, 240, 248, 256
Frazier, Joe, 105
Free Press, 37
Friends (film), 67–68
Frio, Rick, 40, 52
From the Inside, 226
"Fun, Fun, Fun," 176
"Funeral for a Friend / Love Lies Bleeding," 126, 129, 176, 185, 204, 218, 239, 251
Funk Brothers, 170
Furnish, David, 265

Garbo, Greta, 163, 186
Garden Party festival, 71
Garland, Judy, 110, 128
Gasoline Alley, 145
Gaye, Marvin, 208, 218

Geffen, David, 154
"Georgia," 233
Gere, Richard, 265
"Get Back," 41, 59
"Get Down," 112
"Get It On," 70
Gibb, Robin, 32
Gilbert, Lewis, 67
"Give Peace a Chance," 57
Goats Head Soup, 104
"Golden Years," 171
Goldsmith, Harvey, 236–37
Gone with the Wind (film), 163
"Goodbye," 85
Goodbye Yellow Brick Road, 104–7, 116–17, 124–31, 143, 145
"Goodbye Yellow Brick Road," 123, 128, 143, 172, 212, 218, 222, 250–51
"Good Vibrations," 45
Goon Show (TV show), 35
Goons troupe, 9
"(Gotta Get a) Meal Ticket," 173
Go West (film), 108
Graham, Bill, 44, 69
Gralto company, 20, 22
Grammy Awards, 139, 183
Grant, Cary, 189, 190
Grant, Peter, 119
Grateful Dead, xxii, 82
"Great Balls of Fire," 8
"Greatest Discovery," 218
Greco, Buddy, 27
Greenaway, Roger, 29, 33–34
"Grimsby," 137, 145
Groundhogs, 33
"Grow Some Funk of Your Own," 181–82, 198, 224
Guercio, Jim, 136
Gunfighter Ballads and Trail Songs, 19–20

Hair (musical), 24
Haley, Bill, 7, 257
Hall, Ken, 219–20
Halley, Bob, 219–20, 234, 237, 252
Hammersmith Odeon concerts, 132, 161
Handel, George Frederick, 8
"Hard Luck Story," 181
Harlow, Jean, 186
Harold and Maude (film), 60
Harris, Emmylou, 189
Harrison, George, 54, 265–66
Harty, Russell, 186
"Heartbreak Hotel," 7, 205
Heath, Edward, 131–32
"Heaven Help Us All," 60
Hefner, Hugh, 183, 208
"He'll Have to Go," 17, 250
Helms, Jimmy, 219
Hendrix, Jimi, xii, 126, 145, 152
Hendryx, Nona, 114
Henry VIII, King of England, 192
Henson, Jim, 222
Hentschel, David, 89, 126
Hepburn, Katharine, xxii, 128
Heptones, 32
"Hercules," 90, 190
Herman, Dave, 58
He Who Rides the Tiger, 248
"Hey Baby," 10
"Hey Jude," 29, 30
"High Flying Bird," 108
Hilburn, Robert, 43–44, 57, 237, 239, 250
Hockney, David, 113
Hodes, Lennie, 33–34
Holden, Stephen, 108, 243
"Holiday Inn," 75
Holly, Buddy, 8
Hollies, 20
Hollywood Bowl, 121–24, 131

Hollywood Vampires, 203
Hollywood Walk of Fame, 186, 187
"Honey Roll," 67
"Honky Cat," 90, 128, 132
Honky Château, 81–84, 90, 93, 95, 172
"Honky Tonk Women," 41, 179–80
Hookfoot, 50
Horton, Johnny, 49
Hot Rats, xxii
"Hound Dog," 206
Houses of the Holy, 112
Houston, Cissy, 152
Howard, James Newton, 168, 175, 223, 251
Hunt, Marsha, 24
Hutton, Danny, 40, 44–46

"I Can't Explain," 165
"I Can't Go on Living Without You," xiii
"I Can't Stop Loving You," 10
"Idol," 212
"I Don't Know How to Say Goodbye," 162
"I Feel Like a Bullet (in the Gun of Robert Ford)," 182, 198
"I Feel Love," 242
If It Was So Simple, 114
"I Guess That's Why They Call It the Blues," 262
"I Heard It Through the Grapevine," 218, 239
"Iko Iko," 87
"I Love You Because," 17
"Imagine," xviii, 252, 256
"I'm Gonna Be a Teenage Idol," 108
"I'm Not in Love," 198

"I'm Still Standing," 262
Incredible String Band, 53
"Indian Sunset," 56
"I Need You to Turn To," 56, 138, 184
Inkpen, Mick, 11
Ink Spots, 14
Internal Revenue Service (IRS), 113
"In the Midnight Hour," 13
Invalid Children's Society, 145
Irish Republican Army (IRA), 86, 201
"I Saw Her Standing There," xx, 177
"Island Girl," 182, 191
It Ain't Easy, 87
Italy, 115–16
"I Think I'm Going to Kill Myself," 90–91, 97–98, 101
"(I Think It's Going to Be a Long, Long Time)," 90
ITV, 130
"I've Been Loving You," 26
I've Got the Music in Me, 152
"I've Got the Music in Me," 208
"I've Seen the Saucers," 138
Ivor Novello award, 217
"I Want Love," 263

Jackie magazine, xvi
Jackson 5, 102
Jackson, Michael, 208
Jagger, Bianca, 209
Jagger, Mick, 110, 131, 179–81, 227
Jahr, Cliff, 210
Jamaica, 105–7
James, Dick, 3–4, 23, 26, 28–30, 32, 34, 39, 75. *See also* DJM
Elton's contracts and, 112–13

Elton's disputes with, 94, 109–10
Elton's name change and, 79
on Elton's personality, 131
MCA contract and, 153–55
Reid as Elton's manager and, 71–72, 74
Taupin's wedding and, 67
James, Stephen, 23, 25–26, 34, 74, 110, 112
Jaws (film), 183, 186
"Jeepster," 103
Jeff Beck Group, 3
Jefferson Airplane, xxii
Jesus Christ Superstar (musical), 96
Jet Lag (proposed film), 221
John, Elton Hercules (Reginald Kenneth Dwight). *See also* Taupin, Bernie; *and specific albums; concerts; and songs*
AIDS foundation of, 266
albums cycles and, 172–73
American tours, xviii, 3–4, 33–45, 51–61, 63, 68–70, 88, 91–92, 97–98, 102–3, 120–25, 148, 157–61, 184–92, 196, 204–10, 243–44, 250–55
appearance and dress and, xv, xviii, 2, 8, 40, 44, 56, 57, 66, 72, 78, 91, 101, 103–4, 110–11, *118*, 120–23, 134, 140, 169–70, 204, 221–22, 232–33, 243, 253, 255
art collection and, xxi, 113, 192, 265
Australian tours, 77–78, *134*, 137, 140–42, 244, 255–56
awards and honors, 139, 186, *187*, 217, 266
band fired by, *168*, 172

begins performing as Elton
John, xii–xvi, *xv*
Bell produces, 224–26, 243–44
Big Picture and, 262
Blue Moves and, 198–200,
208–9, 212–13
Bluesology and, xii, 2, 11–17
bootleg albums and, 59
Captain & the Kid and, 263
Captain Fantastic and, 146,
149–52, 156–57, 173,
173–75
Caribou and, 135–40, 152–53,
178
charity concerts, 183–84
Christmas concerts, 132, 161
comeback of 1978, 231–34
contract with Dick James, 3,
23–24, 26, 74, 109–13
contract with MCA, 153–55
Corvettes and, 10–11
critics on, 43–44, 57, 65,
69–70, 86, 108–9, 130, 141,
153, 201, 209, 211, 243
"Daniel" and, 109–10
difficulties of 1980s and, 259
Diving Board and, 263
documentary films on, 66,
130–31, 237
Don't Shoot Me and, 93–94,
102, 105–6, 108
drugs and, xvii, xxi, 24, 45, 84,
88, 105, 120–21,
135–37, 155, 176, 181,
185–87, 198, 200, 211–12,
218–19, 227, 229, 234,
244–47, 246, 259–61,
265–66
early life and education of,
4–12
early performing by, 9–11,
24, 32

"Ego" and, 228
11-17-70 and, 59
Elton John and, 3, 29–34, 54
"Elton John" chosen as stage
name by, xxiii–xxiv, 2, 26, 79
Empty Sky and, xiv–xvi, 3,
29–30, 33–34
European tours, 235–36
fame and, xxi–xxii, 61,
68–70, 77, 87–89, 111,
123–24, 130, 158, 160, 188,
197–98, 206–7, 212, 214,
264–65
father and, 5–6, 8–9, 213
film *Born to Boogie* and, 103
film *Tommy* and, 164–66, *165*
finances and, 82, 93, 95, 113,
163, 192–94, 261
first single, 26
friendship with Lennon and,
xvi–xxi, *xx*, 155–56,
160–61, 255–56
friendship with royals and, 80,
86, 101–2, 193, 201,
218–19, 256–57, 266
Friends soundtrack and, 67–68
gay identity and, 16, 28,
69–70, 72–74, 76, 92,
110–11, 159, 210–12, 214,
221, 233, 237
Goodbye Yellow Brick Road
and, 104–7, 116–17,
124–30
Greatest Hits and, 162
Greatest Hits Volume II and,
224
health problems and, 43, 65,
94, 182, 234–35, 244–45
Here and There and, 203–4
homes of, 73–74, 93, 103, 115,
128, 130, 163, 184, 186,
192–93, 249–50, 261–62

John, Elton Hercules (Reginald
Kenneth Dwight) (*cont.*)
Honky Château and, 81–84,
88–93, 95
interviews of, 63–64, 69–70,
110, 117, 126, 186, 210–11,
213, 228–29
Italian tour, 115–16
Japanese tour, 137, 140
knighted, 266
Leather Jackets and, 262
Madman Across the Water and,
75–77, 82–83
marriage to Furnish, 265
marriage to Blauel, 260
New Zealand tour, 137,
140–42
Osborne writes with,
225–28
Peachtree Road and, 263
performing style of, xxii,
41–44, 55, 56–57, 65, 74,
85–86, 90–91, 97–98, 101,
111, 121–23, 132, 134
personality and moods of, xvi,
xxiii, 7, 24, 41–42, 63–64,
74, 79, 87–88, 103–4, 123,
126, 131, 137–42, 163, 184,
186–87, 198, 209, 229
"Philadelphia Freedom" and,
170–72
protégé Kiki Dee and,
152–53
recent life of, 264–67
record collection of, xi–xii, xiv,
xxii–xxiii, 7, 38–39, 112
rehab and, 259, 265
Reid as manager and, 71–72,
74–75, 112–13, 200–201
retirement of, 207, 209–12,
218–20, 223–24
Rocket Records and, 113–15,
162–63, 221
Rock of the Westies and,
175–77, 179–82, 184
romances and, 184, 264–65
romance with Reid, 73–75,
160, 161, 211
romance with Reid breaks up,
191–92, 194, 198–99, 216
romance with Woodrow, 24–28
Single Man and, 232–34, 232,
241–42
Songs from the West Coast and,
263
Soviet tour and, 230, 235–42,
254–55
Starship plane and, 119–20,
148, 157, 159
suicide attempts and, 27, 157,
173–74, 186–88
Taupin partnership and,
xiii–xiv, 17–30, 18, 49,
66–67, 69, 72–73, 100
Taupin partnership breaks up,
202–3, 226–28, 233
Taupin partnership resumes,
235, 247–48, 262–64
tennis and, 144, 170–71
thirtieth birthday of, 217
Too Low for Zero and, 262–63
trio with Olsson and
Murray, 48
Troubadour debut of, 33–46,
36, 42, 51–53
Tumbleweed Connection and,
49–51, 53, 55–56
TV appearances, 32, 65–66,
70–71, 77, 145, 163–64,
169–71, 183, 197–98,
222–23, 225, 254–55
21 at 33 and, 247–49
UK tours, 65, 84–87, 103–4,
111, 176–77, 200–201, 204,
211–13, 236
vacations and, 65, 94–96, 194

Victim of Love and, 242–43
WABC-FM live-to-air show, 57–59
Watford Football Club and, 144–45, 188, 213–14, 217–18, 261–62
Wonderful Crazy Night and, 263
John D (boat), 114
John Gardiner Tennis Ranch, 144
"Johnny B. Goode," 243
John Reid Enterprises, 112–13, 193, 200–201, 218
Johnston, Bruce, 139
Johnstone, Davey, 83–85, 89, 92–94, 106–7, 113–14, 116–17, 156–57, 168, 175, 180, 190, 193, 202, 223
Jolson, Al, 17
Jones, Jack, 102
Jones, Mrs. (piano teacher), 6
Jones, Quincy, 40–41
Joplin, Janis, 125
Journey Through the Past, 112

Kanga, Skaila, 50
Kaye-Smith Studios, 225
Keen, Mike, 217
KFRC radio station, 159
KHJ radio station, 54, 88
Khrushchev, Nikita, 237
Kimball, Richard, 158
King, Billie Jean, 170–71, 177, 189, 190
King, Carole, 112
King, Tony, 151
"King Must Die, The," 31
Kinks, 55
Kirshner, Don, 183
Klein, Calvin, 251, 253
KMET radio station, 158
Knechtel, Larry, 31

Knockin' Em Dead Alive (bootleg album), 59
Kokonin, Vladimir, 236
KPPC radio, 58
Krassner, Paul, 96
Kubrick, Stanley, 92
Kunz, Charlie, 5

LaBelle, Pattie, 13–14, 114, 170
Lacey, Peter, 220
LaChapelle, David, 266
Ladies of the Canyon, 31
"Lady Samantha," xiii, xvi, 29
La Frenais, Ian, 237
Laine, Frankie, 5
Laine, Linda, 242
Lance, Major, 13, 170
Larkham, David, 38, 51, 76, 128–29, 174
La Rue, Danny, 102
LaRue, Lash, 49
Las Vegas Convention Center, 184
"Laughter in the Rain," 163
Leather Jackets, 260, 262
Led Zeppelin, xxii, 112, 119, 183
Lee, Byron, 104
Lennon, Cynthia, 151
Lennon, John, *xx*, 57, 101, 123, 128, 151, 158, 173, 192, 202, 252, 262
  friendship with Elton, 155–56, 160–61, 253
  Madison Square Garden concert with Elton, xvi–xxi, 204
  murder of, 255–56
  records *Walls and Bridges* with Elton, 156
  reunited with Yoko, xx–xxi
Lennon, Julian, 151
Lennon, Sean, xx, 255–56
Leonard, John, 183

Let It Be, 228
Let's Make Up and Be Friendly, 91
"Let the Heartaches Begin,"
    24, 26
"Levon," 76, 184, 190
Lewis, Jerry Lee, 7, 10, 12, 44,
    57, 87–88, 114, 141, 239
Liberace, 102
Liberty Records, 16–17, 19–20
Life, 7
Lightfoot, Gordon, 40
Lincoln City Football Club, 217
Lindsay-Hogg, Michael, 228
Little Feat, 158
"Little Jeannie," 249
Little Richard, 7, 12, 15, 103
Live E Jay (bootleg album), 59
London Palladium, 87–88, 101–2
London Weekend Television
    (LWT), 65, 185, 186, 189
Lone Ranger, 49
Longdancer, 114
Long John Baldry Show, 24, 25
Los Angeles Times, 43, 57, 155,
    237
Louder than Concorde tours,
    200–210
Love, Mike, 40
Lovelace, Linda, 121–22, 183
"Love Song," 145, 204
Loving and Free, 115
Low, 84
"Lucy in the Sky with
    Diamonds," xix, 144, 156,
    163, 176–77
Lulu, xiii, 139
Lundstrom, Astrid, 105

Mackie, Bob, 190, 252
Madison Square Garden,
    xvi–xxi, 123, 160–61, 204,
    207, 209–10, 256

Madman Across the Water,
    75–77, 82, 85, 90, 172, 175,
    185, 250
"Madman Across the Water," 76
Madman (yacht), 185, 186
Magical Mystery Tour, 90
Magna Carta folk group, 83
Magne, Michael, 81–82
Maitland, Mike, 153–55
Malouf, Joanna, 39
"Mama Can't Buy You Love,"
    225, 243
Mamas & the Papas, 45, 60
"Mammy," 17
Manson, Charles, 37, 45, 163
Margaret, Princess, Countess of
    Snowdon, xxii, 80, 86, 102,
    145, 193, 201, 256
"Marmion" (Scott), 19
Marx, Groucho, xxii, 95–96, 186
Marx Brothers, 108, 120
MCA Records, 52, 114, 153–55,
    159, 183, 203, 231–32, 252
McCartney, Linda Eastman, 112,
    177
McCartney, Paul, xx, 29, 112,
    128, 173, 177, 227, 262
McLaren, Malcolm, 219
"Medley (Yell Help, Wednesday
    Night, Ugly)," 181
Melcher, Terry, 37
"Mellow," 90
Melodiya records, 242
Melody Maker, 60, 63, 65, 69,
    85, 111, 114, 153, 177, 201
Mendes, Sérgio, 32
Mercer, Keith, 214
Merry Pranksters, 96
"Merry Xmas Everybody," 132
MGM records, 7
Michael, George, 265
"Michelle's Song," 67
MIDEM, 64

Midler, Bette, 70, 164
"Midnight Creeper," 108
Millermen, 5
Mills Music, 12–13
Mind Games, 156
Miracles, 72
Mitchell, Joni, 31, 39, 45, 50,
    154, 183, 202
Modeste Mignon (Balzac), 81
Mojo magazine, xxii
"Mona Lisas and Mad Hatters,"
    52–53, 128
Monkees, 119
Monroe, Marilyn, 125, 126
Moon, Keith, xvii, 176, 203
Moroder, Giorgio, 242
Morris, Jim, 158
Morrison, Jim, 125
Motown, xxiii, 72, 74, 115, 170,
    209
Move, 15
"Mr. Frantic," 16
Muppet Show, The (TV show),
    222–23
Murray, Dee, 32–33, 38, 40, 48,
    58, 83, 102, 123, 172, 175,
    249–51
Musicland record shop, xi–xii
Musicland studios, 242
"My Baby Left Me," 41, 59
"My Father's Gun," 49–50, 60
"My Old Man (Said Follow the
    Van)," 9, 214

Nash, Graham, 20
National Aeronautic and Space
    Administration (NASA), 90
National Union of Mineworkers,
    131–32
National Youth Theatre, 86
NBC TV, 60
"Never Can Say Goodbye," 164

Newcastle concert, 111
"New Guitar Boogie Shuffle," 5
Newman, Del, 139
Newman, Nanette, 94, 128
New Musical Express, 16, 20,
    102–3, 130
New York Times, 155, 183, 244
"Nice and Slow," 225
"Night They Drove Old Dixie
    Down, The," 50
Nilsson, Harry, xvii, 114, 177,
    203
Nixon, Richard M., 37, 76, 96
Nolan, Tom, 153
"North to Alaska," 49
Northwood Hills pub, 9–11
"No Shoe Strings on Louise," 31
Nyro, Laura, xii, 39

O'Connor, Inspector, 86–87
Odetta, 40, 56
Older, Charles, 37
Old Grey Whistle Test, The (TV
    show), 77, 145
Olsson, Kai, 114
Olsson, Nigel, 32–33, 38–40, 48,
    58, 60, 83, 102, 107, 111,
    114, 116, 139, 161, 172,
    175, 249–51
Olympics (Moscow, 1980), 236,
    240
"One Day (at a Time)," 156
O'Neill, Terry, 159, 182, 191
*One Who Writes the Words for
    Elton John, The* (Taupin),
    202
Ono, Yoko, xvii–xviii, xx–xxi,
    253, 255–56
Osborne, Gary, 225–28, 249
Osmond, Donny, 112
O'Sullivan, Gilbert, 112
Oz, Frank, 223

Pacific Coliseum, 160
Page, Gene, 171, 173
Page, Patti, 5
Palasport di Genova, 115
Palladium, 244
Palmer, Robert, 244
Palomino club, 250
Pang, May, xvii–xviii
Papagayo Club, 15
Paramount Pictures, 67
Parkinson, Michael, 197
Parkinson (TV show), 197–98
Parks, Van Dye, 45
Parkside Lutheran Hospital, 259
"Part-Time Love," 233, 242
Passarelli, Kenny, *168*, 175–76,
    180, 182, 188, 199, 201–2,
    207
Paxton's Music, 12
Peachtree Road, 263
Pearls Before Swine, 89
Peebles, Andy, 249
Peel, John, 162
Peking, SS (ship), 253–54
Peters, Linda, 53
"Philadelphia Freedom," 171–72,
    176, 251
Philadelphia Freedoms, 170
Philadelphia Story, The (film),
    128
Philips Records, 26
Phillips, John, 60
Philly Soul, 173, 224
Piaf, Edith, 212
Pickett, Wilson, 13
Piena, Helen, 8
"Pinball Wizard," 165, 177, 190,
    239
Pinkertons, 49
Pink Floyd, xxii, 33
Pinner County Grammar School,
    7–8, 11–12, 103–4
Pin Ups, 84

Pipolo, Pat, 143, 252
Pitney, Gene, 29
Playboy magazine, 210–11
Please Please Me, xx
Poco, 55
Police, 255
Polydor Records, 7
Ponty, Jean-Luc, 90
Pop, Iggy, 124
Pope, Maldwyn, 162
Pope, Roger, 50, *168*, 175–76
Pouteaux, Dr. Pierre, 221
Preservation Hall, 50
Presley, Elvis, xxii, 7, 41, 152,
    204–7, 212, 214, 220
Preston, Billy, 180
Pretty Things, 33
"Pretty Vacant," 217
Phillip, Prince, Duke of
    Edinburgh, 219
Procol Harum, 20
Professional Bull Riders, 264
Proktor, Patrick, 212
"Proud Mary," 164
Pye Records, 29
"Pyjamarama," 112

Quaye, Caleb, 12, 17, 21–24, 50,
    168, 175, 187–88, 202
Queen, 192, 227

Radio Luxembourg, 12
Rainbow Theatre, 103, 218, 235
Ramone, Phil, 58
Range Rider, 49
Ray, Johnnie, 5
"Razor Face," 76
RCA Victor, 7
"Reach Out I'll Be There," 14
Reavey, Annie, 110
Record Plant, xvii

Record World, 112
Redding, Otis, 11, 152
Reeves, Jim, 17, 250
Regan, Russ, 33–35, 40–41,
    51–52, 54, 153
"Regimental Sgt Zippo," 28
Reid, John, 79, 92–93, 96, 123,
    129, 159, 184–86, 207, 225,
    255
    arrested in Auckland, 142, 145
    becomes Elton's manager,
      71–74, 97
    breaks up with Elton, 191–92,
      194, 198, 216
    contract negotiations and,
      112–13, 145, 153–55
    drugs and, 135
    Elton's retirement and, 224
    MCA contract and, 203
    Rocket Records and, 113–15,
      162
    romance with Elton, 73–74, 77,
      93, 160, 161, 184
    Soviet tour and, 236–37
    temper and, 116, 129–30,
      141–42, 200–201, 228
Reid, Keith, 20
Reinhardt, Django, 11
Rembrandt, 113, 193, 249
    Adoration of the Shepherds,
      193
Renault, Mary, 31
Renwick, Rim, 251
"Return to Paradise," 233
Revolution Club, 32, 72
Revolver, 14
Rhymes & Reasons, 112
Richard, Cliff, 237
Richards, Keith, 179–80, 181
"Ride a White Swan," 63
"Rime of the Ancient Mariner,
    The" (Coleridge), 19
Robbins, Marty, 19, 49

Roberts, Tommy, 40
Robertson, Robbie, 49
Robinson, Edward G., 125
Robinson, Smokey, 72
Robinson, Tom, 249
"Rock and Roll, Hoochie Koo,"
    136
Rock and Roll Circus, 228
"Rock and Roll Madonna," 33
"Rock Around the Clock," 257
"Rocket Man," 83, 88–90,
    92–93, 101, 176, 190, 204,
    220, 238, 251
Rocket Record Company,
    113–15, 151–52, 162–63,
    185, 221, 223, 228–29
Rock Music Awards, 183
Rock'n'Roll, xvii
Rock of the Westies, 179–82,
    184, 191, 198
Rock of the Westies Express
    (plane), 185
Rockwell, John, 209
"Rocky Mountain Way," 136
Rogers, Roy, 49, 124–25
Rolling Stone magazine, 42, 69,
    108, 130, 153, 160, 210–11,
    213, 243, 249
Rolling Stones, xiv, xxii, 41, 82,
    104–6, 108, 112, 116,
    179–81, 209, 228, 237, 243,
    262
"Roll Out the Barrel," 9
Ronson, Mick, 190
Ronstadt, Linda, 183
Rose, Don, 159
Rose, Howard, 188, 193
Ross, Diana, 158, 183
Ross-Leming, Eugenie, 210
Rotten, Johnny, 217
"Rotten Peaches," 76
Roxy Music, 103, 112
Royal Academy of Music, 7–8

Royal Albert Hall, 53–54
Royal Festival Hall Show, 65,
    84–85, 126, 145, 203–4
Royal Philharmonic Orchestra,
    85, 204
Royal Variety Performance, 101
Royal Windsor Big Top Show,
    219
Rudis, Al, 153
"Rudolph the Red-Nosed
    Reindeer," 132
Russell, Ken, 165
Russell, Leon, xxii, 31, 43, 55,
    59, 181
Russo, Toni, 248

"Salvation," 90
Sand, George, 81
San Diego Sports Arena, 184
San Francisco Civil Auditorium, 69
Santa Monica Civic Auditorium,
    56–57, 182–83
"Sartorial Eloquence," 249
"Saturday Night's Alright,"
    106–7, 116–17, 123, 141,
    145, 177, 190, 212, 239, 251
"Saturday Sun," 53
"Saved by the Bell," 32
"Scarecrow," 22
Scott, Sir Walter, 19
Séance on a Wet Afternoon
    (film), 94
"Seasons," 67
Seattle Post-Intelligencer, 69
Sedaka, Neil, 162–63, 191
Sedaka's Back, 162–63
Selznick, David O., 163
Sex Pistols, 217, 219
Sgt. Pepper, 121
"Shake, Rattle and Roll," 7
Shankar, Ravi, xxii
Shearing, George, 5

"Sheik of Araby," 5
Shepard, Matthew, 263
Sherman, Bobby, 119
"Shine On Through," 225, 231
"Shooting Star," 231
Shoreditch College, 219–20
Sigma Sound Studios, 225
"Signed, Sealed, Delivered (I'm
    Yours)," 32
Silver, Mike, 114
Simon, Neil, 193
Simon, Paul, 60, 114
Simon & Garfunkel, 31
Simpson, Donnie, 143
Sinatra, Frank, 6
"Sing," 112
"Singin' In the Rain," 92, 145
Single Man, 232–34, 241–42, 251
"Sitting in the Park," 13
"Sixty Years On," 31, 41, 56,
    231
"Skater's Waltz," 4
Skidoo (film), 96
"Skyline Pigeon," xiv–xv, 29,
    145, 204
Slade, 132
"Slave," 90
Smile, 45
Smiling Face, 114
Smith, "Legs" Larry, 90–92,
    97–98, 97, 101–2
Smoker You Drink, the Player
    You Get, The, 136
Snowdon, Antony Armstrong-
    Jones, Earl of, 80, 86
Snyder, Tom, 254
"Social Disease," 126
"Solar Prestige a Gammon," 138
Solzhenitsyn, Aleksandr, 125
"Someone Saved My Life
    Tonight," 156–57, 173–74,
    250, 266
"Someone's Final Song," 212

"Somewhere Over the Rainbow," 14
"Song for Guy," 229, 231, 233
"Song for You, A," 31
Songs for Swingin' Lovers!, 6
Songs from a Room, xii
Songs from the West Coast, 263, 266
"Sorry Seems to Be the Hardest Word," 199–200, 218, 223, 251
Sotheby's, 261
Soul Train (TV show), 169–71
Sound Techniques Studio, 53
Soviet tour of 1979, 236–42, 254–55
"Space Oddity," 30, 89
Spector, Phil, xvii
"Speedy Gonzales," 108
Spinners, 224
Springfield, Dusty, 114
Squires, Dorothy, 249
Stacey, Bob, 38
Stafford, Jo, 5
Stallone, Sylvester, 265
Stanshall, Vivian, 91
Starr, Ringo, 103, 114, 158, 176–77, 183, 192, 202
Starship (jet), xxi, 119–20, 123, 148, 157, 159, 207–8
Stax Records, xxiii
Steampacket, 15–16
Steely Dan, 175
Stein, Jules, 183
"Step into Christmas," 132
Stevens, Cat, 114
Stewart, Billy, 13
Stewart, Rod, 15, 87–88, 114, 139–40, 145, 164–66, 193, 221, 236, 243
Sting, 255
"Stinker," 137
Stockholm Concert Hall, 235

Stone, Sly, 70
Stooges, 124
Strauss, Richard, "Also Sprach Zarathustra," 205
"Street Kids," 181
Streisand, Barbra, 158
Stylistics, 224
Suitable for Framing, 29
Summer, Donna, 242
Sun, The newspaper, 228, 261
Sunday Times (London), 228–29
Sunflower, 44
Sunshine Boys (film), 193
Super Bear Studios, 248
Super-Sonics, 5
"Surfin' U.S.A.," 176
Surf's Up, 89
"Surprise Surprise (Sweet Bird of Paradox)," 156
"Susie (Dramas)," 90
"Swan Queen of the Laughing Lake," 20
"Sweet Little Rock 'n' Roller," 145
"Sweet Painted Lady," 106, 125, 218
Sylvester, Ward, 119

Tabolsky, Marvin, 92
"Take Me to the Pilot," 31, 41, 54, 59, 85
Take One newspaper, 96
Tamla Motown Records, 72, 73
"Tartan-Colored Lady," xiii, 28
Tate, Sharon, 37, 163
Taupin, Bernie
   Ackles's *American Gothic* and, 202
   AIDS foundation and, 266
   Alice Cooper and, 95, 226
   appearance of, 21
   "Bennie and the Jets" and, 144

Taupin, Bernie (*cont.*)
  Blue Moves and, 198–200,
    208, 212, 227
  "Candle in the Wind" and, 125
  Captain & the Kid and, 263
  Captain Fantastic and, 146,
    149–50, 173–74
  Caribou and, 136–39
  "Daniel" and, 109, 110
  drinking problems and, 202–3,
    226
  early life and background of,
    19–21
  Elton John and, 30–31
  Empty Sky and, xiv
  fame and, 66, 69
  Friends soundtrack and, 67
  Goodbye Yellow Brick Road
    and, 105–7, 112, 116–17,
    124–29
  Hollywood Vampires and, 203
  Honky Château and, 82–84
  "Indian Sunset" and, 56
  Madman Across the Water and,
    75–76, 94, 109–10
  marriage to Maxine Feibelman,
    39, 56, 66–67, 76, 198–99,
    203
  marriage to Toni Russo, 248
  "Mona Lisas and Mad
    Hatters" and, 52–53
  partnership with Elton begun,
    xiii–xiv, 17–30, 18, 66, 100
  partnership with Elton breaks
    up, 202–3, 225–27, 233
  partnership with Elton
    resumed, 235, 247–49,
    262–64
  personal relationship with
    Elton and, 28, 72–73,
    263–64
  "Philadelphia Freedom" and,
    171
  publishes *Burning Cold*, 248
  "Rocket Man" and, 83, 89
  Rocket Records and, 113
  Rock of the Westies and,
    181–82
  solo album *He Who Rides the
    Tiger*, 248
  solo album *Taupin*, 202
  "Someone Saved My Life
    Tonight" and, 173–74
  tours and xix, 38–39, 44–45,
    51–53, 58–61, 66, 122–23,
    148, 159, 190–91, 209
  Tumbleweed Connection and,
    49–51
  TV appearances, 65–66
  21 at 33 and, 247–49
  Westerns and, 49
Taupin, 202
Taupin, Maxine Feibelman, 39, 56
  divorces Taupin, 198–99
  marries Taupin, 66–67, 76, 174
Taylor, Elizabeth, 158, 208
Taylor, Graham, 217, 244–45
Taylor-Wood, Sam, xxi
"Teacher I Need You," 108
"Tears of a Clown, The," 72
Teigel, Eliot, 57
"Tell Me When the Whistle
  Blows," 173
Tempest, Roy, 13
10CC, 198
Terrell, Tammi, 208
"There's Still Time for Me," xiii
"(They Long to Be) Close to
  You," 37
"This Train Don't Stop There
  Anymore," 263
Thompson, Linda Peters, 53
Thompson, Richard, 53
Three Dog Night, 29, 40
"Three Way Love Affair," 225
"Thunder in the Night," 243

"Ticking," 139, 145
"Time Has Told Me," 53
Time magazine, 109, 193
"Tinderbox," 263
"Tiny Dancer," 75–76, 250
"To Be Young, Gifted and
    Black," 32
Tommy (album), 183
Tommy (film), 164–66, 165
Tomorrow Show (TV show),
    254
Tonight Show (TV show),
    254–55
Too Low for Zero, 262
Top Forty, 60, 68, 76, 143
Top of the Pops (TV show), 32,
    65, 70–71, 87, 117, 171,
    217, 228
Tormé, Mel, 27
Toussaint, Allen, 90
Toussaint, Jolanna, 170
"Tower of Babel," 173
Tower Records, 113, 158
Townshend, Pete, 165
Traffic, xiv, 82
T. Rex, 63, 70, 103
Trident Studios, 30, 50, 67, 75
Trombley, Rosalie, 143
Troubadour Club, 34–35, 36,
    38–44, 42, 51–56, 183–84,
    237, 250
Troy, Doris, 14
Tucker, Ken, 249
Tumbleweed Connection, 49–51,
    53, 55–56, 58, 60–61, 64,
    67–68, 145, 175, 218
"Tutti Frutti," 103
21 at 33, 247–48, 251, 262
"Twelfth of Never," 112
2001: A Space Odyssey (film),
    205
"Two Rooms at the End of the
    World," 247

UCLA Eye Institute, 183
Uni Records, 33–34, 38–41, 44,
    51–52, 89, 153
Updike, John, 188

Van Gogh, Vincent, 81
Vannelli, Gino, 170
"Velvet Fountain," 22
Very Live (bootleg album), 59
Victim of Love, 242–43
Vietnam War, 38, 109
Village Voice, The, 243
Vinci, Leonardo da, xxi

WABC-FM live radio show
    (1970), 58–59
Wainwright, Rufus, 265
Waits, Tom, 154
Walker, Alan, 16
Walls and Bridges, 156
Walsh, Joe, 136, 175, 189
"Waltzing Matilda," 78
War, 64
Warhol, Andy, xvii, 209, 253
Warlock Music, 53
Watford Football Club, 144–45,
    213–14, 217–18, 233, 244,
    261
Watford Town Hall, 86–87, 201
"We All Fall in Love Sometimes,"
    173, 263–64
Wembley Empire Pool Arena,
    223, 235
Wembley Stadium concert,
    176–77, 181
West, Mae, xxii, 95, 183
Western Springs Stadium, 141,
    142
Weston, Doug, 41
"Whatever Gets You thru the
    Night," xvii–xix, 156

Wheeler, David, 141–42
"When Irish Eyes Are Smiling," 9
"When I Was Tealby Abbey," 28
"When the First Tear Shows," xiii
"Where To Now St. Peter?," 50, 218
Whistle Down the Wind (film), 94
White Album, 30
"White Christmas," 161
"White Lady White Powder," 247, 249
"Whiter Shade of Pale, A," 20
Who, 116, 164–66, 165, 183
"Whole Lotta Shakin' Goin' On," 114
Wigg, David, 237
Williams, Andy, 60
Williams, Hugh, 265
Williams, Kevin, 141
Williams, Ray, 16–17, 20–22, 38–39, 71, 73
Wilson, Brian, 44–45
Wilson, Carl, 139
Wilson, Marilyn, 45
Wing and a Prayer Fife and Drum Corps, 194
Winter, Norman, 4, 38, 41–42
"Wish You Were Here," 5
"Witches' House, The," 22
Witherspoon, Jimmy, 11
WJLB radio station, 143
WNEW-FM radio station, 209

Wolfe, Tom, 259
Wonder, Stevie, xxii, 32, 60, 123
Wonderful Crazy Night, 263
Woodrow, Linda, 24–25, 27, 156, 174
Worden, Al, 90
Worthington, Calvin Coolidge, 189
"Writing," 173
Wyman, Bill, 105

Yardbirds, 3
"Year of the Teddy Bear, The" (Taupin verse), 20
Yencess, Hubert, 149
Yes, 71
York, Kay Sutton, 248
Yorkshire Folk, Blues & Jazz Festival, 33
"You'll Be Sorry to See Me Go," xiii
Young, Neil, 39, 112, 115
"Your Song," 30–31, 40, 44, 54, 56, 58–60, 64–65, 85, 101, 123, 155, 162, 189, 193, 220, 238, 253
"You Wear It Well," 88

Zappa, Frank, xxii
Zito, Richie, 251

ABOUT THE AUTHOR

TOM DOYLE is an acclaimed music journalist, author, and long-standing contributing editor to *Q*. His work has also appeared in *Mojo, The Guardian, Billboard, The Times,* and *Sound on Sound.* Over the years he has been responsible for key magazine profiles of Paul McCartney, Elton John, Yoko Ono, Keith Richards, U2, Madonna, Kate Bush, and R.E.M., among many other artists. He is the author of *The Glamour Chase: The Maverick Life of Billy MacKenzie,* and *Man on the Run: Paul McCartney in the 1970s.* He lives in London, England.

@Tom_Doyle_

ABOUT THE TYPE

This book was set in Sabon, a typeface designed by the well-known German typographer Jan Tschichold (1902–74). Sabon's design is based upon the original letterforms of sixteenth-century French type designer Claude Garamond and was created specifically to be used for three sources: foundry type for hand composition, Linotype, and Monotype. Tschichold named his typeface for the famous Frankfurt typefounder Jacques Sabon (c. 1520–80).